ENGAGING WRITING 1

Essential Skills for Academic Writing

Mary Fitzpatrick

College of Marin

PEARSON
Longman

Engaging Writing 1, Essential Skills for Academic Writing

Pearson Education, 10 Bank Street, White Plains, NY 10606 USA

Staff credits: The people who made up the *Engaging Writing 1* team, representing editorial, production, design, and manufacturing, are Pietro Alongi, Rhea Banker, Gina DiLillo, Oliva Fernandez, Nancy Flaggman, Gosia Jaros-White, Amy McCormick, Linda Moser, Mary Perrotta Rich, Debbie Sistino, Jennifer Stem, Paula Van Ells, and Patricia Wosczyk.

Cover image: Colin Anderson/Getty Images
Text composition: Rainbow Graphics
Text font: New Aster
Illustrations: Linda Bittner (pages 25–26); Patrick Merrell (page xxiii)
Technical art: Tinge Design Studio
Photo credits: see page xxii
Text credits: see page xxii

Library of Congress Cataloging-in-Publication Data

Fitzpatrick, Mary, 1953–
    Engaging writing. 1 : essential skills for academic writing / Mary Fitzpatrick. — 2nd ed.
        p. cm. — (Engaging writing 1 Essential skills for academic writing.)
    ISBN 0-13-608518-0 — ISBN 0-13-248354-8 1. English language—Rhetoric. 2. Report writing. I. Title.
    PE1408.F467 2010
    808'.042076—dc22

                                                    2010022162

ISBN-13: 978-0-13-608518-8
ISBN-10: 0-13-608518-0

PEARSON LONGMAN ON THE WEB

Pearsonlongman.com offers online resources for teachers and students. Access our Companion Websites, our online catalog, and our local offices around the world.

Visit us at **www.pearsonlongman.com**.

Printed in the United States of America
1 2 3 4 5 6 7 8 9 10—V011—15 14 13 12 11 10

Contents

CHAPTER 1 **Accomplishments: Writing a Process Paragraph**   1

This chapter focuses on academic achievements and how they are accomplished. Students will work with paragraphs on topics such as giving a speech, memorizing terminology, and overcoming procrastination. The chapter-opening reading is a first-person narrative by a "Lost Boy" of Sudan, who recounts some of the steps that took him from his war-torn homeland to graduating from college.

CHAPTER 2 **Places and Events: Writing a Descriptive Paragraph**   24

This chapter focuses on writing about places and events. Students will describe a location or event that is special to them, from a tranquil campsite to a thrilling soccer game. In the chapter-opening reading, a wildlife biologist describes a unique national park in Bolivia that he is dedicated to protecting.

CHAPTER 3 **Pastimes and Entertainment: Writing a Reason Paragraph** 50

This chapter focuses on all types of entertainment, from mahjong to detective dramas. Students will compose paragraphs in which they identify and explain two or three reasons for their entertainment preference. The chapter-opening reading is by a blogger who lives in Bahrain and has used blogging to learn about the Middle East.

CHAPTER 5   **Growing Up in Different Cultures: Writing a Contrast Paragraph**

This chapter looks at child rearing, child development, and family structure in countries around the world. Students will work on paragraphs focusing on the differences between two cultures or two age groups as they learn to manipulate comparison/contrast patterns. In the chapter-opening reading, an international team of social scientists presents some findings of their cross-cultural research on the phenomenon of putting a baby to bed.

CHAPTER 6 **Making Communities Better: Writing an Opinion Paragraph and Essay** 148

This chapter focuses on quality of life. Students will choose an issue they believe is important, from recreation and health to justice and equality, and recommend a related improvement to their town or city. First, they will support their point of view in a paragraph. Then they will expand their ideas in an essay. In the chapter-opening reading, a sociologist discusses urban crime and presents solutions from Tanzania, Japan, Uganda, and France.

To the Instructor

Engaging Writing 1 and *2* teach students the concepts and skills of academic writing, from paragraphs to essays. These books grew out of the need for materials with thematic lessons, ample modeling, and instruction that is fully integrated with the students' writing process. *Engaging Writing 1* and *2* are user-friendly texts that fully support the needs of intermediate (level 1) and high-intermediate-to-low-advanced (level 2) ESL learners.

Features of *Engaging Writing 1*

- *Well-crafted instructional sequence with clear applications.* The chapter components are carefully articulated to allow for both progressive skill building and varied learning experiences. Students begin with reading and discussion as they engage with the chapter theme. Vocabulary exercises then serve as a bridge to the writing portion of the chapter. So that students have a clear sense of how they will use the rhetorical instruction, writing prompt(s) precede the presentation of the mode. In the middle of each chapter, students are asked to produce a first draft so that they can apply subsequent instruction to revision. Following each rhetorical or grammar teaching point, revision checkpoints remind students to apply the new information to their evolving drafts. Across chapters, the instructional sequence is arranged so that students can draw upon previously acquired knowledge and skills as they encounter new information and master new skills.

- *Appealing and appropriate range of themes and topics.* *Engaging Writing 1* offers a range of chapter themes that are both stimulating and accessible to the diverse ESL audience. Themes include personal accomplishments, reasons for entertainment preferences, the effects of jobs, cross-cultural comparisons of child-rearing practices, and quality-of-life improvements to towns and cities. The chapter-opening readings, most of which were written specifically for this volume, are written by authors whose lifework is closely associated with the subject matter of their texts. Student writers will find a range of topic suggestions within each chapter theme. This allows them to tailor each assignment to their own interests.

- *Multiple realistic models.* Each chapter has a number of writing models illustrating a range of approaches to the prompt(s). The subject matter and language of these models reflect actual student writing. Exercises ask learners to mark and manipulate the models so that they become familiar with the features of expository writing. A central piece of each chapter is a step-by-step demonstration of how an individual student completed the chapter assignment. This sequence not only demystifies the process, but—because it includes a first and final draft—demonstrates that revision is essential to effectively completing an assignment.

- *Student-centered, communicative approach.* Because social engagement promotes learning, the chapters of *Engaging Writing 1* contain interactive activities throughout: Students discuss readings, collaborate to complete exercises, and, at the end of each chapter, share their final drafts using the Peer Review Forms found in Appendix II. In addition, *Engaging Writing 1* emphasizes the social nature of writing itself by repeatedly advising students to be aware of their audience. Students who understand that writing is not just a performance but real communication are more motivated to write and to become better writers.

- *Critical thinking.* *Engaging Writing 1* guides students in the use of analysis in both post-reading and prewriting activities. It familiarizes students with cognitive functions such as making comparisons and analyzing causation; it encourages questioning; and it teaches students to apply intellectual standards such as clarity, relevance, and logic as they evaluate models and their own drafts.

- *Academic vocabulary.* Words from the Academic Word List (Coxhead, 2000) are identified in the vocabulary exercises and in the glossing of the chapter-opening readings with this symbol (∗). The instruction highlights parts of speech and suffixes so that students gain a better understanding of the words at hand and the broader nature of the lexicon. Students are encouraged to use new vocabulary in their writing in order to facilitate acquisition.

- *A complete foundation for student success.* Each chapter in *Engaging Writing 1* contains rhetorical principles and language concepts that students will need to fulfill the chapter assignment. In addition, Appendices IA and IB address gaps in student knowledge by providing thorough instruction in the rules of grammar, capitalization, and punctuation. Appendix IA begins with the basic building blocks that many intermediate students have not fully learned—parts of speech, subjects and verbs, word order—and builds progressively toward more complex aspects of the language. Students can study this appendix from the beginning onward or dip into it as they need to. The instruction and exercises are suitable for classroom use or as resources for individual students.

- *Flexibility.* Instructors may select the chapters in *Engaging Writing 1* that best suit their students' needs. Groups with less writing experience can start with the process paragraph in Chapter 1, while those with more background might begin with a later chapter so that they will have time to finish Chapter 6, in which they learn how to expand a paragraph to an essay. Instructors may choose not to complete every part of every chapter; instead, they can select the parts best suited to their students. In later chapters, teachers of more advanced students will find aspects of writing that are not usually included in books at this level, such as pronoun point of view and real and unreal conditionals.

- *Teacher's manual.* The teacher's manual has suggestions for using the text, as well as an answer key, and will be available online @ www.pearsonlongman.com/engagingwriting.

How a Chapter Works

Engaging Writing 1 fully integrates instruction with the students' writing process. Each part of a chapter is designed to meet students' needs at a specific stage of writing. At first they become familiar with the theme and the mode, and then they work through the prewrite, draft, and revise sections until they complete the assignment.

■ READING FOR WRITING

Before You Read   This brief segment introduces the topic or ideas students will encounter in the reading. Discussion activities encourage an exchange of information and promote reflection on the ideas and issues in the text.

Reading   Students encounter a wide variety of texts representing authors and issues of global interest. The readings introduce students to the chapter's theme and rhetorical focus.

Understanding the Reading   The follow-up discussion questions not only give students a chance to relate to the subject matter and express their ideas about it, but also focus their attention on aspects of the writing assignment that lies ahead.

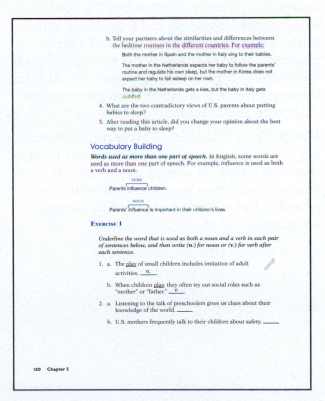

Vocabulary Building   Students learn and practice vocabulary related to the chapter theme and pick up words they can use in their writing assignment. As students proceed through the text, they learn about broad features of the lexicon, such as word families, words that are more than one part of speech, and relationships among categories of words (for example, *-ing* adjectives that come from verbs). Short exercises encourage dictionary use and serve as warm-ups to the chapter writing assignment.

■ WRITING

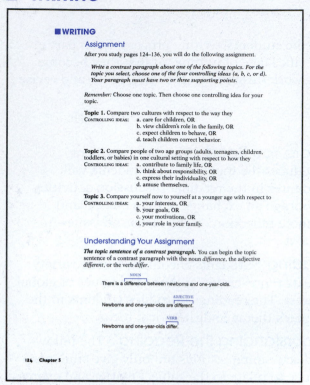

Assignment Students choose one of several topics related to the chapter theme. While all the topics in a chapter require the use of a single rhetorical mode, they vary enough to accommodate multiple interests and ability levels.

Understanding Your Assignment This key section develops aspects of each writing assignment, from understanding the mode to writing topic sentences and supporting details. With clear, concise explanation and simple modeling, it gives students the conceptual tools they need to begin the assignment and introduces them to various prewriting strategies, such as clustering and outlining.

The Writing Process This section presents easy-to-follow steps that guide students from choosing a topic to writing a first draft. It also incorporates a case study showing how an individual student completed the chapter assignment.

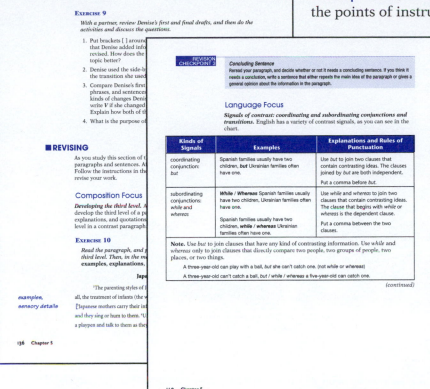

EXERCISE 9

With a partner, review Denise's first and final drafts, and then do the activities and discuss the questions.

1. Put brackets [ ] around ... that Denise added info... revised. How does the ... topic better?
2. Denise used the side-b... the transition she used...
3. Compare Denise's first... phrases, and sentences... kinds of changes Denis... write *V* if she changed... Explain how both of t...
4. What is the purpose of...

■ **REVISING**

As you study this section of t... paragraphs and sentences. A... Follow the instructions in the... revise your work.

Composition Focus

Developing the third level. ... develop the third level of a p... explanations, and quotations... level in a contrast paragraph...

EXERCISE 10

Read the paragraph, and ... ... *third level. Then, in the m...* ... *examples, explanations, ...*

Jap...

examples, sensory details

¹The parenting styles of J... all, the treatment of infants (the w... ²Japanese mothers carry their in... and they sing or hum to them. ⁴U... a playpen and talk to them as they...

136   Chapter 5

REVISION CHECKPOINT 3	*Concluding Sentence*

Reread your paragraph, and decide whether or not it needs a concluding sentence. If you think it needs a conclusion, write a sentence that either repeats the main idea of the paragraph or gives a general opinion about the information in the paragraph.

Language Focus

Signals of contrast: coordinating and subordinating conjunctions and transitions. English has a variety of contrast signals, as you can see in the chart.

Kinds of Signals	Examples	Explanations and Rules of Punctuation
coordinating conjunction: *but*	Spanish families usually have two children, *but* Ukrainian families often have one.	Use *but* to join two clauses that contain contrasting ideas. The clauses joined by *but* are both independent. Put a comma before *but*.
subordinating conjunctions: *while* and *whereas*	*While / Whereas* Spanish families usually have two children, Ukrainian families often have one. Spanish families usually have two children, *while / whereas* Ukrainian families often have one.	Use *while* and *whereas* to join two clauses that contain contrasting ideas. The clause that begins with *while* or *whereas* is the dependent clause. Put a comma between the two clauses.

Note. Use *but* to join clauses that have any kind of contrasting information. Use *while* and *whereas* only to join clauses that directly compare two people, two groups of people, two places, or two things.

A three-year-old can play with a ball, *but* she can't catch one. (not *while* or *whereas*)

A three-year-old can't catch a ball, *but / while / whereas* a five-year-old can catch one.

(continued)

140   Chapter 5

Peer Review Form

■ **CHAPTER 4—Occupations**   **EFFECT PARAGRAPH**

WRITER: _____   READER: _____

Read a classmate's paragraph and answer the questions.

1. What is the topic of the paragraph? _____

   Does the topic need to be defined or explained?   ☐ yes ☐ no

   If yes, is there a clear definition or explanation?   ☐ yes ☐ no

2. How many effects does the paragraph discuss? _____

3. Does the paragraph contain three levels?   ☐ yes ☐ no

   How did the writer develop the supporting points?

   ☐ with sensory details   ☐ with examples   ☐ with explanations   ☐ with quotations

   Do you see any problems with unity or focus?   ☐ yes ☐ no

   If yes, explain. _____

4. Did the writer use repeated and related words to create connections within the paragraph?   ☐ yes ☐ no

   If yes, what are some of them? _____

5. Which verb tenses did the writer use in the paragraph?

   ☐ the present perfect   ☐ the simple present   ☐ the simple past

250   Appendix II

Composition Focus   This section reinforces the points of instruction in Understanding Your Assignment, by revisiting concepts such as topic sentence, controlling idea, and development. It also introduces rhetorical concepts that relate directly to review and revision, such as unity and focus. Varied models and interactive exercises maintain student interest, and advice boxes remind learners to apply each teaching point to their own drafts.

Language Focus

Students learn and practice sentence skills appropriate to the chapter assignment. This section emphasizes sentence development and combining—key skills for intermediate writers. Advice boxes remind students to apply each piece of instruction to their own drafts.

■ **FINAL DRAFT AND PEER REVIEW**

Students exchange papers with classmates and fill out the assignment's Peer Review Form, which is located in Appendix II. This activity not only reviews the main teaching points of the chapter, but also reminds students that they are writing for an audience. After receiving feedback from their peers, students make final changes and proofread their compositions before submitting them to their instructors.

About the Author and Reviewers

About the Author

Mary Fitzpatrick teaches ESL at the College of Marin in California. She has also taught with the San Francisco Community College District, the Academy of Art University in San Francisco, and Santa Rosa Junior College. Her particular interest is teaching writing to English language learners.

Reviewers

Pearson Education is grateful to the following individuals who reviewed the manuscript:

Kitty Barrera, University of Houston, Houston, TX; **Leslie Biaggi**, Miami-Dade College, Miami, FL; **Jan Bowes-Marek**, Norwalk Community College, Norwalk, CT; **Sharon Cavusgil**, Georgia State University, Atlanta, GA; **Anthony Halderman**, Cuesta College, San Luis Obispo, CA; **Steve Horowitz**, Central Washington University, Ellensburg, WA; **Greg Jewel**, Drexel University, Philadelphia, PA; **Ana Jusino**, Norwalk Community College, Norwalk, CT; and **Suzanne Overstreet**, West Valley College, Saratoga, CA.

Acknowledgments

I want to express my thanks to all the people at Pearson Longman who helped to make this book possible including Debbie Sistino, Mary Perrotta Rich, and Malgorzata Jaros-White.

I am particularly grateful to the writers who contributed original texts to this volume—to Panther Alier, Robert Wallace, Ayesha Saldanha, Anthony Campaña, and Sara Harkness and her co-authors. I want to thank all of them for their patience, generosity, creativity, and passion for their subject matter.

Credits

Text Credits

Pages 2–4: "Healing and Learning to Learn." Panther Alier, 2009.

Pages 25–27: "A Biological Treasure Chest," adapted from "Madidi National Park." Robert Wallace, PhD., 2009.

Pages 52–53: "How Blogging Changed My Life." Ayesha Saldanha, 2009.

Pages 85–86: "Being a Firefighter." Anthony Campaña, 2009.

Pages 117–119: "Putting the Baby to Bed in Five Cultures." Sara Harkness, Charles M. Super, Jong-Hay Rha, Marjolijn Blom, Blanca Huitrón, Ughetta Moscardino, Saskia van Schaik, and Margreet de Looze, 2009.

Pages 149–151: Adapted from Franz Vanderschueren, "From Violence to Justice and Security in Cities," *Environment and Urbanization* 8. 93 (1996): 93–112.

Photo Credits

All photos are from Shutterstock.com except for the following: Page 3, Roger Hutchings/Alamy; 26, Bhandol/Alamy; 50 (bottom right), Oliver Knight/Alamy; 65, AfriPics.com/Alamy.

About *Engaging Writing 1*

To **engage** (or to be engaged) means to be very interested, to be active, to be a part of something, or to make something a part of your life.

Look at the pictures. Then discuss this question with a partner: In which pictures are the mice engaged?

As you start this book, *Engaging Writing 1*, think about all the ways you will be engaged—both in and out of class. With a partner, check off (✓) ways to be engaged that can help you learn and improve your writing.

- ☐ think about what you read
- ☐ be active in class discussions
- ☐ ask yourself questions about what you read and what your teacher says
- ☐ follow directions carefully
- ☐ review your compositions often
- ☐ complete assignments on time
- ☐ get to know your classmates
- ☐ spend time thinking about writing assignments outside of class before beginning to write

If you checked all the ideas above, you are ready to engage in learning more English and becoming a better writer. Welcome to *Engaging Writing 1*!

Accomplishments

Writing a Process Paragraph

What are your goals? Do you want to learn to cook, find a better job, or improve your English? Have you reached some of your goals? When someone achieves a goal, other people are naturally curious about how the person did it. In this chapter you will write a process paragraph explaining step-by-step how you accomplished a goal.

This chapter will help you

- use lists to prepare to write a paragraph.
- write a topic sentence and supporting sentences.
- use explanations to help the reader understand your supporting ideas.
- use transition signals to make your paragraph easy to read.
- review past tense irregular verbs.
- use conjunctions to connect ideas.

■ READING FOR WRITING

Before You Read

A. *Complete the tasks with a partner or a small group.*

1. Look at the people in the photographs on page 1. Tell what you think each person has accomplished. Then tell about something that you accomplished recently.

2. Some students have faced major challenges in their lives, and they consider themselves lucky to be in school. Make a list of two or three things that can interfere with a person's goal of getting an education.

B. *You are about to read an article about a person who received some of his education in Kenya and some in the United States. Education is a little bit different in every culture. Read the following items, and think about your own experiences in elementary school and high school. Then compare answers with a partner's.*

1. What subjects or skills did the teachers think were most important in your schools? How did they show you that they considered those subjects important?

2. When do you believe you learned the most—when you were listening to the teacher, reading textbooks, talking with classmates, or doing assignments on your own?

3. Imagine going to school in East Africa. Write down one way that schools in this part of the world are probably different from the schools you attended.

Reading

HEALING AND LEARNING TO LEARN
by Panther Alier

1   If I had stayed in my village in southern Sudan, my life would be completely different from what it is today. I would be a cattle keeper or farmer, or both. I would probably also be a traditional singer and a wrestler. I would be **illiterate**. This is a typical lifestyle that a Dinka tribesman has. In addition, I would probably still believe that the world was as big as my eyes could see and that only Dinka people lived in it.

illiterate: *unable to read*

2   I was born in 1977 in Dinka Bor, Sudan. My village had no clean water, electricity, medicine, or modern schools. Both of my parents died when I was about four years old. My aunt raised me along with her children in her small grass-roofed mud hut. She cared for us until 1987, when the civil war began.

3   When I was ten years old, the Sudanese army of northern Sudan attacked our village and many other villages in the South. Along with great numbers of other children, some as young as five years old, I became separated from my loved ones. For a month and a half we walked toward safety in Ethiopia. We lived there for four years until a civil war in Ethiopia forced us to wander through East Africa for another year. Finally, those of us who were still alive were able to settle in a **refugee camp** in Kenya in 1992.

4   There, after so many **traumatic** experiences, I began to see that education was necessary for my survival. I began going to classes under trees on the dry riverbanks. I was determined to get educated at all costs. Neither dust nor hunger nor diseases would stop me. I went right through all the grades and graduated with a high school diploma.

5   In 2001, I moved to Boston, Massachusetts. So many things—the food, the weather, the customs—were different all at once. But within my first year in the United States, I passed my **GED** test, received my driver's license, enrolled at a community college, and was accepted into the University of Massachusetts Boston. I realized that education is one thing that no one can take away from me. Despite the challenges, this deep **commitment** to my own education helped me **prioritize** my time and continue.

6   The university was where I really learned how to learn. In Africa, doing well in school meant memorizing what was in the books and what the teachers said. On tests we had to be able to reproduce what we had memorized. At the University of Massachusetts, though, the required reading for each course was far too much to memorize. That meant I had to **concentrate** on the ideas expressed in a text.

7   How did I learn to do this? I think my professors helped most. They encouraged me to express my thoughts. They discussed ideas with me. They guided me when I did not understand and sent me back to my books to read again. They taught me to question, and questioning made me think more clearly.

8   Changing the way I learned was not easy. First, I spent many, many hours with tutors and talking with professors during office hours and after class. In addition, because my English was not adequate, I had to study much more

* **text:** *part of a book, article, or other reading*

than most of my American classmates. I did not take time out for fun. Since I read slowly, I had to spend more time reading. I had to read **texts** over and over until I understood.

9   Fortunately, I found that almost everyone at the university was responsive to a student like me who worked hard and was so eager to learn. I became comfortable with expressing my ideas and feelings. Through this process, I was able to heal my traumas and improve my English. At the end of four years of hard work, I graduated with a bachelor's degree **magna cum laude** in political science.

magna cum laude: *Latin for "with high honor"*

ABOUT the **AUTHOR**   After graduating from the University of Massachusetts Boston, Panther Alier worked as a research assistant with an environmental consulting firm. He then studied international sustainable development at Brandeis University. Panther Alier now works for a nonprofit organization that is strengthening local communities and local governments in his native homeland, Sudan.

Understanding the Reading

With a partner or a small group, discuss the following items.

1. Describe the place where Alier lived in his early childhood.

2. How did Alier spend the years of his life between ages ten and fifteen?

3. At what age did Alier probably first attend school? How did he feel about education at that time?

4. How was the University of Massachusetts different from the first school Alier attended? How do you think going there changed his life?

5. How did Alier learn a new way to learn at the university? Who helped him with this accomplishment?

6. What does Alier mean when he writes in paragraph 7, ". . . questioning made me think more clearly"? Do you think questioning is a necessary part of learning? Why or why not?

Vocabulary Building

Academic vocabulary and word families. As you write, you will discover that you need to build your **academic vocabulary** (longer, more formal words used in college textbooks and lectures). You can find academic words in the dictionary, and you will see that many of them belong to word families such as the ones below.

   * achieve (*v.*), achievement (*n.*)
   * respond (*v.*), response (*n.*), responsive (*adj.*)

In this book, words that belong to the **Academic Word List** (a list of the 570 most common word families found in college texts) are identified with a star (✳) symbol.

EXERCISE 1

A. *Use your dictionary to complete the word-family chart.*

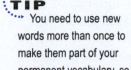

TIP
You need to use new words more than once to make them part of your permanent vocabulary, so try to use some of this new vocabulary in your writing assignment.

		Nouns	Verbs
1.		accomplishment	*accomplish*
2. ✳			commit
3. ✳		comprehension	
4. ✳			concentrate
5.		expression	
6.			improve
7.			manage
8.		memorization memory	
9. ✳			motivate
10.		organization	
11. ✳			prioritize

B. *In the following exercise, replace informal vocabulary with more formal, academic vocabulary. Change the underlined word or phrase to one of the words from the chart.*

　　　　　　organize my books
1. If I ~~put my books in order~~, I can find them whenever I need them.

2. After I took my listening-speaking class, I was able to <u>understand</u> people's conversations better.

3. How did you <u>learn</u> all those people's names?

4. Be sure you can <u>handle</u> the homework before you sign up for extra units.

5. I congratulated my friend on his <u>getting better</u> in English.

6. I wanted to <u>tell</u> my thoughts, but I couldn't find the right words.

7. I made a <u>very serious promise</u> to myself that I would do all my homework assignments.

8. When I read in the library, my <u>ability to pay attention</u> is greater.

9. I have several duties in my role as a student, but right now, getting good grades on my tests is my <u>number one responsibility</u>.

10. Passing a hard class is a big <u>achievement</u>.

11. Whether you are playing music, speaking a foreign language, or playing a sport, you need <u>the strong desire to reach your goal</u>.

C. *Answer the following questions on another piece of paper. Use at least one word from the chart in each answer. Underline all the words from the chart that you use.*

1. Where do you prefer to study? Why?

2. What is your number one academic goal?

3. What makes you want to reach that goal?

4. In your opinion, what are the keys to academic success?

■WRITING

Assignment

On pages 2–4, you read Panther Alier's article, which explains the steps he took to successfully graduate from a U.S. university. After you study pages 7–13, you will do the following assignment.

Write a one-paragraph composition about something you have accomplished. Tell about the steps you took to reach your goal.

Suggested Topics

- getting a passing grade in a difficult class
- getting accepted to a school or training program
- having a satisfactory job interview
- learning a new skill, such as driving or using a computer program
- finding a trusted friend
- making a lifestyle change (such as starting to cook for yourself, saving money for the future, being a neater person, or getting up earlier in the morning)

Understanding Your Assignment

First, let's look at the parts of a paragraph.

The paragraph. A **paragraph** is a group of sentences about a single topic. A paragraph has two parts:

- topic sentence
- supporting sentences

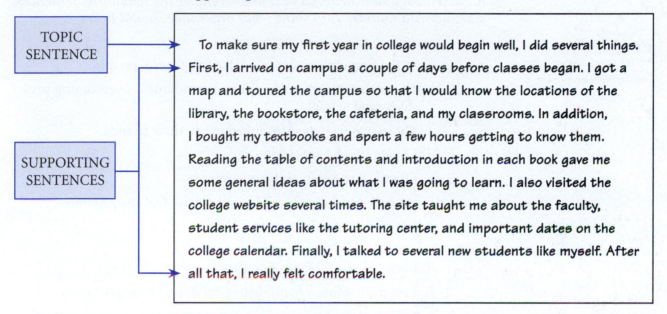

TOPIC SENTENCE

SUPPORTING SENTENCES

To make sure my first year in college would begin well, I did several things. First, I arrived on campus a couple of days before classes began. I got a map and toured the campus so that I would know the locations of the library, the bookstore, the cafeteria, and my classrooms. In addition, I bought my textbooks and spent a few hours getting to know them. Reading the table of contents and introduction in each book gave me some general ideas about what I was going to learn. I also visited the college website several times. The site taught me about the faculty, student services like the tutoring center, and important dates on the college calendar. Finally, I talked to several new students like myself. After all that, I really felt comfortable.

A paragraph usually begins with the **topic sentence**. The topic sentence gives the main idea of the paragraph, and it tells the reader what kind of information to look for in the rest of the sentences. It is usually the most general sentence in the paragraph.

The rest of the sentences in the paragraph are called the **supporting sentences**, or the **support**. The supporting sentences develop the idea or ideas in the topic sentence. In the process paragraph that you will write, the supporting sentences will tell the steps you took to reach your goal.

EXERCISE 2

*Read the following paragraph. Circle the topic sentence, and write **topic sentence** in the margin next to it. Then circle the supporting sentences, and write **supporting sentences** in the margin next to them.*

Learning to Stand Up Straighter

[1]In order to improve my posture (the way I hold my body), I followed a series of steps. [2]First, I started checking my posture two or three times a day by standing with my back against a wall. [3]When I do this, I make sure that my ears, shoulders, hips, knees, and ankles are in a straight line. [4]Second, I began doing exercises to strengthen my back every

morning and night. [5]For example, in one exercise I extend my arms out, hold them at shoulder height, and count to ten. [6]Finally, I took a yoga class. [7]Yoga not only strengthens my back and chest but also helps me relax, which is very important for good posture.

EXERCISE 3

*Each group of sentences is a scrambled process paragraph. Find the topic sentence, and write **TS** next to it. Number the remaining sentences, starting with number 2, to show what order they should be in.*

TIP
The topic sentence is the most general sentence in the paragraph.

1.

_____ a. At the first club meeting, I talked to several people.

_____ b. The accomplishment I am happiest about is overcoming my shyness at school.

_____ c. Those two friends introduced me to their friends.

_____ d. I made two friends in the club.

_____ e. I decided to join a club on campus.

_____ f. Now I know lots of people, and I don't feel shy anymore.

2.

_____ a. I kept a record of my "fun expenses."

_____ b. I set aside money for housing, food, and transportation.

_____ c. I reached my limit for "fun expenses."

_____ d. The remainder was "fun money" that I could spend on gifts, clothes, and entertainment.

_____ e. I stopped spending.

_____ f. In order to stay within my budget, I followed a series of steps.

3.

_____ a. I found the library website.

_____ b. I went into the stacks to get the book.

_____ c. I typed in the name of the book I was looking for.

_____ d. The computer told me that the book was on the shelf.

_____ e. Last week I learned how to find a book in my college library.

_____ f. I located the catalog on the website.

_____ g. I selected "Title."

_____ h. I wrote down the call number.

Notice the patterns used in the topic sentences in Exercise 3.

The accomplishment I am happiest about / I am proudest of is
_____ing _____.

In order to _____, I followed a series of steps.

Last week / Last year / Recently I _____.

NOTE
You will learn more
about topic sentences in
Chapter 2.

EXERCISE 4

Use all three sentence patterns to practice writing topic sentences about one of the following accomplishments or a different accomplishment of your choice. Use another piece of paper.

- learning to speak English
- enrolling in this class

The Writing Process

To get the best results when you write, break a writing assignment down into a series of steps and focus on one step at a time. The first step is **choosing a topic**. The second step is **brainstorming**, or gathering ideas. The third step is **organizing**, or putting your ideas in order. When you organize, you figure out what the main idea and supporting points are. The next step is writing the **first draft**. The final step is rewriting, or **revising**—which means rereading, checking, and improving your work to achieve a satisfactory **final draft**.

1. Choosing a topic
2. Brainstorming
3. Organizing
4. Writing the first draft
5. Revising

In each chapter in this book, you will see how one student completed the chapter assignment by following steps, from choosing a topic to writing the first draft. As you read through the following steps, you will see how Miriam, a student from Israel, prepared to write a paragraph about one of her accomplishments.

Complete steps 1 to 3, do Exercise 5 on page 13, and then write your first draft.

Miriam's Steps

STEP 1 *Choosing a topic.* Make a **list** of things you have accomplished. Put a check (✔) next to the accomplishment that you think you can explain clearly in three to five steps.

Miriam made the following list. She chose the last item to write about because it would be the easiest to explain in three to five steps.

I graduated from the cooking academy in Tel Aviv.
At my job at the hotel, I learned to cook meals for 200 people.
I learned how to use e-mail.
I got a visa to come to the United States.
I made a study plan for myself to get an associate's degree in dietetics technology.
On the first day of school, I learned the first names of all twenty of my classmates.
✔ I set up a study place in my apartment.

STEP 2 *Brainstorming.* For the accomplishment you have checked, list the steps that you followed to reach it. You should have three to five steps.

Steps:
I chose a quiet place.
I found a comfortable table and chair.
I cleaned the area and took away my CD player and other things.
I put my school supplies where I could reach them easily.
I pinned my weekly study schedule on the wall where I could see it from my chair.

STEP 3 ***Organizing.*** Look over your list of steps, and make sure that they are in the correct order and that you have not left anything out. At the top of the list, write a sentence that tells what you accomplished. This will be your topic sentence. You can use one of the patterns on page 9.

Miriam checked her list, and then she drafted a topic sentence:

> *To improve my study habits, I set up a study place in my apartment.*

STEP 4 ***Writing the first draft.*** After reading Miriam's first and final drafts and doing Exercise 5 on page 13, begin your first draft. Start with your topic sentence, and complete the paragraph with supporting sentences that tell each step you took to reach your goal.

Miriam's First Draft

Draft #1   Miriam Pappan

Creating a Place to Study

To improve my study habits, I set up a special place in my apartment. I chose a place with good light and the right temperature. I cleaned the area and removed my CD player and other stuff, and I put my school things there. I put my study schedule on the wall so that I can look at it when I am sitting at the desk. Having a nice place to study has made me want to do my homework and succeed in school.

As Miriam studied the rest of this chapter, she made some changes to her first draft. After finishing the chapter, she typed her final draft.

Miriam's Final Draft

Miriam Pappan
November 7, 2010

Creating a Place to Study

¹To improve my study habits, I set up a special place in my apartment. ²First, I chose a quiet place with good light and the right temperature. ³I can concentrate more easily in cool temperatures. ⁴Then I found a comfortable table and chair. ⁵Next, I cleaned the area of clutter and removed distractions like my CD player, photograph albums, and magazines. ⁶Then I arranged my textbooks, dictionary, paper, pens, and pencils where they are easy to reach. ⁷Finally, I pinned my weekly study schedule on the wall so that I can look at it when I am sitting at the desk. ⁸The study schedule shows the hours I attend class, the blocks of time when I study, and the times when I relax. ⁹It reminds me of my goals and responsibilities. ¹⁰Having a clean, functional place to study has made me more motivated to do my homework and succeed in school.

Paragraph form. Whenever you write a paragraph to hand in to your teacher, follow these guidelines.

- Put the title on the top line in the middle of your paper. Always use a capital letter for the first word in the title. Use capital letters for all other words except for articles, prepositions, and conjunctions, such as *and* and *but*.

An Important Accomplishment for Me

- Indent the first line of the paragraph five spaces.
- Use a capital letter for the first letter of the first word in each sentence.
- End each of your lines at about the same place on the right side of the page.
- If you are writing by hand, use lined paper with a margin line on the left. Except for the first line of your paragraph (which is indented), your writing should start next to the margin line.
- If you are typing, double-space and use a 12-point type size.

EXERCISE 5

Study Miriam's first and final drafts on pages 11 and 12. Then do the following to each draft.

1. Draw an arrow pointing to the five-space indentation at the beginning of each paragraph.

2. Look at the first letter in each word in the title. Put one line under the lowercase (small) letters and three lines under the capital letters. Look at this example.

How I Learned to Be an Effective Writer

3. Put three lines under all the capital letters in the paragraph, and discuss why they are capital with your teacher and classmates.

 For more on capital letters, see Appendix IB, page 241.

■ REVISING

The final step in the writing process is **revising**. Revising means changing your writing to make it better. Successful writers review, or reread, their writing often and check for ways to make it clearer and more interesting to readers. Producing an effective piece of writing takes time and attention.

As you study this section of the chapter, you will learn more about paragraphs and sentences. Keep your first draft on your desk in front of you as you go through the chapter. As you finish each exercise or section, look at your draft and try to use what you have learned to improve your writing. Follow the instructions in the Revision Checkpoint boxes to become skilled at reviewing and revising.

Composition Focus

As you read on page 7, a paragraph has two parts: the **topic sentence** and the **support**. Let's look again at these two parts in order to find ways to improve and develop your first draft.

Placement of the topic sentence. Although the topic sentence is usually the first sentence in a paragraph, it can come in other positions. For example, you may need to begin your paragraph by explaining the topic or by telling why you are writing about the topic. In this case, your topic sentence will follow the explanation.

EXERCISE 6

A. In the two paragraphs below, the topic sentence is not the first sentence. Find and underline the topic sentence in each paragraph.

1.

How I Learned to Manage Stress

¹A little stress is helpful—it makes us stay alert and put forth our best effort in school—but too much stress can make it hard to concentrate. ²I used to feel so much stress that I couldn't study well. ³However, I learned how to manage my stress by following a few simple steps. ⁴First, I made sure to get enough sleep, to eat a healthy diet, and to exercise regularly. ⁵Then I organized my schedule so that I had enough time for classes, homework, work, family responsibilities, and relaxation, and I stuck to that schedule consistently. ⁶Next, I tried to think positively. ⁷For example, I stopped thinking about a test as a chance to fail. ⁸Instead I saw it as a chance to show what I know. ⁹I also imagined myself after I had reached my goals. ¹⁰I visualized myself graduating from college and getting a wonderful job. ¹¹Finally, when I felt overly nervous, I talked to a friend or my college counselor. ¹²Usually just talking to someone reduced my stress.

2.

Getting Rid of a Bad Habit

¹Procrastination is the practice of putting off something you do not want to do. ²I used to be a procrastinator. ³I would not start my homework assignments, pay my bills, or even buy gas for my car until the very last minute. ⁴This caused some serious problems in my life. ⁵Therefore, my most important accomplishment was stopping my procrastination. ⁶To change my bad habit, first I made a list of my reasons for procrastinating. ⁷I discovered that I was procrastinating because studying wasn't my top priority. ⁸I changed my priorities, and now studying is number one on my list. ⁹Second, I decided to turn big assignments into little ones. ¹⁰That means instead of trying to read a whole chapter in one sitting, I read a section of a chapter every day until I'm done. ¹¹Then I go back and review—every day I cover larger portions of the chapter. ¹²Finally, I reward myself for achievements like finishing a chapter or doing well on a test by doing something I enjoy, such as going for a walk, calling a friend, or watching a TV show.

B. Tell your partner how you identified the topic sentence in these two paragraphs. Then discuss the purpose of the sentences before the topic sentence with your teacher and classmates.

The Topic Sentence
Check your paragraph. Make sure it has a clear topic sentence that presents the main idea and prepares the reader for what is to follow.

The support. As you recall, in a process paragraph, the supporting sentences describe and explain the series of steps you followed to reach your goal.

EXERCISE 7

With a partner, look at the two paragraphs in Exercise 6. How many supporting sentences does each paragraph have?

Supporting points. A **supporting point** is an *individual idea* or *separate step* in a process. The number of supporting points in a paragraph is not always the same as the number of supporting sentences. For example, paragraph 2 in Exercise 6 has seven supporting sentences (sentences 6 through 12) but only two supporting points. It is easy to see which sentences give a supporting point because the writer used *transitions* (*first* and *second*) to mark the supporting points.

Transitions. To help readers recognize the steps in your paragraph, you can use these transitions and time expressions.

Transitions That Signal a Time Sequence	Transitions That Signal Addition	Time Expressions That Can Be Used as Transitions

first, first of all
second
then, next, after that,
    afterward
finally
	also
	in addition
		one day
		two weeks later
		at the same time
		when I had finished
		    that step

EXERCISE 8

How many supporting points does paragraph 1 in Exercise 6 have? How did you identify them? Underline the transitions, and draw brackets [ ] around each supporting point.

Read the following two paragraphs and locate the supporting points.
Write the number of supporting points on the line below the paragraph.
Insert a transition before each supporting point.

1. **Finding the Right Hairstyle**

> ¹When I started college, I wanted to have a new look, so I decided to change
> *First,*
> my hairstyle. ²I collected newspaper and magazine pictures of women with hairstyles
> that appealed to me. ³I chose pictures showing round faces like mine. ⁴I thought
> about my budget and my schedule and decided I needed a simple, easy-care hairstyle.
> ⁵As a student, I would not have much time or money to spend on my hair. ⁶I took the
> photographs to a hairstylist, and she advised me to wear my hair shoulder length and to
> blow-dry it so that it looked a little higher on top. ⁷She said doing that would make my
> face look less round. ⁸She was right—my new look is the right one for me.

Number of supporting points: _____

2. **Taking Good Notes in College Lectures**

> ¹During the first couple of weeks in my history class, I had trouble taking notes.
> ²So I asked the teacher for advice. ³She made some suggestions, and I gradually became
> an efficient note taker. ⁴I always finished the reading before class. ⁵Being familiar with
> the material made it so much easier for me to pay attention during class. ⁶To take notes
> more quickly, I created a set of abbreviations like "hist." for *history* or *historical* and
> "WWII" for *World War II*, and I started using symbols like "+" for *and*, "b/c" for *because*,
> and "*" for *important*. ⁷I tried to listen as closely as possible every minute I was in class.
> ⁸When I noticed myself thinking about another class, my friends, or lunch, I pulled my
> attention back to the lecture immediately. ⁹I copied everything the teacher wrote on
> the board, and I learned how she identified key points. ¹⁰For example, when I heard the
> words *major* or *critical*, I made sure to write down what she was saying. ¹¹I reviewed my
> notes right away after class to see if everything made sense and to begin storing the new

information in my memory. [12]If I noticed that anything was unclear, I discussed it with my classmate before the next class or went to see the teacher during office hours.

Number of supporting points: _____

Supporting Points and Transitions
Read over your draft and decide how many supporting points it contains. Make sure that each supporting point is marked with a transition or time expression so that the reader can find it easily.

Additional explanation. Sometimes you will need to add explanations to your supporting points (steps). For example,
- you have to explain why a particular step was necessary.
- you have to explain how you completed a step.
- you have to explain what happens if a particular step is (or is not) done a certain way.
- you have to explain your vocabulary.
- you have to give examples.

EXERCISE 10

A. *Reread the paragraphs in Exercise 9, and put brackets [ ] around the explanations that follow some of the steps.*

B. *With your teacher and classmates, discuss why these explanations were necessary. Refer to the list of reasons for adding explanations above.*

EXERCISE 11

Read the paragraph and the sentences of explanation that follow it. Copy the paragraph on another piece of paper, and add the sentences of explanation to it in the appropriate places.

Paragraph

Looking Cool on the Dance Floor

[1]I have found that dancing is a great way to get out and meet people, but to enjoy the fun, I needed to become a better dancer. [2]To improve my style on the dance floor, I followed a series of steps. [3]First, I practiced dancing to different types of music at home so that I could find out what kinds of music suited me. [4]Second, I got some dancing clothes that gave me confidence and made me comfortable. [5]Then, the next time I was at a party, I watched the dancers for a while to find potential partners whose styles and abilities were like mine. [6]When I started dancing, I paid attention to my partner and everyone around us. [7]I had a great time, and I plan to go out dancing often.

Sentences of Explanation

- Everyone responds differently to rhythms. For some, salsa is best, and for others, soul music feels right. I found that rock and roll fits my inner rhythms.
- I chose colors and styles that look good on me, and I picked clothes that fit well and let me move comfortably.
- I found someone who was having fun but who did not have the fanciest steps on the floor.
- I tried to synchronize my steps with my partner's. I also made sure to avoid stepping on anyone's toes.

REVISION CHECKPOINT 3

Adding Explanations

Read over your draft, and decide if it needs any more explanation. If any of your supporting points need explanation, add it now.

Put brackets around all the explanations in your paragraph. Show the paragraph to a partner, and ask him or her if the explanations are clear.

Language Focus

Past tense irregular verbs. Regular English verbs end in *-ed* in the past tense (for example, work*ed*, start*ed*, laugh*ed*). However, many of the most common verbs in English are not regular (for example, *wrote, began, thought*). You need to memorize these irregular verbs.

EXERCISE 12

Read the following paragraph and underline all past tense verbs. Find and correct <u>four</u> mistakes with irregular past tense verbs.

Memorization

[1]Last semester I had to learn 750 scientific terms for my final in anatomy. [2]It was a monumental task, so I started weeks before the test and broke it down into various steps. [3]First, I organized the material. [4]I put the words in lists—parts of the leg, parts of the foot, parts of the digestive system. …[5]Then I looked for connections between the words on each list. [6]For example, the *aorta* is part of the heart, and the *clavicle* is connected to the breastbone and the shoulder blade. [7]For each list I made a study sheet showing these relationships. [8]I am a visual learner, so on each sheet I used various colored pens to write the terms. [9]I draw pictures of the body parts in corresponding colors. [10]Next, I began

testing myself by looking at a sheet and looking away, trying to remember what it said. [11]At first, I could only remember about a quarter of the words, but I didn't let that upset me. [12]I spend about forty-five minutes reviewing the lists and testing myself every day. [13]I usually drank a cup of lemon or peppermint tea while I studied because those two scents improve memory and attention. [14]I noticed that each day I remembered a little bit more. [15]Gradually I increased the amount of time between looking at the list and testing myself, and I find I could still recall nearly everything. [16]When the day of the final arrived, I feel fully ready to demonstrate what I knew.

 For a list of irregular verbs and additional practice, see Appendix IA, pages 238–240.

REVISION CHECKPOINT 4

Past Tense
Check your draft to see if you have used verb tenses correctly. Pay special attention to irregular verbs.

Combining sentences. When you write only simple sentences, you cannot show the connections between ideas very clearly. Look at these two sentences.

> I went to the computer lab. I practiced typing.

You can use the **coordinating conjunction** *and* to combine these sentences.

> I went to the computer lab, *and* I practiced typing.

You can also use the **subordinating conjunctions** *when* or *after* to combine the sentences.

> *When / After* I went to the computer lab, I practiced typing.

Coordinating and subordinating conjunctions show meaningful relationships between ideas. In the examples above, *and* shows **addition**—one idea is added to another—and *when* and *after* show **time sequence**—one action happens before another.

In process paragraphs, two kinds of relationships are very useful: **time sequence** and **purpose** (the reason for doing something).

You can show **time sequence** in the following ways.

COORDINATING CONJUNCTION

and + (transition)   I finished my paper, *and then* I handed it in.

SUBORDINATING CONJUNCTIONS

when / after   *When* I finished my paper, I handed it in.

                                        After I finished my paper, I handed it in.

The sentences with the subordinating conjunctions *when* and *after* can also be written this way.

I handed my paper in *when / after* I finished it.

EXERCISE 13

Combine the following pairs of sentences using **when** *or* **after**. *Write your sentences on another piece of paper.*

1. I decided to buy a laptop computer. I went online to do some research.

   When / After I decided to buy a laptop computer, I went online to do some research.

   OR

   I went online to do some research when / after I decided to buy a laptop computer.

   OR

   I decided to buy a laptop computer, and then I went online to do some research.

2. I became familiar with the different sizes and prices on several websites. I went to a store near my house to get some hands-on experience.

3. I tried a few desktop computers. I finished looking at the laptops.

4. I saw a desktop on sale at a very low price. I decided to get it instead of a laptop.

In process paragraphs, sometimes you need to explain the **purpose** of a step, or why a particular step was necessary. You can show purpose in the following way.

SUBORDINATING CONJUNCTION

so that   I bought a table *so that* I could set up my new computer.

                                        I bought a table *so that* I would not have to put my new computer on the floor.

Notice that the modal verbs *could* and *would* are used after *so that*. This is because *so that* expresses something you want to happen in the future.

EXERCISE 14

Combine the following pairs of sentences using the subordinating conjunction **so that.** *Be sure to put* **could** *or* **would** *in the clause following the conjunction. Write your sentences on another piece of paper.*

1. I typed my composition on the computer. I wanted it to look neat and professional.

   I typed my composition on the computer so that it would look neat and professional.

2. I added some explanations to my paragraph. I wanted all of my points to be clear.

3. I used the spell-checker. I wanted to fix my misspelled words.

4. I reviewed my work several times. I did not want to overlook any mistakes.

EXERCISE 15

Complete the following paragraphs with **and then, after, when,** *or* **so that.**

1. **Giving a Successful Speech**

   Public speaking was not something I looked forward to, but a fifteen-minute speech was required in my marketing class, so I prepared very carefully. First of all, I did a lot of research (a) __*so that*__ I would not bore the class by talking about things they already knew. Then I chose three related ideas to focus on. I did not want to cover more than three points. I thought the audience might lose interest if I included too many ideas. (b) _____ I had researched those three points and taken some notes, I timed myself talking about them. Next, I asked my roommate to help me pronounce some difficult words, (c) _____ I practiced the body of the speech several more times until I could deliver it smoothly in about ten minutes. Finally, I worked on the introduction and conclusion. For the introduction, I chose a funny story about my father because it was related to the main ideas of my talk. I practiced the whole speech ten or more times. (d) _____ I thought I knew the speech by heart, I added gestures and practiced using them as I talked. On the day of my speech, I was a little nervous at the beginning, but (e) _____ the audience laughed at the story, I relaxed. The rest of the speech went very well because I was so well prepared.

2.

How I Became More Fit

In order to build up my muscles, I started a weight-lifting program at home and began jogging. First, I bought some free weights. Second, I made an exercise schedule for myself (a) _____ I would work all parts of my body equally. For example, I work on my upper body on Mondays and my lower body on Tuesdays, (b) _____ on Wednesdays I go jogging. Third, at the beginning of my program, I used lighter weights, (c) _____ I changed to heavier weights later, (d) _____ I was ready. Finally, every week I add at least one new exercise (e) _____ I do not get bored. One day, (f) _____ I had been working out for a couple of months, my girlfriend said I looked "buff," (g) _____ I knew that I would continue weight lifting and jogging.

EXERCISE 16

On another piece of paper, write the groups of sentences in Exercise 3 on page 8 in correct order in paragraph form. Use at least one coordinating or subordinating conjunction to combine sentences in each paragraph. Add transitions. Underline the topic sentence in each paragraph.

 For information about simple, compound, and complex sentences, see Appendix IA, pages 200–201.

 **REVISION CHECKPOINT 5**

Sentence Combining
Check your draft to see if you can make the connections between your ideas clearer by using coordinating or subordinating conjunctions to combine sentences.

■ FINAL DRAFT

Before you write your final draft, look back at Miriam's first and final drafts.

EXERCISE 17

Reread Miriam's first and final drafts on pages 11–12. Then make a list of the differences between them. Discuss the list with your classmates and teacher.

1. Prepare a final draft of your own composition. Make sure that you have used capital letters at the beginnings of your sentences and periods at the end, and check your spelling.

2. Exchange papers with one or two classmates. Read each other's papers carefully. Turn to page 247 in Appendix II, and fill out the Peer Review Form.

3. Check your paper again and make any necessary corrections. Turn in your paper to your teacher.

■ CHAPTER REVIEW

Look back at what you have accomplished in Chapter 1. Check off (✓) what you have learned and what you have used while writing and revising your composition.

Chapter 1 Topics	Learned	Used
using academic vocabulary (page 4)		
brainstorming and organizing before writing (page 9)		
writing a topic sentence (page 9)		
using correct paragraph form (page 12)		
writing supporting sentences that describe the steps in a process (page 15)		
using transition signals to make the supporting points easy to recognize (page 15)		
adding explanations to make clear why a step was necessary, how a step was done, or what a word means (page 17)		
using past tense irregular verbs correctly (page 18)		
combining sentences to show sequence and purpose (pages 19–20)		

CHAPTER
TWO

Places and Events

Writing a Descriptive Paragraph

Picture a place you have been. Why does it stay in your memory? Do you remember certain sights, sounds, smells, tastes, and feelings? Memories of places and events are like movies. When we write about places and events we have experienced, we can bring these "movies" back to life for ourselves and share them with others. In this chapter you will write a paragraph describing a place you have visited or a public event in which you have participated.

This chapter will help you

- write a descriptive paragraph.
- use a cluster to prepare to write.
- write a topic sentence with a controlling idea.
- support your topic sentence with facts.
- add details with specific nouns, adjectives, and prepositional phrases.
- understand and use present and past time frames.

■ READING FOR WRITING

Before You Read

With a partner or small group, discuss the questions.

1. You are about to read an article about a national park in Bolivia. Have you visited any national parks in your own country or in other countries? If yes, what do you remember about your visit? Do you have memories of unusual sights, sounds, or smells? Is the park home to any unusual animals or plants?

2. When countries choose natural areas to create national parks, they often look for lands where *species* (kinds of animals and plants) that are *endangered* (in danger of disappearing) live. Do you know of any animal or plant species that is endangered? (If you know of one, but don't know its English name, draw a picture.)

Reading

A BIOLOGICAL TREASURE CHEST

Adapted from "Madidi National Park" by Robert Wallace

biodiversity: *the variety of plants and animals in a particular place*

explore: *to travel around an area in order to find out about it*

geography: *land forms*

habitat: *the environment in which a plant or animal lives*

1   Madidi National Park in Bolivia is quite simply one of the most amazing places on Earth: It is where the Andes Mountains meet the Amazon River basin. Madidi has more **biodiversity** than any other national park in the world, so it is appropriate to call it a global treasure. However, much of the park, which was created in 1995, has not been **explored**. In fact, about 70 percent of Madidi—which is the size of a small country—is unknown, although more than fifty scientists have explored the park over the last fifteen years.

2   Madidi's special **geography** is the reason for its biodiversity. Madidi includes almost the entire eastern side of the Andes, from 180 meters in the lowlands to just over 6,000 meters in the highlands. This large area contains fifteen major **habitat** types such as Andean grasslands, mountain forest, and lowland tropical forest. Madidi protects one of the largest sections of untouched tropical mountain forest left in the Tropical Andes, making the recipe for record-breaking biodiversity complete. For example, almost 300 species of mammals, including deer,

Jaguar

bears, jaguars, and giant otters, live there. Madidi is also home to at least 1,050 species of birds and almost 700 fish, amphibian, and reptile species. Finally, more than 12,000 species of plants are also found within this biological

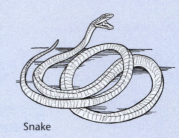

treasure chest. About 30 percent of these animal and plant species live only in the Tropical Andes.

3

Madidi's size is particularly important because many of its animal species need large areas of land to live in. However, the park's large size also makes it difficult to protect it from those who want to harvest the forests, explore the area for oil and gas, and build dams to collect water. Fortunately, the **indigenous** groups who live in small communities inside or just

Tree Frog

outside the park, including the Leco and Takana, have played a **key** role in defending the park against illegal logging and settlements.

4   In addition, the Wildlife **Conservation** Society, which works to save wild places around the world, has contributed to Madidi's protection. In order to understand how to protect the park, the society sent my wife and me to explore the area in 1999. We spent six months getting to know the different habitats and the local people. On this trip, we found woolly monkeys and white-tailed deer, which were not known to live in Bolivia. On later trips, I was lucky enough to discover a new species

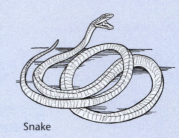

Snake

of titi monkey. Titi monkeys are **secretive**, eat fruits and leaves, and often hide in thick vegetation. Observing them is very difficult, except early in the morning when adult pairs make **territorial calls**: *luca luca luca luca luca.*

These calls are the origin of their local names, *lucachi* or *luca luca.*

5   My discovery of the new species of titi monkey gave Madidi an opportunity to raise money. The Wildlife Conservation Society, with the Bolivian government, raised $650,000 with an online **auction** to name the newly discovered monkey. The monkey is now known as *Callicebus aureipalatii.* This money has allowed Madidi to hire 50 percent more park guards than was possible before. The auction also helped people around the world learn about Madidi National Park. Madidi

Tiki monkey

National Park **deserves** to be recognized as a global treasure, and it will need global support to ensure the future protection of its amazing biodiversity.

indigenous: *describing people who have always lived where they are*

key: *very important*

conservation: *the protection of a natural resource from harm*

secretive: *preferring to hide*

territorial calls: *sounds that animals make to guard their area from other animals*

auction: *a sale in which the person who offers the highest amount of money buys the item*

deserve: *to be important or good enough for something to happen*

Understanding the Reading

With a partner or a small group, complete the activity, and discuss the following questions.

1. This article about Madidi National Park contains both facts and opinions. Mark each sentence **F** if it represents a fact or **O** if it represents an opinion.

   __O__ a. Madidi National Park in Bolivia is one of the most amazing places on Earth.

   _____ b. Madidi includes almost the entire eastern side of the Andes, from 180 meters in the lowlands to just over 6,000 meters in the highlands.

   _____ c. Madidi is also home to at least 1,050 species of birds and almost 700 fish, amphibian, and reptile species.

   _____ d. Madidi National Park deserves to be recognized as a global treasure.

   _____ e. Madidi contains fifteen major habitat types such as Andean grasslands, mountain forest, and lowland tropical forest.

2. Do you think facts are important in an article that describes a place like Madidi National Park? Why or why not?

3. Why does Madidi National Park have so much biodiversity? Do you think it is important to preserve this biodiversity?

4. Why did Robert Wallace go to Madidi National Park? What did he do there?

5. Would you be interested in going to Madidi National Park? Why or why not?

Vocabulary Building

Nouns and adjectives. You can recognize many *nouns* and *adjectives* by looking at their *suffixes* (word endings). Here are some common noun and adjective endings.

Words that belong to the Academic Word List are indicated with a star (✱) symbol.

For more on nouns and adjectives, see Appendix IA, page 185.

Adjective Suffixes	Adjectives
-al	architectural, biological, ✳financial, historical, national, regional, ✳traditional, tropical
-ant / -ent	brilliant, elegant, important, ✳significant, silent
-ful	beautiful, colorful, peaceful, skillful, wonderful
-ing	amazing, charming, exciting, fascinating, moving
-ive	active, attractive, impressive, massive
-ous	✳enormous, gorgeous, indigenous, marvelous, spacious

Noun Suffixes	Nouns
-ance / -ence	importance, performance, ✳significance, silence
-ity	activity, ✳complexity, ✳diversity, ✳variety
-ment	amazement, excitement, government, management
-ness	coolness, darkness, happiness, peacefulness
-tion / -ion	attraction, celebration, fascination, ✳region, tradition, ✳transportation

 For a more complete list of noun and adjective suffixes, see Appendix IA, page 237.

TIP

To find out which suffix to use for a word, check the dictionary. When you look up a word, be sure to notice its word family. That way you will increase your vocabulary and your knowledge of suffixes.

With a partner, read the following postcard. Underline the correct word form (noun or adjective) for each pair of words in parentheses. Then discuss whether each correct answer is a noun or an adjective. The first one has been done for you.

Hi Ruben,

I'm in the center of Basseterre, the capital of St. Kitts, an island in the Caribbean. I will try to give you a (1. <u>description</u>, descriptive) of this (2. fascination, fascinating) place. In the center of Basseterre there is a (3. tradition, traditional) square. It is a pleasant open (4. space, spacious) with a lot of (5. activity, active) both day and night. Across the square I can see the (6. elegance, elegant) green clock tower. Behind the clock tower is the National Museum, which has old photographs that explain the (7. history, historical) of the island. The (8. architecture, architectural) here is quite simple but very (9. attraction, attractive).

More later,
Sonia

Ruben Torres
58 N.W. Broadway
Portland, OR 97232
USA

EXERCISE 2

The following sentences have noun or adjective word-form errors. Find the error in each sentence and correct it. If necessary, use your dictionary to find the correct word form.

TIP
You need to use new words more than once to make them part of your permanent vocabulary, so try to use some of this new vocabulary in your writing assignment.

                diverse
1. Madidi National Park is home to ~~diversity~~ species of animals.

2. Many species of monkeys live in tropics forests.

3. Siberia is in the northernmost regional of Russia.

4. The Swiss Alps have beauty scenery.

5. Chichen Itza is a marvel place in southern Mexico.

6. The construction of the Great Wall of China was an importance achievement.

7. The focus of the New Year's parade was the color dragon.

8. Live Aid, a benefit rock concert to feed hungry people in Africa, was an amazement event.

9. Tourists in London can get lost because of the complex of the London subway system.

■WRITING

Assignment

After you study pages 30–39, you will do the following assignment.

Write a one-paragraph composition that describes two or three parts or qualities of a place or event.

You can write about a place or event that you experience often or that you have been to just once. If possible, go back to the place or event before you write to observe people, activities, colors, sounds, and smells. Take notes or draw a sketch of the scene. If you can't return to the place or event, you will need to depend on your memory, so you should choose something that you can remember very clearly.

Understanding Your Assignment

Description. Good description helps readers imagine what the writer is writing about even if they have never experienced it themselves. Good descriptive writing has

- specific information or vocabulary (words that name exact things).

    I served my guests *cinnamon rolls*, *scrambled eggs*, and *coffee*.

    A *1966 Volkswagen* and a *2009 Honda Accord* are parked in Sam's driveway.

- sensory information about how something looks, sounds, smells, feels, or tastes.

    I *smelled seaweed* and *heard the waves crashing on the rocks*.

    Police sirens and *flashing lights* approached from behind me.

EXERCISE 3

A. *Read the pairs of sentences, and place an **S** next to the more specific sentence in each pair. Then underline the words or phrases that make that sentence more specific.*

1. _____ There are a few pieces of furniture in the room.

   __S__ There is a <u>single bed</u>, a <u>tiny desk</u>, and a <u>simple chest with a mirror over it</u> in the <u>upstairs bedroom</u>.

2. _____ The band set up microphones and amplifiers before the rock concert.

   _____ The men set up some equipment before the show.

3. _____ The nine- and ten-year-olds play basketball and soccer between 3:00 and 4:00 P.M.

   _____ The children play games after school.

4. _____ An expert in energy systems gave a talk.

   _____ An engineer who specializes in wind energy systems gave a talk about windmills in the Netherlands.

B. *The following sentences do not have any specific vocabulary. Rewrite the sentences on another piece of paper, and make them more specific. Replace general words with more specific ones, and add specific information to each sentence. Underline the specific words and phrases in your sentences.*

1. Some people were in the park.

   Some <u>elderly men in overcoats</u> were <u>sitting on benches</u> in the <u>city park</u>.

2. I have things in my backpack.

3. The garden has flowers.

4. Food is available at the sporting event.

5. Several people brought things to the party.

C. *Now compare your answers with your classmates'. Notice how many different ways you can make a sentence specific.*

With a classmate, identify the kind of sensory information in each sentence by writing **sight**, **sound**, **smell**, **touch**, *or* **taste**. *Then underline the words or phrases that express that sensory information.*

1. The kitten's <u>fur</u> was <u>light and soft</u>, but the <u>bones under its skin</u> told me the poor creature was hungry. _____*touch*_____

2. Smokers had used the hotel room, and no one had opened the windows for a long time. _____

3. As a flock of crows passed overhead, they called to each other like family members who were happy to see each other after a long time apart. _____

4. The branches of the peach trees were turning reddish and the round buds were growing, so I expected lovely pink blossoms to appear in a few days. _____

5. The musicians tuned their violins as they waited for the signal to begin to play. _____

6. The tomato sauce was spicy and a little sweet. _____

7. On winter mornings, the cement floor felt like a block of ice, and the tap water made my nose, cheeks, and fingers numb. _____

8. The rainbow made a complete arc across the sky, reaching from the mountaintop to the valley. _____

9. My neighborhood has a vinegar factory, and the air is always heavy and sour. _____

EXERCISE 5

*Read the paragraph. With a classmate, underline words and phrases that give (1) specific vocabulary and (2) sensory information. In the margin next to each word or phrase you underline, write **specific information or the name of the sense (sight, sound, smell, touch, or taste)** that the sentence refers to.*

Camping in the Laurentian Mountains

sound

¹The campsite in the mountains north of Montreal that I went to last fall was tranquil and beautiful. ²The forest was silent except when <u>a bird sang</u>, <u>the wind blew</u>, or we stepped on the dry leaves on the ground. ³We didn't see any other campers. ⁴The beauty of the fall colors was breathtaking. ⁵The leaves of the maple, birch, and beech trees were brilliant red, orange, yellow, and purple. ⁶When the wind blew, colored leaves drifted through the air against the background of the bright blue sky. ⁷I felt so thankful for every day I spent in this peaceful, gorgeous spot.

Finding focus points for your paragraph. You need to choose two or three points related to your topic to write about in your paragraph.

- If you are writing about a place, you can focus on *areas*.

  place: <u>Madidi National Park</u>

      grasslands

      lowland tropical forest

      mountain forest

- If you are writing about an event, such as a public festival, you can focus on the most important or memorable *parts of the experience*.

  event: <u>Hong Kong's dragon boat festival</u>

      large, happy crowd of spectators

      colorful dragon boats

      the competition between the boaters

- For either a place or event, you can focus on *qualities*.

  place: <u>Tsukiji Fish Market in Tokyo</u>

      busy

      well organized

      economically important

  event: <u>the Egyptian spring festival</u>

      family oriented

      simple

      fun

The controlling idea of a topic sentence. The topic sentence of your descriptive paragraph will name the place or event you have chosen and the points you want to describe. It will have two parts.

- **The topic.** This first part names the *place or event* that you are writing about. It identifies the subject of your paragraph.
- **The controlling idea.** This second part names the *important points* of your topic. It is called the controlling idea because it determines what you will write about in the paragraph and how you will organize that information.

Here are three topic sentences for descriptive paragraphs. Notice that in each sentence the controlling idea is made of two or three supporting points.

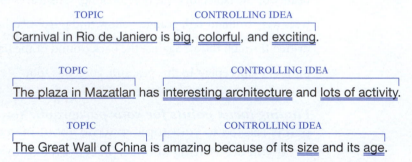

TOPIC		CONTROLLING IDEA

Carnival in Rio de Janiero is big, colorful, and exciting.

The plaza in Mazatlan has interesting architecture and lots of activity.

The Great Wall of China is amazing because of its size and its age.

EXERCISE 6

A. *Read each topic sentence. Put one line under the topic and two lines under each part of the controlling idea.*

1. Disney World has a great deal of variety and entertainment.

2. Jaipur, India, is beautiful and historical.

3. The farm where I grew up has mango trees and a 100-year-old house.

4. The singer's performance was skillful and moving.

5. The fashion show had elegant models, intriguing new clothing designs, and well-chosen music.

6. The beach at Maresias is wonderful because of its soft sand, beautiful sunsets, and good waves for surfing.

7. Puebla, Mexico, has interesting architecture and outgoing people.

8. The Russian Winter Festival in Moscow is fun because of its ice sculptures and snowmen.

B. *The controlling idea in each of the sentences in Exercise A consists of either nouns or adjectives. With your class, discuss whether the controlling idea in each sentence consists of nouns or adjectives, and mark each sentence (**n.**) or (**adj.**).*

Three sentence patterns are used in the topic sentences in Exercise 6. You may use any of these patterns in the topic sentence of your descriptive paragraph.

[topic] is / was (adj.) and (adj.)

[topic] has / had (n.) and (n.)

[topic] is important / wonderful / exciting / amazing because of (n.) and (n.)

EXERCISE 7

On another piece of paper, write sample topic sentences for the places and events listed on page 33. Use the patterns shown above.

The Writing Process

Clustering. In Chapter 1, you prepared to write by making lists. In this chapter, you will use another brainstorming technique, **clustering**.

A **cluster** is a drawing with words and phrases in it. When writers make a cluster, they think about the topic and then write down ideas as they come. The topic goes in the circle in the middle, and the main points of the topic go in the circles around it. Look at the sample cluster for the topic Puebla, Mexico.

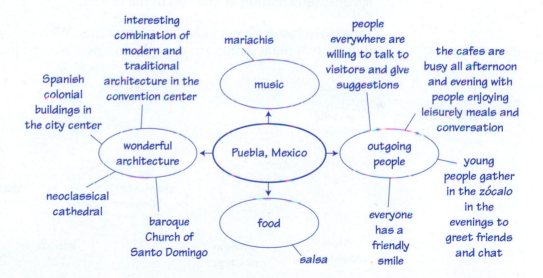

- How many main points about Puebla are shown in the cluster?
- What are the main points?
- How many of the main points have enough specific details to include in a paragraph?

Read through the steps. You will see how Rogerio, a student from Brazil, prepared to write a paragraph about a public event—a soccer game he had attended in his hometown of Salvador.

Complete steps 1 to 3 to prepare to write your first draft.

Rogerio's Steps

STEP 1 To choose a topic, make a **list** of places and a **list** of public events that you might like to write about. Circle the place or event that you think you can describe very well with specific vocabulary and sensory information.

Rogerio made the following lists of topics. He chose to write about the championship soccer game he had seen a few months ago because he still had very clear memories of it.

Places	Events
• café	• Carnival in Bahia
• college campus	• rock concert
• park	• state championship in Salvador

STEP 2 For the place or event you have circled, make a **cluster**. Add as much specific information as you can to the cluster.

Rogerio's cluster shows only two main points. With enough supporting details, two main points are enough to write a paragraph.

STEP 3 Number each part of your cluster to show what you will discuss first and what you will discuss second. Then draft your **topic sentence**. Make sure your topic sentence has a controlling idea that includes the numbered points in your cluster. (You may want to review the topic sentence patterns on page 34.)

As you see in the cluster, Rogerio put a number 1 above *the players*, which he planned to describe first, and a 2 above *the fans*, which he planned to describe second. Then he drafted the following topic sentence.

> The 2008 soccer championship for the state of Bahia, Brazil, had the best players and fans.

STEP 4 Use your cluster to write a first draft of your paragraph.

Rogerio's First Draft

A Soccer Game

[1]The 2008 soccer championship for the state of Bahia, Brazil, had the best players and fans. [2]The players of the two teams showed great skill. [3]They all played with great strategy and coordination. [4]They were graceful. [5]They seemed to dance with the ball as they ran with it and passed. [6]The fans showed their enthusiasm for the sport and their loyalty to their teams. [7]They came wearing fan club T-shirts, and they started playing samba drums and dancing before the game began. [8]When the players appeared on the field, the fans set off fireworks. [9]Every time a team scored, the fans sang songs of praise and held up banners. [10]In this match, the players showed the best Brazilian-style soccer, and the fans showed their passion for the game and for the players.

EXERCISE 8

Compare Rogerio's first-draft paragraph on page 37 with his cluster on page 36.

1. Put brackets [ ] around the topic sentence of the paragraph, and circle the two parts of the controlling idea. Are they the same as the two parts of Rogerio's cluster?

2. Compare the details in the paragraph with the details in the cluster. Put a check (✔) over each word in the paragraph that appears in the cluster. Did Rogerio add more specific information as he wrote the paragraph? Underline the specific information he added as he wrote his first draft.

As Rogerio worked through the rest of this chapter, he reviewed and revised his paragraph. Then he wrote the final version you see here.

Rogerio's Final Draft

A Marvelous Game

¹Last year's soccer championship for the state of Bahia, Brazil, was amazing because of the skillful players and the enthusiastic, loyal fans. ²The players of both teams, Vitória and Bahia, showed great skill. ³They played with marvelous offensive strategy and great team coordination. ⁴Their movements were graceful and unpredictable. ⁵They seemed to dance with the ball as they ran with it and passed. ⁶They shot for the goal when no one expected them to. ⁷In addition, the 96,000 fans in Fonte Nova Stadium showed their enthusiasm for the sport and their loyalty to their teams. ⁸They came wearing fan club T-shirts, and they started playing samba drums and dancing before the game began. ⁹When the players appeared on the field, the fans exploded fireworks that sent up puffs of smoke in the team colors. ¹⁰Every time a team scored, the fans sang songs of praise and held up massive banners that covered entire sections of the stadium. ¹¹In this match, the players showed the best Brazilian-style soccer, and the fans showed their passion for the game and for the players.

EXERCISE 9

With a partner, review Rogerio's final draft, and then do the activities and discuss the questions.

1. Compare the topic sentence of Rogerio's final draft with the topic sentence of his first draft. What parts of the topic sentence did Rogerio change? Circle the two parts of the controlling idea in Rogerio's final draft.

2. Compare the rest of Rogerio's final draft with his first draft. Find and underline the specific information that Rogerio added to his final draft.

3. Make a big circle around the part of the paragraph that corresponds to the first part of the controlling idea; make another big circle around the part of the paragraph that corresponds to the second part of the controlling idea. Underline the signal in the paragraph that marks the beginning of the second part.

4. What kinds of sensory information did Rogerio include? Identify the kinds by writing the words *sight, hearing, smell, touch,* or *taste* in the margin next to the lines where you find the sensory information.

■ REVISING

Now that you have completed your first draft, you are ready to begin revising. Revising is just as important as writing a first draft, and it can take about the same amount of time. The time you put into revising is well spent because, by revising, you make your paper better and improve your skills as a writer.

As you study this section of the chapter, you will learn more about paragraphs and sentences. After you finish each section, review your draft. Follow the instructions in the Revision Checkpoint boxes to check and revise your work.

Composition Focus

The controlling idea. You learned on page 34 that a controlling idea is the part of the topic sentence that tells the reader what the main points of your paragraph will be.

EXERCISE 10

The topic sentences of the paragraphs below do not have controlling ideas. Read each paragraph, and decide what aspects of the topic the paragraph discusses. Then revise the topic sentences to include a controlling idea. (See the patterns for topic sentences on page 35.) Write the revised topic sentence on the lines below each paragraph.

1.
Grand Central Terminal

[1]Grand Central Terminal is in New York City. [2]This station was designed in 1903 to be an elegant place for travelers. [3]When visitors look around, they see a white marble floor, 70-foot-high windows, and a 120-foot-tall ceiling with stars painted on it. [4]Large brass lamps hang from the ceiling. [5]In addition, the station is well planned. [6]If travelers have questions, they can easily find the information booth in the center of the great hall. [7]If they are hungry or they need to buy a hat or umbrella, they can find what they need in the many restaurants and shops that line the walkways leading to the trains. [8]Because the station was designed so that hundreds of trains can enter and leave underground, the city was able to build streets over the train tracks, and traffic was able to flow around the station. [9]Grand Central Terminal, now close to 100 years old, is an elegant public space and a well-designed transportation center.

_____

_____

2.
The Blue Mosque

[1]I visited the 400-year-old Blue Mosque in Istanbul, Turkey. [2]Its architecture makes a deep impression on visitors. [3]The prayer space is huge, and the ceiling is very high. [4]Tall columns support the ceiling, which consists of domes—one very large dome in the center with many smaller ones around it. [5]Tall, narrow, colored, glass windows bring in sunlight. [6]Also, the Blue Mosque is very peaceful. [7] Within the mosque, it is very quiet because carpets on the floor absorb the sound of footsteps, and visitors remain silent out of respect. [8]But the main reason for its calm, peaceful effect is its color. [9]The mosque gets its name from the 20,000 blue tiles that cover its high walls, columns, and domed ceiling. [10]The impressive design and serene color make the Blue Mosque a wonderful place to experience.

_____

_____

The Topic Sentence and Controlling Idea
Check your paragraph. Make sure the topic sentence has a clear controlling idea that presents the aspects of your topic that your paragraph discusses.

Transitions. In Chapter 1, you used transitions such as *first*, *second*, and *finally* to mark the steps in your process paragraph. (See page 15.) You can use these and other transitions in your descriptive paragraph to help the reader identify the supporting points.

Transitions for a Descriptive Paragraph	
First, + (*first supporting point*)	
Second, + (*second supporting point*)	Also / In addition, + (*second or third supporting point*)
Third / Finally, + (*third / last supporting point*)	

EXERCISE 11

Reread "Grand Central Terminal" and "The Blue Mosque" in Exercise 10, and underline the transitions.

EXERCISE 12

The paragraphs below do not have transitions to identify the supporting points. Read each paragraph, and insert one or more transitions from the chart.

1.   **The National Library of China**

[1]The National Library of China (NLC), which is located in Beijing, is important to China because of the services it provides to the nation and its size. [2]The NLC serves the Chinese parliament, scholars, and the general public. [3]It also trains librarians for the whole country and preserves ancient documents and rare books. [4]The library is vast. [5]It has over 20 million books and about 11 million periodicals, as well as over 5,000 electronic publications. [6]It contains over 30 reading rooms, which 8,000 to 13,000 people use every day.

2.   **The Two Bridges Coffeehouse**

[1]The Two Bridges Coffeehouse is known for its food, music, and clientele. [2]The food is delicious. [3]Soups, salads, and sandwiches are prepared daily from fresh

ingredients, and the pizzas are excellent. ⁴The café has international music. ⁵Sometimes one hears Italian songs, sometimes Arabic, and sometimes Spanish. ⁶All kinds of people visit the Two Bridges Coffeehouse. ⁷College students, actors, artists, and tourists sit side by side at small round tables sipping coffee or eating lunch. ⁸At midday, men and women from nearby offices and construction sites line up to buy pizza and sandwiches.

Transitions
Check your draft to see if adding transitions will make your paragraph easier to read. If you need transitions, add them now.

Specific support: Using facts. Readers prefer writing that contains specific factual information. If you can say exactly how big something is, how old it is, or how much it costs, readers will appreciate your effort to be accurate and will have more confidence in your writing. So when facts are available to you, use them.

EXERCISE 13

Reread "A Biological Treasure Chest" on page 25. Look for facts and specific details, and underline them. Then compare your underlining with a partner's.

EXERCISE 14

On another piece of paper, rewrite the following paragraph. Add the facts from this list:

> *age:* around 4,500 years old
> *number of blocks:* 2.5 million
> *weight of one block:* as much as 5,000 pounds
> *biggest gap between blocks:* 0.02 inches
> *length of each side:* 756 feet
> *weight of all the stone in the pyramid:* 5 million tons

The Great Pyramid of Giza

¹The Great Pyramid of Giza is amazing because of its age and its precise construction. ²First, there is no exact record of the pyramid's age, but most experts agree that it is very old. ³Second, its construction is so precise that builders with today's technology cannot copy it. ⁴Each of the Great Pyramid's many stone blocks weighs a lot. ⁵The blocks fit together so well that the biggest gap between them is tiny. ⁶The four sides

are exactly the same length, and they point precisely to the north, south, east, and west. [7]No one knows how the Egyptian builders of the third millennium B.C.E. moved so many tons of stone to build such a perfect monument.

Specific support: Using questions to fill information gaps. Readers expect each part of a paragraph, or each supporting point, to be complete. If one part of a paragraph is not fully developed, readers can become confused or may feel that their questions are unanswered. An **information gap** is a part of a paragraph that does not meet readers' needs because it does not contain enough specific information. Read the sample paragraph, which has information gaps, and look at the questions on the sides, which address those gaps.

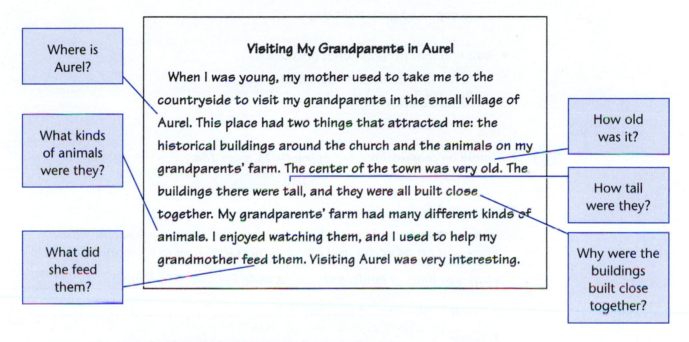

Where is Aurel?	**Visiting My Grandparents in Aurel**
What kinds of animals were they?	When I was young, my mother used to take me to the countryside to visit my grandparents in the small village of Aurel. This place had two things that attracted me: the historical buildings around the church and the animals on my grandparents' farm. The center of the town was very old. The buildings there were tall, and they were all built close together. My grandparents' farm had many different kinds of animals. I enjoyed watching them, and I used to help my grandmother feed them. Visiting Aurel was very interesting.
What did she feed them?	

How old was it?

How tall were they?

Why were the buildings built close together?

EXERCISE 15

A. *Exchange draft paragraphs with a classmate. Read your classmate's draft, and look for information gaps. If you find any, use a pencil to write questions in the margins of your partner's paper. Be sure to write clearly so that your partner can read your questions.*

B. *Review your partner's questions. Add questions of your own if you can.*

REVISION CHECKPOINT 3

Specific Support
After studying the questions, revise your paper. Add as many facts and specific details as possible.

Language Focus

Expanding the noun phrase. As you add details and make your writing more specific, your sentences will become more *sophisticated*—that is, more advanced or mature. In particular, you will improve the *noun phrases* (nouns and the words that modify them) in your sentences.

- You will use more specific nouns.

    a building → a house

    an animal → a dog

- You will add descriptive adjectives.

    a house → a *tiny pink* house

    a dog → a *big old black* dog

- You will add prepositional phrases.

    a tiny pink house *on a busy street*

    a big old black dog *with sad eyes*

 For more on prepositions, see Appendix IA, page 186.

EXERCISE 16

With a partner, replace each general noun with a more specific noun. Then add an adjective and a prepositional phrase to each specific noun.

1. street   *boulevard*   *a wide boulevard in Miami*

2. event   _____   _____

3. place   _____   _____

4. person   _____   _____

5. machine   _____   _____

6. tree   _____   _____

7. performance   _____   _____

You can also use noun modifiers to modify nouns. In the examples below, the nouns *city*, *government*, and *school* are used as noun modifiers. Just like adjectives, noun modifiers are placed before the noun they modify.

- a *city* street
- a *government* building
- a *school* event

EXERCISE 17

The noun modifiers in the following paragraph are in bold type. Draw an arrow from each noun modifier to the noun it modifies.

A Pleasant Room

¹My sister's living room is attractive and comfortable. ²There is a large tropical plant in a shiny **brass** planter near the window. ³Sunlight comes through the white **lace** curtains and shines on the red **tile** floor. ⁴The walls are light blue. ⁵**Family** photographs hang on one wall, and **landscape** paintings are on the others. ⁶A **glass** vase of fresh flowers sits on a central table. ⁷The other good quality the room has is comfort. ⁸The **leather** sofa with soft **silk** pillows is a relaxing place to read or to talk. ⁹The **wood** stove makes the room cozy in winter, and a big **chestnut** tree outside keeps it cool in summer.

To learn more about noun modifiers, see Appendix IA, page 226.

> ### Using Specific Vocabulary
> Review your writing, and ask yourself how specific your vocabulary is. Check to see if you can use more specific nouns and add adjectives, prepositional phrases, and noun modifiers to your paragraph to make your writing more specific.

Time frames. There are three basic time frames, or ways to talk about time: *past*, *present*, and *future*. For this writing assignment, you probably used either the past or the present time frame.

- *Past time frame.* Use the past time frame in a paragraph about an event that you experienced at a specific time in the past or about a place you visited at a specific season or time. For those topics, all or most of the verbs will be in the simple past tense. For example, "I *went* to the museum and *learned* about the city's history." Two examples of paragraphs in the past time frame are "Camping in the Laurentian Mountains" on page 33 and "A Marvelous Game" on page 38.

  A paragraph written in the past time frame needs at least one *time signal* (adverb or adverb phrase), such as *yesterday* or *two years ago*. The first time signal usually comes in the first sentence of the paragraph. Can you find the time signals in "Camping in the Laurentian Mountains" and "A Marvelous Game"?

- *Present time frame.* Use the present time frame in a paragraph about a place as it usually appears or about an event that occurs regularly (every year, every month, etc.). For those topics, all or most of the verbs will be in the simple present tense. For example, "The New Year's parade *starts* when the drummer *begins* to pound the drum." Two examples of paragraphs in the present time frame are "The National Library of China" on page 41 and "The Two Bridges Coffeehouse" on pages 41–42.

A paragraph written in the present time frame has a *time signal,* such as *every day* or *once a year,* if it describes an activity or event that repeats regularly. Can you find the two time signals in "The Two Bridges Coffeehouse"?

EXERCISE 18

A. Read the following paragraphs and underline all the verbs. Notice what tense each paragraph is written in. Then, on another piece of paper, rewrite each paragraph changing the past-tense paragraph to present tense and the present-tense paragraph to past tense. The first sentence of each paragraph has been done for you. Notice the change in the time signals.

1. ### *Noche de Rabanos* (Night of Radishes)

¹On December 23 every year, the *zócalo*, or central plaza, in Oaxaca, Mexico, is the site of a beautiful traditional event. ²In the middle of the day, people begin arriving and setting up tables. ³They carefully unpack charming figures that they carve from a large root vegetable—the radish, or *rabano*. ⁴The figures represent holy people such as the mother of Jesus, historical figures such as Emiliano Zapata, and literary personalities such as Don Quijote. ⁵The artists set their figures in little scenes made of painted cardboard, dried corn husks, and dried flowers. ⁶In the late afternoon, the Christmas lights come on, and townspeople and tourists gather to view the display. ⁷Later in the evening, the makers of the best carvings receive prizes. ⁸Finally, everyone enjoys the fireworks which go off over the city.

First sentence: <u>*On December 23 last year, the zócalo, or central plaza, in Oaxaca, Mexico, was the site of a beautiful traditional event.*</u>

2. ### New Year's Eve at Times Square

¹Last year's New Year's Eve event at Times Square in New York City <u>thrilled</u> spectators with its entertainment and its beautiful glass ball. ²Starting at 7:00 P.M., the crowd of nearly 1 million people enjoyed the performances of singers and rock bands and watched well-known TV personalities on a giant screen as they counted down the hours and minutes to midnight. ³At a minute before 12:00, the mayor of New York led the crowd in the final countdown as a six-foot cut-glass ball slowly descended from

the top of a tall building down into the square. ⁴Thousands of colored lights within the transparent ball created changing patterns during the minute the ball took to come down. ⁵When the ball reached Times Square, spectators shouted "Happy New Year" to one another, and over a ton of confetti came down from the tops of the surrounding buildings.

First sentence: <u>Each year's New Year's Eve event at Times Square in New York City thrills spectators with its entertainment and its beautiful glass ball.</u>

B. *With a partner, read each paragraph aloud two ways. One of you should read the past-tense version, and the other should read the present-tense version. Be sure to pronounce all the verb endings correctly. If you remember to pronounce the sound of the final -s or -ed, you will remember to write it.*

Changing the time frame. Usually, if a paragraph is written in the present time frame, all the verbs in that paragraph will be in a present tense. Similarly, if a paragraph is written in the past time frame, all the verbs in that paragraph will be in a past tense. Yet sometimes a writer needs to add some information that requires a different time frame. In that case, the writer uses time signals such as *now, today, years ago*, or *in the past* to mark the change of time frame.

EXERCISE 19

Reread "The Great Pyramid of Giza" on pages 42–43, and underline all the verbs in the paragraph.

1. What is the time frame of most of this paragraph? _____
2. What phrase signals a change in time frame in the last sentence?

   _____

EXERCISE 20

A. *Read the following paragraph, and underline all the verbs. Identify the time frame of the first and second sentences, and write **present** or **past** next to them. Put brackets [ ] around the sentences in which the time frame changes. Circle the time signals that mark the two places where the time frame changes.*

Tet Trung, the Children's Festival

¹In Vietnam, there <u>is</u> a harvest festival during the full moon in August. ²This festival, *Tet Trung*, is famous for its demonstration of love for children and its beautiful procession of lights. ³Originally, people celebrated Tet Trung after the harvest. ⁴Parents

had been busy with the harvest and wanted to remind their children that they still loved them, so they created a celebration for them. [5]To prepare for Tet Trung, parents made lanterns with candles inside for the children. [6]Today most parents buy the lanterns, which are in the shapes of stars, the moon, fish, and butterflies. [7]The main part of the festival is the procession, which takes place at dawn or dusk. [8]Children walk through the streets singing and holding their bright lanterns while the older people watch them. [9]Everyone enjoys sweet moon cakes made of lotus seeds, beans, and a round egg yolk, which represents the full moon.

B. With your teacher and classmates, discuss the reason that the writer needed to change the time frame in this paragraph.

 For more on verb tenses and time frames, see Appendix IA, pages 214–217.

 **Time Frames**
Check the verb tenses in your draft to see if you used the present or the past time frame consistently. Make sure that if you changed time frames, you had a reason for doing so and you clearly marked each shift with a time signal.

■ FINAL DRAFT

1. Before you write your final draft, look over your paragraph one last time to decide if you want to make any further changes.

2. Prepare a final draft of your composition. Make sure that you have used capital letters at the beginnings of your sentences and periods at the end, and check your spelling.

3. Exchange papers with one or two classmates. Read each other's papers carefully. Turn to page 248 in Appendix II, and fill out the Peer Review Form.

4. Check your paper again and make any necessary corrections. Then turn in your paper to your teacher.

■ CHAPTER REVIEW

Look back at what you have accomplished in Chapter 2. Check off (✔) what you have learned and what you have used while writing and revising your composition.

Chapter 2 Topics	Learned	Used
recognizing noun and adjective suffixes (page 28)		
finding focus points for a paragraph (page 33)		
writing a topic sentence with a controlling idea (page 34)		
using a cluster to brainstorm and plan before writing (page 35)		
using transitions within a paragraph to introduce supporting points (page 41)		
using facts as specific support and using questions to fill information gaps (page 42)		
using specific nouns and adjectives and prepositional phrases (page 44)		
using the present and past time frames and time signals (pages 45–46)		

CHAPTER THREE

Pastimes and Entertainment

Writing a Reason Paragraph

Fun is important. Some people like being with their friends and family, some like developing a skill or talent such as playing the piano, and others enjoy competitive games such as tennis or chess. What do you do for fun? Which of the activities shown in the pictures look interesting to you? In this chapter you will write a reason paragraph explaining why a pastime or kind of entertainment is enjoyable for you or for people in general.

This chapter will help you

- write a paragraph that gives reasons.
- use an outline to prepare to write.
- write a brief definition to explain a word or idea to your readers.
- develop your paragraph with details, examples, and explanations.
- use gerunds and infinitives to talk about activities and pastimes.
- use cause-and-effect signals.

■ READING FOR WRITING

Before You Read

In this chapter, you will read about various leisure activities, or things people do to relax in their free time. Think about the questions, and then discuss your answers with a small group.

1. People choose different leisure activities because their personalities and talents are different. Look at the diagram. How would you describe yourself? What do you prefer to do in your free time?

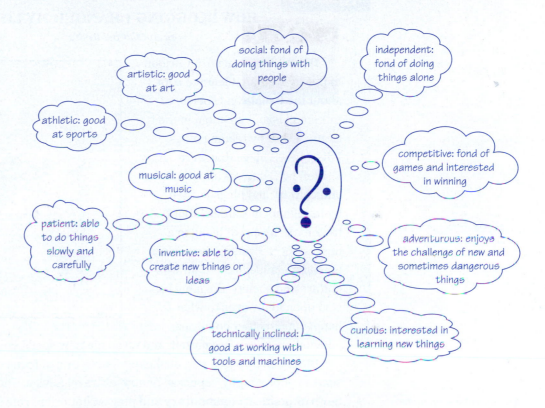

artistic: good at art

social: fond of doing things with people

independent: fond of doing things alone

athletic: good at sports

musical: good at music

competitive: fond of games and interested in winning

patient: able to do things slowly and carefully

inventive: able to create new things or ideas

adventurous: enjoys the challenge of new and sometimes dangerous things

technically inclined: good at working with tools and machines

curious: interested in learning new things

With your group, share information about your personality traits and talents as well as your favorite pastimes. Look at these examples.

I'm curious. I like to go to museums.

I'm adventurous. I enjoy hiking and climbing mountains.

I'm musical. I like to play the keyboard.

2. Some people like to read and write *blogs* online. A blog is a journal in which a person writes information, ideas, opinions, or questions about any topic that interests him or her. When other Internet users read someone's blog, they sometimes write back to share information or express their own ideas.

Why do you think people spend their free time reading, responding to, and writing blogs? Does blogging interest you as a pastime? Why or why not?

Reading

HOW BLOGGING CHANGED MY LIFE
by Ayesha Saldanha

1   When I first came from Britain to live in Bahrain, I learned a lot about the people and society of this small island kingdom in the Arabian Gulf by reading blogs. I discovered blogs that were written by Bahrainis about politics and culture, and blogs written by foreigners in Bahrain about their experiences of living in a new country. Reading these blogs helped me understand Bahrain's culture and society. Blogging has also opened my eyes to what is happening in other countries, allowed me to express myself, and given me new social contacts.

2   Blogs can be about personal experiences or can focus on specific topics such as photography, Japanese poetry, or travel advice. They also provide news or political **commentary** and play an important role in countries where the **mainstream media** are not free to discuss everything. Blogs can give readers a clearer idea of what is happening than official newspapers or TV channels can, even in countries where the media are free. That is why bloggers are sometimes called **citizen journalists**. Blogs can reach hundreds, even thousands, of readers, who can write back with comments or questions. I enjoy reading blogs from different countries in the Middle East. Even though I may never get the chance to visit the countries, I have learned a lot about them from their bloggers.

✳**commentary:** *opinions or an opinion essay*

✳**mainstream media:** *television, newspapers, and magazines that most people accept*

citizen: *a member of a society or country*

✳**journalist:** *a writer or reporter for newspapers, magazines, or television*

3   Why did I start writing my own blog? I felt that as a British woman living in Bahrain, my experiences would be interesting for people outside Bahrain so that they could learn about life in an Arab country. However, I soon found that most of the people reading my blog were actually Bahrainis and that they enjoyed the new **perspective** I gave them of their own society and culture. They left comments on my **posts** and shared their ideas and experiences. Sometimes they corrected me if they felt I had misunderstood something about their culture.

4   These days I write about many things: a book I have read, a poem I like, an experience I have had, my ideas on a recent event in Bahrain or abroad. I enjoy blogging because it gives me opportunities to exchange ideas with people all around the world. An unexpected reward of blogging is that I have made a lot of friends, both in Bahrain and in other countries. In Bahrain a group of bloggers meets regularly, and some of my closest friends now are people I know through blogging.

5   To find blogs you might be interested in, you can use any one of a range of blog search engines, such as blogsearch.google.com or technorati. com. Technorati says it **tracks** more than 130 million blogs. An interesting way to discover blogs from different parts of the world is to explore globalvoicesonline.org, a website which gives a voice to people and places that are not well represented in the Western media. If you want to start a blog, you can choose from many blogging platforms such as Blogger or Wordpress, which are available on the Internet in many languages.

6   I expect to continue blogging so that I can keep in touch with my new friends and continue sharing my ideas. It is not an exaggeration to say that blogging is a very important part of my life.

ABOUT the **AUTHOR**   Ayesha Saldanha was born in India and grew up in Britain, but she now lives in Bahrain. She works as a translator and English teacher. She calls her blog *Bint Battuta*, after the fourteenth-century Moroccan scholar Ibn Battuta, whose travels took him through western and northern Africa, Europe, China, and India.

Understanding the Reading

With a partner or a small group, discuss the questions and complete the activities.

1. Why did Saldanha begin to read blogs after she moved to Bahrain? Why did she start to write her own blog? Why will she continue?

2. How do blogs benefit people around the world?

3. Compare writing a blog and writing in a traditional diary or journal. Write down as many similarities and differences as you can think of.

Similarities	Differences
Both blogs and diary entries can be about the events of daily life.	

4. Did reading "How Blogging Changed My Life" make you interested in reading or writing blogs? If yes, what topics would you like to read or write about? Review Saldanha's article, and underline the details that convinced you that reading and writing blogs might be interesting.

Vocabulary Building

Verbs and -ing adjectives that describe feelings. When we talk or write about pastimes and activities, our reactions and feelings are important. Certain verbs and *-ing* adjectives describe people's reactions to and feelings about their experiences. Here is an example.

VERB   ADJECTIVE

Blogs *interest* me. = Blogs are *interesting*.

Words that belong to the Academic Word List are identified with a star (✹) symbol.

EXERCISE 1

A. *The chart shows some common verbs and adjectives that describe feelings. Use your dictionary to complete the chart, and then discuss the differences in meaning with your classmates and teacher.*

	Verbs	-ing Adjectives
1.	*amuse*	amusing
2.		annoying
3.	appeal (to)*	
4.	bore	
5.		engaging
6.	entertain	
7.		exciting
8.	inspire	
9.		interesting
10.✹	relax	
11.		stimulating
12.	uplift	

*Note that the verb *appeal* is followed by the preposition *to*: Mystery stories appeal *to me*.

The other verbs in the chart are followed by direct objects: Mystery stories relax *me*.

B. *Complete the statements using both the adjective and the verb. After you finish writing, compare sentences with a partner or small group.*

1. Chess is ___*stimulating*___. ___*Chess stimulates me.*___

2. Card games are _____

_____

3. Televised sports are _____

_____

4. TV sitcoms (short comedy shows that usually appear weekly on U.S. TV) are _____

_____

5. TV soap operas (dramatic programs that have continuing stories) are _____

_____

6. Classical music is _____

_____

7. Rock music is _____

_____

Vocabulary that describes entertainment. As you read through this chapter, you will read about various pastimes and kinds of entertainment. Some of the vocabulary you will see appears in the chart in Exercise 2.

EXERCISE 2

A. Use your dictionary to complete the word-family chart.

	Nouns	Verbs	Adjectives
1.	*competition*		competitive
2.			entertaining
3.	escapism		
4.		exercise	
5.		inform	
6.			inspiring
7.	socializing		
8.✱	suspense		

TIP

Each event has several possible answers. For example, ice-skating can be social or competitive. It is also physical exercise.

B. With a small group, look at the list of weekend events from a newspaper and match each event with a word family in the chart. Then, using **all** the vocabulary in the word family, explain why some people will choose that event.

Some people will go to the ice-skating rink because they like *exercise*. (noun)

Some people will go to the dance lesson because they like *to exercise*. (verb)

Some people will go to the science lecture because they like to get *information*. (noun)

Some people will go to the science lecture because it is *informative*. (adjective)

Some people will go to the science lecture because it will *inform* them about the universe. (verb)

WEEKEND EVENTS	
Saturday	**Sunday**
a. __4__ **Ice-skating rink.** Open 10–5, Central Park.	**Foot race,** cash prizes, open to everyone. 9 A.M., corner of Brant and Harper Streets. e. _____
b. __5__ **Science Lecture:** "The Origin of the Universe." 11 A.M., Science Hall.	**Gospel Singers' Performance:** songs of faith. Noon, Community Center. f. _____
c. _____ **Dance Lesson:** Learn to samba. 2 P.M., Community Center.	**Movie:** *The Lord of the Rings*, a classic fantasy film. 2 P.M., Community Center. g. _____
d. _____ **Movie:** *Psycho*, a psychological thriller. 4 P.M., Downtown Theater.	**Stand-up Comedy Show:** Joe Stoddard and Michelle Woods. 8 P.M., Creekside Room. h. _____

C. On another piece of paper, write answers to the following questions. Use complete sentences, and use as many members of a word family as you can.

1. Which weekend event would you choose, and why?

2. Which events would your family members (parents, brothers, sisters, etc.) choose, and why?

3. If you are a parent now or you plan to have children in the future, what kinds of entertainment would you like to introduce your children to? Why?

■ WRITING

Assignment

After you study pages 58–69, you will do the following assignment.

Write a one-paragraph composition that gives two or three reasons that either you or people in general enjoy a specific pastime or kind of entertainment.

Understanding Your Assignment

Choosing a topic. You can choose either a general topic or a specific topic for this assignment. Here are some examples.

General Topics		Specific Topics
playing team sports	⟶	playing second baseman with my softball team, the Rangers
listening to popular music	⟶	listening to the rock band Radiohead sing their song "Karma Police"
watching movies	⟶	watching the 2006 movie *The Golden Door*

For either a general topic or a specific topic, you will need to provide (1) reasons to support your preference and (2) specific details, examples, or explanations to support each reason.

The topic sentence. The topic sentence of your paragraph can focus on your own experiences, other people's experiences, or the activity itself.

I enjoy playing team sports for three reasons.

People enjoy playing team sports for three reasons.

Playing team sports is enjoyable for three reasons.

Finding supporting reasons for your paragraph. Your paragraph will list two or three supporting reasons. The reasons can focus on (1) you or people in general or (2) the activity itself.

TOPIC SENTENCE: I like Agatha Christie's detective stories for two reasons.

REASON 1: I enjoy trying to solve mysteries.
REASON 2: Christie's detective stories are very well written.

TOPIC SENTENCE: Internet shopping is a popular pastime for two reasons.

REASON 1: People like learning about new products and comparing product features.

REASON 2: Internet shopping takes only a few minutes, but going to stores can take hours.

A reason must show a clear logical connection to the topic sentence and must answer the question *Why?* In the following examples, the statements following the topic sentences do not provide clear reasons.

TOPIC SENTENCE: I enjoyed the movie *Casablanca*.

NOT A REASON: It cost $1,039,000 to make *Casablanca* in 1942.
(This doesn't explain why the writer liked the movie.)

TOPIC SENTENCE: Stamp collecting is a popular hobby.

NOT A CLEAR REASON: New stamps are issued every day.
(This sentence isn't a clear reason, but if the writer adds *so collectors have many to choose from*, the logic will be clear.)

EXERCISE 3

A. *Read the four topic sentences. Each topic sentence is followed by three statements. Not all the statements are reasons that support the topic sentence. Identify the supporting reasons by writing **SR** next to them.*

1. Many people enjoy playing video games for several reasons.

    _SR_ a. Some video games allow players to pretend to be fantasy characters.

    _____ b. Games and game consoles are expensive.

    _SR_ c. People can play with their friends and share information about winning strategies.

2. Table tennis, or ping-pong, is a good sport.

_____ a. Table tennis is not hard to learn. Beginners can play right away and have fun.

_____ b. Advanced players find table tennis challenging. They can learn special ways to hit the ball, such as spins and chops.

_____ c. A decent paddle costs only about $40.

3. Many people enjoy reading magazines for entertainment.

_____ a. Most magazines have a lot of advertising.

_____ b. Magazines provide information about popular culture.

_____ c. Magazines usually have appealing photographs.

4. Rock music is popular.

_____ a. The beat of rock music is stimulating, so it gives listeners energy to dance or to exercise.

_____ b. The lyrics, or words, of rock songs are usually about love— a topic that is hard to talk about in daily life.

_____ c. Rock music has spread U.S. and British culture around the world.

B. *Now discuss your answers with your classmates.*

The Writing Process

Outlining. So far you have learned that writers use brainstorming to collect ideas before they write. After brainstorming, writers need to organize their ideas. **Outlining** is an efficient way to organize ideas. An outline shows the structure of a paragraph in three levels.

TOPIC SENTENCE (first level)

    I. FIRST SUPPORTING POINT (second level)

        A. Detail, Example, OR Explanation (third level)

        B. Detail, Example, OR Explanation (third level)

    II. SECOND SUPPORTING POINT (second level)

        A. Detail, Example, OR Explanation (third level)

        B. Detail, Example, OR Explanation (third level)

    III. THIRD SUPPORTING POINT (second level)

        A. Detail, Example, OR Explanation (third level)

        B. Detail, Example, OR Explanation (third level)

Here is an example of (1) a list of a writer's brainstormed ideas, (2) the writer's outline, and (3) the paragraph the writer produced from that outline.

1. BRAINSTORMING NOTES

Watching Finding Nemo

- *great movie*
- *love, friendship, loyalty*
- *This animated movie is not about people but about fish who are like people.*
- *The faces of the fish are fun to watch; they look and talk like people.*
- *Marlin is loyal to Nemo when a scuba diver catches Nemo.*
- *Marlin is loyal to Dory when a fisherman catches her.*
- *This movie is really funny.*
- *I liked the time when other fish asked Marlin to tell a joke because he is a clown fish.*
- *Marlin didn't know how to tell a joke—he told a joke so badly that it was funny.*

2. OUTLINE

One way I like to relax is by watching a movie. <u>Finding Nemo</u> is my favorite movie for three reasons.

  I. It has the universal themes of love, family, and friendship.

    A. It is about a humanlike fish named Marlin, his son Nemo, and his friend Dory.

    B. Through difficult and dangerous situations, Marlin shows great loyalty to Nemo, and Dory is very loyal to Marlin.

  II. The animated characters in this movie are charming.

    A. The faces of Marlin, Nemo, and Dory show distinct personalities.

  III. There is lots of humor in this movie.

    A. Because Marlin is a clown fish, the other fish expect him to be funny, so they ask him to tell a joke. But Marlin doesn't know how to tell a joke, and he tells it so badly that it is funny.

3. PARAGRAPH

Watching *Finding Nemo*

[1]One way I like to relax is by watching a movie. [2]*Finding Nemo* is my favorite movie for three reasons. [3]First, it has the universal themes of love, family, and friendship. [4]It is about humanlike fish who show great loyalty to one another. [5]The central character is a fish named Marlin whose only son, Nemo, is caught by a scuba diver. [6]Marlin then starts on a very difficult journey to find Nemo, and on his way he meets another fish, Dory, who becomes his friend. [7]Marlin and Dory encounter many dangerous situations, such as the time when Dory is caught in a fisherman's net, but by helping one another, they survive. [8]Second, the animated characters in this movie are charming. [9]Their faces show distinct personalities. [10]Nemo is an innocent youngster, Marlin is an overly concerned parent, and Dory, who is forgetful, often looks confused. [11]Finally, there is lots of humor in this movie. [12]Because Marlin is a clown fish, other fish expect him to be funny. [13]However, Marlin is much too serious, and when he tries to tell a funny story, he ruins it—in a way that is very entertaining.

EXERCISE 4

Read the two paragraphs, and complete the outline that follows each one. The first level of an outline (the topic sentence) must be a complete sentence. The second and third levels do not have to be complete sentences.

1.   **Listening to Classical Music**

¹People listen to classical music for two reasons. ²First, classical music lets listeners explore a full range of human emotions. ³For example, Berlioz's *Symphonie Fantastique* expresses the power of romantic love, Haydn's "Joke" quartet expresses playfulness, and Tchaikovsky's Symphony no. 6 (the *Pathétique*) expresses deep sadness. ⁴Second, listening to classical music stimulates the brain and can make listeners think better. ⁵In fact, research has shown that listening to Mozart's music before a test can help students get higher scores.

People listen to classical music for two reasons.
_____

   I. Classical music lets listeners explore a full range of human emotions.

      A. Berlioz expresses romantic love.

      B. Haydn expresses playfulness.

      C. Tchaikovsky expresses deep sadness.

  II. _____

      A. Research has shown that Mozart's music can help students get higher test scores.

2.   **TV Talk Shows**

¹TV talk shows are popular for three reasons. ²First, the talk-show hosts have warm, appealing personalities. ³For example, the show *Oprah* has been on the air for over twenty years largely because of the charm and skill of its host, Oprah Winfrey. ⁴Second, viewers like seeing real people talk about real-life problems. ⁵Most of the people who appear on TV are rich or powerful, but talk shows invite as their guests ordinary people with real-world problems. ⁶For example, one day viewers meet Mrs. Smith, who suffers with a mean boss, and another day it is Mr. Roy, who doesn't get along with his family members, or Ms. Rossi, who can't stop smoking. ⁷Finally, talk shows educate viewers about social and personal problems and how to solve them. ⁸Most talk shows have experts, such as psychologists, who advise the audience about how to lose weight, get

along with their spouses, or solve other common problems. [9]Viewers come away from the show feeling good because they see that problems can be solved.

_____

    I. Talk-show hosts have warm, appealing personalities.

        A. _____

           _____

   II. Talk-show guests are ordinary people with real-life problems.

        A. _____

           _____

        B. _____

           _____

        C. _____

           _____

  III. _____

        A. Experts advise the audience about how to lose weight.

        B. Experts advise the audience about how to get along with their spouses.

        C. a positive feeling

Defining the topic. Topics such as movies, television, and team sports are familiar to most readers, so they don't need to be explained. Other topics are less familiar and should be defined or explained. If your topic is not widely known, you should include a definition sentence before your topic sentence. Here is an example.

> *Sudoku* is a number puzzle that requires finding the correct numbers to complete a number grid. I enjoy *sudoku* for three reasons.

Sometimes you may need more than one sentence to explain your topic.

> Graphic novels are fictional stories that have pictures on every page. They are similar to children's comic books, but they are for adults. I enjoy graphic novels for two reasons.

EXERCISE 5

The following paragraphs need definitions. Read each paragraph, and identify the topic. On the lines above the paragraph, write a definition. (You may need to use a dictionary.)

1.   **Aerobic Exercise**

_____

_____

    People enjoy aerobic exercise, such as running or jogging, for two reasons. First, in order to exercise, people get out of their houses and on the streets. There, they can see other people and observe changes in the natural world. Simply saying hello to the same neighbor every morning and noticing the flowers and trees help connect people to their surroundings, and therefore they feel happier. Second, aerobic exercise releases the hormones in the body that make a person feel better. These hormones, called serotonin and endorphin, are the reason for the positive change in mood known as "runners' high."

2.   **Choral Singing**

_____

_____

    I enjoy choral singing for three reasons. First, in a chorus, I feel I am a part of something larger than myself. My voice is just a tiny part of the great and varied sound that thirty-five singers make together. Second, choral singing has improved my musical knowledge and skills. I have grown to understand and appreciate classical, jazz, and gospel music. I have also learned to read musical notes, to remain focused on the conductor and other singers, and to notice and correct my own mistakes. Third, as part of a local chorus, I contribute to my community. My chorus participates in school and community events and gives free concerts in hospitals.

As you read through the steps, you will see how Salina, a student from Greece, prepared to write a paragraph about a favorite pastime.

Complete steps 1 to 3, and then write your first draft.

Salina's Steps

STEP 1

To select a topic, make a **chart** like the one below showing pastimes or kinds of entertainment that you enjoy. **List** as many reasons as you can for each one. Then put a check (✔) next to the pastime or kind of entertainment that you think has the best supporting reasons. Good supporting reasons are clear, and they are ideas you can develop with an explanation or an example.

Salina made the following chart. She put a check next to "taking dance classes" because she had more to say about that topic than the others.

Pastime or Kind of Entertainment	Reason 1	Reason 2	Reason 3
watching DVDs with my boyfriend	share our opinions and feelings about the movies	escape from our daily routine	
pop singer Katie Melua	great voice	good songs	
watching the program <u>Everybody Loves Raymond</u> on TV	funny		
✔ taking dance classes	make friends	music and traditions of other cultures	make my mind and body work together

STEP 2

If your topic needs to be defined, write a **definition**. Then draft a **topic sentence** for your paragraph. Remember that you can begin the topic sentence with *I*, with *people*, or with the name of the activity. (See page 58.)

Salina's topic did not require a definition, so she began by drafting the topic sentence three ways, as you see here. Then she put a check (✔) next to the one she wanted to use.

✔   *I enjoy taking dance classes for three reasons.*

     People enjoy taking dance classes for three reasons.

     Taking dance classes is enjoyable for three reasons.

STEP 3

Make an **outline**. The first level is the topic sentence you drafted, and the second level includes the reasons you listed in your chart. To develop the third level of your outline, write explanations or examples.

Salina made the following outline.

I enjoy taking dance classes for three reasons.

     I. Dance classes are great places to make friends.

        A. met my best friend Karina

        B. also met my boyfriend Phillip

     II. Dance classes introduce me to the music and traditions of other cultures.

        A. Russian music

        B. African music

        C. Latin music

     III. Dancing makes my mind, body, and spirit work together.

        A. helps me in all parts of my life

Using your outline, write a first draft of your paragraph.

Salina's First Draft

Dance Classes

¹*I enjoy taking all kinds of dance classes for three reasons.*
²*Dance classes are great places to make friends.* ³*I met my
best friend Karina and my boyfriend in dance classes.* ⁴*Dance
classes introduce me to the music and traditions of other
cultures.* ⁵*I have danced to Russian, African, and Latin music.*
⁶*Dancing makes my mind and body work together.* ⁷*This helps
me in all parts of my life.*

As she studied the rest of the chapter, Salina made changes to her draft. Then she completed the draft you see here.

Salina's Final Draft

Why I Love Dance Classes

¹I enjoy taking all kinds of dance classes for three reasons. ²First, dance classes are great places to make friends because people who dance usually have healthy lifestyles and positive attitudes. ³I met my best friend Karina in a modern dance class and my boyfriend Phillip in a jitterbug class. ⁴Second, dance classes introduce me to the music and traditions of other cultures. ⁵For example, doing ballet steps to Prokofiev gives me a taste of Russian culture, doing African dance steps to the drummer Mamady Keita gives me the feeling of African culture, and learning to salsa dance to Gloria Estefan's music brings Latin culture into my life. ⁶Finally, dancing makes my mind and body work together. ⁷This gives me self-confidence, which helps me do better at work, in school, and in my personal life.

With a partner, review Salina's first and final drafts. Then do the activities and discuss the questions.

1. Compare Salina's final draft with her first draft. Find and underline the specific information that Salina added to her final draft. What is the effect of these added details?

2. Can you find three levels in Salina's final draft? Above the sentences in the paragraph, write a **T** for the topic sentence, a Roman numeral (**I, II,** or **III**) to indicate the major supporting points on the second level, or a plus sign (**+**) to indicate the third level.

3. Look at the sentences on the third level. Which ones give examples? Which one gives an explanation? Write *example* or *explanation* in the margin next to each of those sentences.

4. Circle the transitions Salina added to her final draft. Why did she add them?

■ REVISING

As you study this section of the chapter, you will learn more about paragraphs and sentences. As you finish each exercise or section, review your draft and use what you have learned to improve your writing. Follow the instructions in the Revision Checkpoint boxes to improve your work.

Composition Focus

Paragraph structure. Academic writing in English always begins with general ideas and moves toward specific supporting information. As you saw when you worked with outlines in Exercise 4 on page 63, in a three-level paragraph, the first level is the most general, and the third is the most specific. The second level is more specific than the first and more general than the third.

You have learned that an outline is helpful when you are organizing your ideas and planning a three-level paragraph. You can also use an outline when you are revising. Checking your paragraph and the outline you made before writing, or making a new outline based on your draft, can help you evaluate whether your paragraph has a complete three-level structure.

EXERCISE 7

A. *The draft paragraphs below are incomplete. Read the paragraphs. On another piece of paper, make an outline of each one to find out what is missing. After you know what part of the outline is missing, add a sentence of your own to make it complete.*

TIP

If you find a definition at the beginning of a paragraph, do not put it in the paragraph outline. Also, do not include transitions in an outline. The purpose of an outline is to show only the structure of main and supporting ideas.

1.
Bike Riding

¹Riding bicycles is a popular pastime for three reasons. ²First, bike riders get physically stronger. ³Riding a bicycle strengthens the muscles in the legs and torso and improves the efficiency of the heart and lungs. ⁴Therefore, bike riders are able to do other physical activities like climbing steps without tiring or getting out of breath. ⁵I have taken many bike rides on country roads near where I live. ⁶I have seen how strawberries, onions, and tomatoes grow in the fields and have noticed what kinds of birds and other wildlife live in the trees and bushes. ⁷Third, bike riders can join clubs and meet new friends. ⁸Like many cities, mine has a bike club. ⁹I joined the Westlake Bicycle Club two years ago, and I met my good friends Miki and Tom there.

2.
Top 40 Radio

¹"Top 40 Radio" refers to almost any radio station that plays contemporary popular music. ²Stations are called Top 40 because they play the forty most popular songs at the time. ³I like listening to Top 40 radio for three reasons. ⁴First, I enjoy knowing what is popular now. ⁵The radio station I listen to has a countdown every weekend, and I always tune in near the end so that I know which songs are in the top ten. ⁶That way I can discuss the music scene with my friends. ⁷Second, I like to learn facts about my favorite pop stars from the announcers. ⁸For example, I learned that Madonna was listed in the *Guinness Book of Records* as the world's most successful musician and that Rihanna was born in Barbados. ⁹I know the words of dozens of songs, and some of my favorite ones to sing along with are "Rain," "When I Fall in Love," and "Girlfriend."

B. *Compare your outlines with a partner's. Discuss what was missing from each paragraph and what you did to solve the problems.*

In the two draft paragraphs in Exercise 7, sentences from the second level are missing. You probably noticed the missing transitions and a gap in each paragraph where the sentences did not fit together well. The second level in a paragraph is important because it serves as a bridge between the general topic sentence and the specific examples.

REVISION CHECKPOINT 1

Paragraph Structure
Review your paragraph and the outline you made before you wrote it, and revise them if you need to. Make sure that your paragraph has a second level that names all the supporting points. Check to make sure that your second level is more specific than the first and more general than the third. If you need help with the second level, ask your teacher for advice.

Developing the third level: Sensory details, examples, and explanations.
A paragraph with a clear topic sentence and logical supporting reasons has
a solid beginning, but to be complete, it needs a well-developed third level.
Only a paragraph with a fully developed third level is convincing to readers.
Here are three ways you can develop the third level of your paragraph.

1. You can add **details about your sensory experiences**. You have five
   senses—sight, hearing, smell, touch, and taste. Sensory information—
   information about what you see, hear, smell, feel, and taste—makes your
   writing much more interesting for readers because it stimulates their
   imaginations. Sensory information also helps readers understand and
   remember your supporting points.

   > SUPPORTING POINT: Roller-skating makes a person feel good.

   > SENSORY INFORMATION: Skaters enjoy the sense of moving rhythmically, traveling
   > smoothly over the pavement, and feeling the cool breeze
   > on their faces.

2. An **example** is a description of a specific thing, person, situation, or
   event that supports a general idea. You can use examples to help readers
   understand and remember your supporting points.

   > SUPPORTING POINT: Roller-skating is social.

   > EXAMPLE: I skate once a week with a friend and, as we skate, we talk about
   > what is going on in our lives.

3. **Explanations** do various things: They can tell what something means,
   how or why something happens, or what the results of something are. You
   can use explanations to add to readers' understanding of general ideas.

   > SUPPORTING POINT: Roller-skating increases physical fitness.

   > EXPLANATION: Roller-skating burns fat and builds muscle. It also improves the
   > efficiency of the heart and lungs.

EXERCISE 8

A. *Read the following two paragraphs, and put brackets around all the
   sentences on the third level. In the margin next to each bracketed
   sentence, write* **sensory information**, **example**, *or* **explanation**.

1.   **Mumbai Restaurant**

   ¹Mumbai Restaurant is a great place to go for three reasons. ²First, it is a beautiful

   place. [³As diners enter through the front door, they see a large gold statue and lush green

   plants. ⁴Then, as they walk to their table on the soft red carpets, they appreciate the fresh

   flowers that decorate the room.] ⁵Second, the menu has various delicious choices. ⁶There

   are spicy meat curries, a fragrant bread called *naan*, and cool and slightly sour yoghurt

*sensory
information*

raita. [7]Third, Mumbai Restaurant provides continuous entertainment to diners. [8]There is a big movie screen on the wall which shows scenes from films made in Mumbai, India. [9]Actors and actresses on the screen sing and dance in rich, colorful costumes. [10]I think an evening at Mumbai Restaurant is a great way to experience Indian culture.

2.   **Comedies**

[1]Comedies are movies or TV programs that contain humor. [2]People choose comedies over serious programs for two reasons. [3]First, laughing relaxes the body. [4]When we laugh, we take deep breaths and release them in bursts. [5]This causes our whole body to shake. [6]Our heart rate increases, and endorphins are released in our blood. [7]Endorphins are also released in the blood during physical exercise, so laughter produces an effect in the body similar to the effect of mild exercise. [8]Second, and probably more important, humor has a psychological effect. [9]A joke asks people to let go of their normal serious point of view and be silly, just as they were when they were children. [10]For example, in the animated movie *Ratatouille*, a rat controls the actions of a chef in a restaurant. [11]The movie invites us to accept this ridiculous idea, and once we do, we find the bossy rat and the hopelessly inexperienced chef funny. [12]Escaping from seriousness into pure, childlike silliness releases tension and lightens our mood.

B. *Compare your markings of the paragraphs with a partner's, and then discuss them with your teacher and classmates. For any sentences that you marked* **sensory** **information**, *discuss which senses are involved— sight, hearing, smell, touch, or taste.*

REVISION CHECKPOINT 2

Developing the Third Level
Review your paragraph, and put brackets around all the sentences in the third level. Notice whether you used sensory information, examples, or explanation. Look for ways to improve the development of the third level by adding more sensory information, examples, or explanations. Revise the third level of your paragraph now.

Transitions. Supporting points in a reason paragraph are usually introduced with *first, second,* and *third* or *finally*. These transitions are particularly helpful to readers when a writer has put quite a bit of information in the third level and the paragraph is long.

You can also use transitions to signal examples in your paragraph. There are two kinds of transitions that introduce examples.

For Examples That Are Complete Sentences	For Examples That Are Parts of Sentences
For example, For instance,	like such as

EXERCISE 9

In the following two paragraphs, fill in the blanks with appropriate transitions to introduce examples.

1.   **Police or Detective Dramas on TV**

People find watching TV police or detective dramas satisfying for three reasons. For one thing, these programs give people an escape from their daily worries. The problems caused by serious crime make the problems of daily life, (a) ___*such as*___ catching a cold or losing a key, seem unimportant. Second, viewers get a sense of security from these shows because they always know who the good and bad guys are. They also know that, in the end, the good guys (the police) are going to succeed. (b) _____, *CSI* (*Crime Scene Investigation*) is about Las Vegas investigators who always succeed in solving unusual crimes. Third, these programs provide suspense to viewers because of the way they are written. While watching, viewers have many questions (c) _____ *Who committed the crime? Did he or she act alone?* and *When did the crime occur?* The feeling of suspense usually continues until the very last minute of the show, when all the questions are answered and the bad guys are locked up. At that point, viewers experience a pleasant release of tension.

2.   **Reading Novels**

I enjoy reading novels for three reasons. First, novels take me to faraway places and distant times. (a) _____, *The Call of the Wild* took me to Alaska in the 1890s, *Gate of the Sun* took me to Palestine in 1995, and *A Wrinkle in Time* took me on a journey through space and time. Second, reading novels helps me understand human nature. When a novel describes a character's behavior, tells me the character's spoken words, and gives me clues about his or her inner thoughts, I begin to understand people in the real world better and even to understand myself more thoroughly. Novels (b) _____ *A Separate Peace*, *The Old Man and the Sea*, and *The Catcher in the Rye* have especially interesting and memorable characters. Third, I enjoy reading novels because their plots, or storylines, interest me and sometimes surprise me. (c) _____, the novel *Holes* is unusual because it has two plots—one set in the present and one set in the past—and I discovered a number of surprising connections between them. I also enjoy books with surprise endings because they often lead me to see things in a new way. (d) _____, at the end of *The Big Wave*, the people return to the place where their village had been destroyed by a tidal wave. This shows me that maintaining their tradition can be more important to people than living in safety. Because of their unique settings, characters, and plots, novels stimulate my imagination and enrich my life.

REVISION CHECKPOINT 3

Transitions to Introduce Supporting Points and Examples
Review your paragraph and look at the supporting points and the examples. Make sure that you marked them with transitions. If you need transitions, add them now.

Language Focus

Gerunds. Gerunds are *-ing* verb forms, such as *watching* and *playing*, that are used as nouns in sentences. A gerund can be in any position that a noun can be in a sentence: subject, object of the verb, and object of a preposition.

SUBJECT

Swimming is fun.

OBJECT OF
THE VERB

I enjoy *swimming*.

OBJECT OF A
PREPOSITION

I took a class in *swimming*.

A gerund can be followed by a noun object or a prepositional phrase. A gerund together with the words following it is called a gerund phrase.

Reading magazines is enjoyable.

Maintaining their tradition can be more important to people than living in safety.

Reading in the café is pleasant.

Escaping from seriousness into pure, childlike silliness releases tension and lightens our mood.

Exercise 10

*Complete the paragraph using gerunds. Under each gerund, write **S** if it is the subject of a sentence, **O** if it is the object of a verb, and **OP** if it is the object of a preposition.*

Entertaining Friends

I love (1) ____*entertaining*____ (entertain) friends for two reasons. First,
        (*O*   )

I like (2) _____ (cook). I love (3) _____ (look) at
      (   )   (   )

recipes and (4) _____ (plan) meals. I enjoy (5) _____
      (   )   (   )

(combine) ingredients and (6) _____ (see) a beautiful, delicious meal
      (   )

develop before my eyes. Afterward, (7) _____ (serve) the food I have
      (   )

prepared to appreciative friends makes me very satisfied. Second, I enjoy conversation.

I have noticed that guests at my parties usually start (8) _____ (talk)
      (   )

in a conventional way ("How have you been?" "The weather's been great, hasn't it?").

But (9) _____ (predict) where the conversation will go after that is
      (   )

impossible. For example, someone may begin (10) _____ (talk) about
      (   )

her pet, another might remember (11) _____ (have) a pet as a child,
      (   )

another will share a childhood memory about (12) _____ (visit) a zoo,
      (   )

and yet another person will talk about (13) _____ (see) a scene in a
      (   )

movie about an animal. Every conversation develops differently as the participants take

turns sharing their experiences and ideas.

Verb + Gerund. Verb + Infinitive. Some verbs are followed by gerunds, and others are followed by infinitives (*to* + the base form of a verb). A few verbs are followed by both gerunds and infinitives.

> I enjoy cooking. (*enjoy* + gerund)
>
> I learned to cook. (*learn* + infinitive)
>
> I like cooking. / I like to cook. (*like* + gerund or infinitive)

 For lists of verbs followed by gerunds, by infinitives, and by both, see Appendix IA, page 223.

EXERCISE 11

Fill in the blanks in the paragraph with gerunds or infinitives.

Playing Mahjong

Mahjong is a traditional Chinese game that families often play during the New Year's celebration. It is similar to the card game rummy, but mahjong is played with little tiles. I enjoy (1) __*playing*__ (play) mahjong at the Chinese New Year for two reasons. First, the tiles are pretty, and they feel and sound good, too. They have pictures of bamboo, flowers, Chinese characters, or symbols on one side. Before we start (2) _____ (play), we need (3) _____ (turn) all 144 tiles over and (4) _____ (mix) them. I like (5) _____ (touch) the cool, smooth tiles and (6) _____ (hear) the click-clack sound they make as we shuffle them. Second, getting ready and playing the game brings the whole family together, so there is always plenty of conversation and laughter. Even my little nephew, who is six, joins the game. He manages (7) _____ (remember) and (8) _____ (follow) the rules and loves (9) _____ (be) with the "big people." After we play for a while, some members of my family tend (10) _____ (tease) each other. For example, if my brother is having bad luck, I might suggest (11) _____ (get) up and (12) _____ (walk) around his chair, and if that fails (13) _____ (change) his luck, I tell him (14) _____ (wash) his hands. He doesn't really mind (15) _____ (be) teased this way. It's all part of the fun. I think mahjong remains popular with Chinese families like mine because it is an appealing game and it gives us a way to spend the holiday together.

When *and* joins two infinitives, you can omit *to* from the second infinitive.

> We need to turn all 144 tiles over and (to) mix them.

> I like to touch the cool, smooth tiles and (to) hear the click-clack sound.

REVISION CHECKPOINT 4

Gerunds and Infinitives
Reread your draft, and underline the gerunds and infinitives you used. If you are unsure about the use of gerunds or infinitives in your paper, write a question to your teacher in the margin.

Coordinating conjunctions. Using conjunctions to combine sentences is a way to make your writing both more sophisticated (advanced and mature) and easier to understand. Conjunctions help readers understand what you write because they show relationships between your ideas.

In Chapter 1, you used the coordinating conjunction *and* to connect independent clauses (see page 19). Other common coordinating conjunctions are *so* and *but*. Each of these coordinating conjunctions has a different meaning.

When a coordinating conjunction joins two clauses, a comma comes at the end of the first clause, just before the coordinating conjunction.

Coordinating Conjunctions	Examples	Meaning
and	Rowing is good exercise, **and** it offers a way to be on the water.	signals addition of a similar idea
so	Rowers use their strength to move a boat, **so** they develop strong muscles.	introduces a result
but	Two rowers are more powerful than one, **but** they must work together.	introduces a contrasting idea

EXERCISE 12

A. *Fill in the blanks with the coordinating conjunction* **and**, **so**, *or* **but**. *In some sentences, two choices are possible.*

Golf—a Rewarding Sport

People like playing golf for several reasons. First, golf courses are pleasant places to enjoy the outdoors. Golf courses are beautiful, (1) ___*and*___ looking at the green grass and blue sky is relaxing. Golf is a good-weather game. Golf courses are open all year, (2) _____ most golfers don't play when the course is wet. Second, golf offers a wonderful opportunity to socialize. Because a game of golf requires two, three, or four players, groups of golfers often play together regularly, (3) _____ they get to know each other well. Third, golf is stimulating to players of various interests and skill levels. Some golfers enjoy just being part of the game, (4) _____ they give little or no thought to their scores. Others are competitive, (5) _____ they like the challenge of getting the lowest score. (In most sports, the player with the highest score wins, (6) _____ in golf, the player with the lowest score wins.) Finally, golf is an international sport, (7) _____ golfers who travel can find courses all over the world.

B. *Circle the commas before the coordinating conjunctions in the paragraph in part A.*

 For more on coordinating conjunctions, see Appendix IA, pages 196–197.

 **REVISION CHECKPOINT 5**

Coordinating Conjunctions

Review your draft to see if you used any coordinating conjunctions. If you did, put a check (✔) in the margin next to those sentences. If you think you can combine any more sentences with coordinating conjunctions, make those changes now. Finally, make sure that you used commas correctly.

Subordinating conjunctions. In Chapter 1, you learned to use the subordinating conjunctions *after*, *when*, and *so that* to show logical relationships between clauses (see pages 19–20). This chart shows these and two other common subordinating conjunctions, *because* and *although*.

Subordinating Conjunctions	Examples	Meaning
after	MAIN CLAUSE SUBORDINATE CLAUSE I watch TV **after** I finish my work. SUBORDINATE CLAUSE MAIN CLAUSE **After** I finish my work, I watch TV.	signals a time sequence, with the action following *after* happening first
when	MAIN CLAUSE SUBORDINATE CLAUSE I watch TV **when** I am too tired to study. SUBORDINATE CLAUSE MAIN CLAUSE **When** I am too tired to study, I watch TV.	signals (1) two actions happening at the same time, or (2) a sequence, with the action following *when* happening first
because	MAIN CLAUSE SUBORDINATE CLAUSE I watch TV **because** I want to escape. SUBORDINATE CLAUSE MAIN CLAUSE **Because** I want to escape, I watch TV.	introduces a reason
although	MAIN CLAUSE SUBORDINATE CLAUSE I watch TV, **although** I should exercise instead. SUBORDINATE CLAUSE MAIN CLAUSE **Although** I should exercise instead, I watch TV.	introduces a contrasting idea
so that	MAIN CLAUSE SUBORDINATE CLAUSE I watch TV **so that** I can relax. SUBORDINATE CLAUSE MAIN CLAUSE **So that** I can relax, I watch TV.	introduces the purpose of an action

When the subordinating conjunction is in the middle of the sentence, do not use a comma, except before *although*. When the subordinating conjunction is at the beginning of the sentence, always put a comma at the end of the subordinate clause.

EXERCISE 13

A. Fill in the blanks with the subordinating conjunction after, when, because, although, or so that. In some places, two choices are possible.

Laughing with My Family in Front of the TV

America's Funniest Home Videos is a popular TV program that shows film clips that people make at home and send in (1) ___*so that*___ they can win prizes. (2) _____ my family and I want to relax and have some fun together, we like to watch this show for three reasons. First, we like *America's Funniest Home Videos* (3) _____ it presents cute and sometimes funny film clips of children and pets. For example, in one clip, a little boy falls asleep (4) _____ he is eating an ice cream cone and continues to lick the cone (5) _____ he is asleep. In another, a baby gets scared (6) _____ she sees her own shadow. We have seen many clips of dogs and cats doing tricks like "playing the piano," but our favorite was the dog that refused a treat (7) _____ it was "from the dog catcher." The second reason that we like the show is the film clips of *bloopers*, or embarrassing mistakes that people make. (8) _____ we feel a little guilty laughing at others' clumsiness or foolishness, we still enjoy it. For instance, we all laughed hard (9) _____ we saw a woman throw a bowling ball into the ceiling of a bowling alley. In another embarrassing but funny clip from a wedding, the groom accidentally called the bride by the wrong name. Finally, we like the last part of every show (10) _____ the host asks viewers to guess the winning film clip. We all pick our favorites and then wait to see which one wins. (11) _____ the host announces the winning clip, we laugh about it again.

 For more on subordinating conjunctions, see Appendix IA, pages 198–200.

 **REVISION CHECKPOINT 6**

Subordinating Conjunctions
Review your draft to see if you used any subordinating conjunctions to combine sentences. If you did, put a check (✔) in the margin next to those sentences. If you think you can combine any more sentences with subordinating conjunctions, make those changes now. Finally, make sure that you used commas correctly.

Cause-and-effect signals. *So* (a coordinating conjunction), *because* (a subordinating conjunction), and *therefore* (a transition) all show cause-and-effect relationships. Although these signals express the same meaning, their punctuation is different.

Cause-and-Effect Signals	Cause-and-Effect Sentences	Punctuation Notes
so	CAUSE OR REASON / EFFECT Pelé was a great soccer star, **so** I loved to watch him play.	Put a comma before *so*.
because	CAUSE OR REASON / EFFECT **Because** Pelé was a great soccer star, I loved to watch him play. EFFECT / CAUSE OR REASON I loved to watch Pelé play **because** he was a great soccer star.	When *because* starts the sentence, put a comma after the dependent clause.
therefore	CAUSE OR REASON / EFFECT Pelé was a great soccer star. **Therefore,** I loved to watch him play.	Put a period before and a comma after *therefore*.

EXERCISE 14

On another piece of paper, use **so,** **because,** *and* **therefore** *to combine each of the following pairs of sentences in three ways.*

1. Some people enjoy watching sports on TV. They dream of becoming stars themselves someday.

   Some people dream of becoming stars themselves someday, so they enjoy watching sports on TV.

   Some people enjoy watching sports on TV because they dream of becoming stars themselves someday. OR Because some people dream of becoming stars themselves someday, they enjoy watching sports on TV.

   Some people dream of becoming stars themselves someday. Therefore, they enjoy watching sports on TV.

2. Some viewers hope to learn skills from the pros. They watch televised sports.

3. Some people support their national teams. They are patriotic (proud of their countries).

4. Televised sports almost always provide suspense. No one knows who will win a game.

Cause-and-Effect Signals
Review your draft to see if you used any cause-and-effect signals. If you did, think about how they sound. Sometimes *because* sounds best, and sometimes *so* or *therefore* sounds better. If you want to change any of your signals, make those changes now. If you have questions about the best choice of signal, write a note to your teacher in the margin.

◼ FINAL DRAFT

1. Before you write your final draft, look over your paragraph one last time to decide if you want to make any further changes.

2. Prepare a final draft of your composition. Make sure that you used capital letters at the beginnings of your sentences and periods at the end and that you used commas with coordinating and subordinating conjunctions. Finally, check your spelling.

3. Exchange papers with one or two classmates. Read each other's papers carefully. Turn to page 249 in Appendix II, and answer the questions on the Peer Review Form.

4. Check your paper again and make any necessary corrections. Turn in your paper to your teacher.

■ CHAPTER REVIEW

Look back at what you accomplished in Chapter 3. Check off (✔) what you learned and what you used while writing and revising your composition.

Chapter 3 Topics	Learned	Used
exploring general and specific topics (page 58)		
writing a topic sentence for a reason paragraph (page 58)		
identifying reasons (page 59)		
outlining a three-level paragraph to help with prewriting and revising (page 61)		
writing a brief definition (page 64)		
using sensory details, examples, and explanations to develop the third level of a paragraph (page 71)		
using transition signals to introduce examples (page 73)		
using gerunds and infinitives (pages 74 and 76)		
using coordinating and subordinating conjunctions (pages 77 and 79)		
using cause-and-effect signals (page 81)		

CHAPTER FOUR

Occupations

Writing an Effect Paragraph

Jobs change lives. Work demands time and energy—mental, physical, and emotional—and in return, it provides a salary. It also offers new social contacts and valuable learning experiences. Have you noticed how a job affects you or someone you know? In this chapter you will write a paragraph about how working at a job has affected you, a member of your family, or a friend.

This chapter will help you

- write a paragraph that lists and explains effects.
- use an interview to prepare to write.
- use quotations to develop the third level of a paragraph.
- use transitions, repeated words, and related words to create connections in a paragraph.
- use the present perfect with the simple present and simple past tenses.
- use participial adjectives to express reactions and feelings.

Before You Read

Complete the activities.

1. With a partner, look at the photographs of people at work on page 84, and answer these questions: What are the people's occupations? How do you think their jobs affect them?

2. On your own, answer this question: What do you think the life of a firefighter is like? Write your answer on the lines, and then share your ideas with a partner.

_____

_____

3. Read through "Being a Firefighter" quickly without stopping to look up unfamiliar words. Get a general impression of what the writer is telling you about his occupation. After you finish reading, tell a partner what you remember from the reading. Then read the article again.

Reading

BEING A FIREFIGHTER
by Anthony Campaña

1   I am often asked the question, "What's it like being a firefighter?" My response is always the same: "Firefighting can be a challenging, exciting, and personally fulfilling career." It is also very different from many other types of work.

2   Like most people, firefighters usually start work at eight o'clock in the morning. However, because the firehouse is open twenty-four hours a day, seven days a week, firefighters stay at work from twenty-four to seventy-two hours at a time. **Shift work** can span weekends and holidays, and while at work, firefighters are always ready to stop whatever they are doing to respond to an emergency. It's not uncommon for firefighters to receive a call for an emergency while they are eating, showering, or sleeping.

3   Firefighters answer a variety of emergency calls that can be physically demanding. In addition to responding to various types of fires, firefighters assist with vehicle accidents, **hazardous materials spills**, downed electrical lines, and medical emergencies. Fighting fire can be the most physically difficult, requiring firefighters to carry and operate equipment weighing about 50 pounds and to wear personal protective equipment of an additional 50 pounds. The weight of the equipment, combined with the task of performing very **strenuous** physical activities, can be incredibly hard on the average human body, especially in an extremely hot environment.

(continued)

✶**shift work:** *time periods that employees work*

hazardous materials spill: *an accidental dropping of dangerous material*

strenuous: *needing great effort or strength*

4   The emotional demands on firefighters can be significant as well. Firefighters must make quick decisions and act rapidly during emergencies, which produces great emotional stress. Even when firefighters do their jobs perfectly, there is always some form of loss. Loss of property, **contamination** of the environment, injuries, and possibly death to both citizens and firefighters are all possible results of emergencies. How firefighters **deal with** loss varies, but they often rely on peer support and humor.

5   Firefighters' duties don't end with responding to emergencies. The firehouse is home to firefighters as they work their shift. They do all the housework, yard work, grocery shopping, cooking, and repairs. Additionally, firefighters check all the equipment to make sure it is in working condition. Everything on the fire engine must be checked or tested, including the fuel and fluids, air brakes, emergency lights, and fire pump. Medical equipment, including medical oxygen and an automatic external **defibrillator**, need to be checked as well.

6   Many aspects of being a firefighter can be very rewarding. Most firefighters would probably say that making a difference in people's lives is the most fulfilling part of their job. Whether it's putting out a fire that is destroying someone's home, providing **CPR** to a patient in **cardiac arrest**, or teaching children about fire safety, most firefighters feel very proud of what they've accomplished during their shift. Training and education available to firefighters is another rewarding aspect of the career. Firefighters can earn **certifications** and licenses by taking courses in special areas such as emergency medical procedures. Not only is becoming specialized personally satisfying, it also develops the individual into a more **capable** firefighter.

7   Even though I have found firefighting physically and mentally challenging, it has been personally **enriching**. At times, people will come by the firehouse to thank us for a job well done, or I will see someone that I helped during a medical emergency who now seems happy and healthy. Moments like these make me proud to be a firefighter and make up for the difficulties of this work.

contamination: *harm caused by releasing dangerous materials*

deal with: *handle, manage*

defibrillator: *a machine that corrects a person's heartbeat*

CPR: *an emergency medical procedure on a person whose heart has stopped*

cardiac arrest: *the stopping of the heart*

certification: *official papers that say a person is ready to work in a certain way*

✳**capable:** *able to do something*

enriching: *beneficial, rewarding*

ABOUT the **AUTHOR**: Anthony Campaña is a fire captain for San Mateo City Fire Department and teaches emergency medical care at the Santa Rosa Junior College Public Safety Training Center.

Understanding the Reading

With a partner or a small group, discuss the following questions.

1. In paragraph 1, what adjectives does Campaña use to describe his occupation?

2. In what ways is firefighting like other jobs? In what ways is it different?

3. In paragraphs 3 and 4, Campaña says that a firefighter's work can be physically and emotionally demanding. What aspects of the job make it physically demanding? What aspects make it emotionally demanding? Look for details in the reading, and complete the chart.

Physical Demands	Emotional Demands
Firefighters assist with vehicle accidents, hazardous materials spills, downed power lines, and medical emergencies.	Firefighters must make quick decisions and act rapidly during emergencies.

4. When firefighters are not responding to emergencies, what keeps them busy?

5. After reading this text about firefighting, what qualities do you think a person needs to be a good firefighter?

6. In paragraph 7, Campaña says that people sometimes come back to thank firefighters for saving their lives or their property. He says, "Moments like these . . . make up for the difficulties of this work." Can you think of any other occupations that have both significant challenges and meaningful rewards?

Vocabulary Building

TIP To find out how to use each member of a word family in a sentence, look up the word in your dictionary and read the examples in its entry. For example, by reading the examples in the entry for the noun *satisfaction*, you will notice that *satisfaction* can be used with the verb *get*.

Word families and choices for writers. Because a word family like *satisfy* (v.), *satisfaction* (n.), and *satisfying* (adj.) contains words with the same basic meanings but different grammatical functions, it gives you choices as a writer. For example, you can make the three similar—but not identical—sentences that you see here.

Anthony Campaña's job *satisfies* him.

Anthony Campaña gets *satisfaction* from his job.

Anthony Campaña's job is *satisfying*.

Words that belong to the Academic Word List are identified with a star (✻) symbol.

EXERCISE 1

A. *Use your dictionary to complete the word-family chart.*

		Nouns	Verbs	Adjectives
1.	✻	benefit	*benefit*	*beneficial*
2.	✻			challenging
3.	✻	communication		
4.	✻		create	
5.				demanding
6.	✻	flexibility		
7.				fulfilling
8.		independence		
9.	✻			motivational
10.		pressure		
11.		responsibility		
12.			reward	
13.	✻			secure
14.	✻			stressful
15.			support	
16.	✻		vary	

B. *With a partner, rewrite each sentence on another piece of paper. Use a different member of the word family of the italicized word. (In some word families, you have two words to choose from. You can choose one of them.) You may need to look at the examples in your dictionary to find out how the various parts of speech are used in sentences.*

1. My job *demands* a lot of my effort.

   My job is demanding.

   OR

   My job makes demands on me.

2. Ruth has a *variety* of tasks to perform at work.

3. Good teamwork requires that employees be *communicative*.

4. Jose's coworkers put *pressure* on him to meet his deadlines.

5. Masako enjoys having a *flexible* schedule.

6. Neftali and Marina have *support* from their supervisor.

7. A break in routine *motivates* workers.

8. Ji Won is able to show his *creativity* when he designs furniture.

9. My job *fulfills* my needs.

10. Natasha's job as a school bus driver is *challenging*.

11. To be happy in his workplace, Martin needs *independence*.

12. A heavy workload *stresses* workers.

13. When I am looking for a job, being *secure* is my top priority.

14. As a child care provider, Louisa is *responsible for* many things.

15. An employee handbook *benefits* new employees.

C. *Now compare sentences with your classmates'.*

-ly *adverbs*. English has various kinds of adverbs. Among them, the *-ly* adverbs are easiest to recognize. Many *-ly* adverbs are made from adjectives.

   physical → physical*ly*

   mental → mental*ly*

EXERCISE 2

A. *Write an -ly adverb next to each adjective in the chart.*

	Adjectives	Adverbs
1. ✱	creative	*creatively*
2.	efficient	
3.	emotional	
4. ✱	financial	
5.	independent	
6.	intellectual	
7.	social	

You can use *-ly* adverbs in two ways.

TO MODIFY VERBS

                  ADVERB

Sasha does her work *carefully*.

                              ADVERB

Pedro and Tomás complete these tasks *quickly*.

TO MODIFY ADJECTIVES

                ADVERB   ADJECTIVE

Selling automobiles is *financially* rewarding.

               ADVERB   ADJECTIVE

Moving furniture is *physically* demanding.

Put adverbs that modify *verbs* at the end of a sentence.

        SUBJECT + VERB (+ OBJECT) + ADVERB

Carla's employer pays her *generously*.

Put adverbs that modify *adjectives* before the adjectives they modify.

        ADVERB + ADJECTIVE

Carla is *financially* independent.

 For more on the various kinds of adverbs and how to use them, see Appendix IA, pages 186 and 192–193.

B. *On another piece of paper, rewrite the statements, adding an adverb to each one. Use the adjective in parentheses to make the adverb.*

1. (social) Alejandra's job as a teacher's aide has benefited her.

   Alejandra's job as a teacher's aide has benefited her socially.

2. (financial) Working as a Web page designer has made Jacques secure.

   Working as a Web page designer has made Jacques financially secure.

3. (efficient) Rodolfo manages the hotel front desk.

4. (physical) Working as a builder's assistant was demanding.

5. (independent) Eleni likes to work in her own home.

6. (emotional) My job as a soccer coach has been satisfying.

7. (creative) Alex videotapes weddings.

8. (intellectual) César's job as a translator is stimulating.

TIP
You need to use new words more than once to make them part of your permanent vocabulary, so try to put some of this new vocabulary in your writing assignment.

■ WRITING

Assignment

After you study pages 91–102, you will do the following assignment.

Write a one-paragraph composition that discusses two or three effects of a certain occupation on you or another person.

Your own experience provides the best source of ideas for your writing. Therefore, if possible, write about your own work experience and its effects on you. If you have never been employed, write about a friend or family member's job experience.

Interview. To gather information about your friend or family member, you will need to conduct an interview. If you write about yourself, doing a practice interview will help you gather ideas. On pages 96–97, you will read a sample interview and notes from that interview and then follow instructions for preparing for and conducting an interview.

Understanding Your Assignment

Cause and effect. Cause-and-effect thinking is an important part of our everyday lives. For example, there are always causes (reasons) behind a decision.

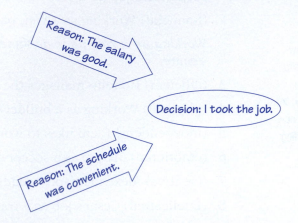

After we make a decision and take action, there are always effects (results).

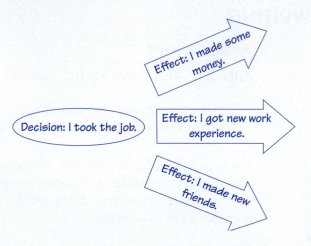

In Chapter 3, you wrote about causes (reasons), and in this chapter, you will write about effects.

The topic sentence of an effect paragraph. Like other topic sentences, the topic sentence of your effect paragraph will have both a topic and a controlling idea. The topic will name a type of job, and the controlling idea will name the effects of the job.

TOPIC   CONTROLLING IDEA

Working in the college bookstore has had two effects on me.

In the controlling idea of the topic sentence, you may use the noun *effect* or the verb *affect*.

NOUN

Working in a bank has had three *effects* on me.

VERB

Working in a bank *has affected* me in three ways.

EXERCISE 3

Read the topic sentences, and then write each one on another piece of paper. If a topic sentence has been written with a noun, rewrite it with a verb. If a topic sentence has been written with a verb, rewrite it with a noun.

1. Being a caterer has affected Sandra in three ways.

    Being a caterer has had three effects on Sandra.

2. Working as a radiology technician has affected Iku in two ways.

3. My job as an apartment manager has had three effects on me.

4. Working as a sound engineer at a radio station has affected Sonia in several ways.

5. Walking dogs for a living has had two effects on Bill.

Positive and negative effects in the topic sentence. You can also identify effects as positive and / or negative in the topic sentence of your outline. Look at the following sample topic sentences.

Working in a fast-food restaurant has had one *positive* and one *negative* effect on me.

Working in a fast-food restaurant has had one *negative* and two *positive* effects on me.

Working in a fast-food restaurant has affected me both *negatively* and *positively*.

EXERCISE 4

A. *Look at the jobs and lists of brainstormed ideas about each job. Only three of the ideas in each list are effects. Cross out the ideas that are not effects.*

1. job: preschool teacher

   - Paula has discovered that some children are better at expressing their feelings than others.
   - ~~Paula gets to work at 6:00 A.M. to get ready for the children, who start arriving at 7:00 A.M.~~
   - Paula has learned to help children when they get frustrated.
   - Working as a preschool teacher has made Paula more flexible because, with small children, sometimes things don't go as adults plan them.
   - ~~Before she got the job as a preschool teacher, Paula had to take a class in first aid so that she could take care of children if they got injured.~~

2. job: fast-food restaurant worker

   - I have learned how to use a cash register.
   - The boss speaks impatiently, so I feel nervous at work.
   - There are many rules in the fast-food restaurant. For example, I have to mop the floor every hour.
   - Some of the customers are friendly, but most of them just want to get their food and go.
   - Because the salary is low, it is hard for me to pay my bills.

3. job: flight attendant

   - Vera has become close friends with her coworkers, and she shares an apartment with two of them.
   - Before flight attendants can work, they have to pass a seven- or eight-week training course.
   - The starting salary for flight attendants is low.

- As a flight attendant, Vera earns free plane tickets, so she has been able to visit her brother in New York and her parents in Lima several times.
- The work schedule is irregular, and the work is physically demanding, so Vera has often felt tired and has gotten sick several times.

4. job: hairstylist

- I have learned to understand customers when they tell me how they want their hair to look.
- I have found that the job is boring when there are no customers.
- My coworker and I look at fashion magazines and try out new hairstyles on each other when we are not busy.
- I went to school and got a license before I started to work.
- I have developed foot problems from standing for eight to ten hours at a time.

B. *On another piece of paper, draft a topic sentence about each job. Put the topic sentence and the effects you have identified in a brief (two-level) outline. Number 1 has been done for you.*

1.

> Working as a preschool teacher has had three effects on Paula.
>
> I. Paula has discovered that some children are better at expressing their feelings than others.
>
> II. Paula has learned to help children when they get frustrated.
>
> III. With small children, sometimes things don't go as adults plan them, so working as a preschool teacher has made Paula more flexible.

C. *Compare your brief outlines with a partner's.*

Organizing supporting points. Readers pay more attention to the first and last supporting points in a paragraph than to the middle point. Think about this when you decide how to organize your supporting points.

The Writing Process

Gathering information through an interview. To get ready for your prewriting interview, read the sample interview in Exercise 5 and the interview notes that follow it. Then complete Exercise 6, a practice interview.

EXERCISE 5

A. *Read the interview between Ahmad, a student from Iran, and his neighbor, Hassan. Ahmad conducted the interview in preparation for the writing assignment in this chapter. As you read it, circle Ahmad's questions, and underline the parts of Hassan's answers that explain the effects of his job.*

Interview

Ahmad: What do you do?

Hassan: I'm a real estate agent.

Ahmad: What is a real estate agent?

Hassan: An *agent* is someone who represents a buyer or a seller or someone who wants to rent. *Real estate* means property—land and buildings.

Ahmad: How long have you been a real estate agent?

Hassan: About a year and a half.

Ahmad: Has being a real estate agent affected you in any way? I mean, have you learned anything? Has the job given you any opportunities? Has it changed your life or changed you mentally, physically, emotionally, or socially?

Hassan: Yes, it has affected me in several ways. First, I have less free time now. I do most of my work on the weekends or during the evenings. That's when clients have time to talk to me, to see properties, to negotiate, or to fill out paperwork. That means that it is hard for me to spend time with my wife and children. Also, I don't have time for tennis anymore.

Ahmad: Umm. Just a minute while I make a note. That's really interesting. Have you experienced any other effects?

Hassan: Sure. I've learned how to really listen to people—not just what they say but how they say it. I asked a client if she liked a house, and she said, "Yes, I like that house," but I could tell she didn't really care for it by her tone of voice.

Ahmad: I see. Do you feel good about your work?

Hassan: Definitely. Real estate has been financially rewarding for me, and that's because I've worked hard. You can't sell houses unless you research the market, advertise, and get out and meet people. I've done all those things, and, as a result, I've been very successful.

Ahmad: Did you say that you research the market?

Hassan: Yes.

Ahmad: What do you mean by "research the market"?

Hassan: Oh, that means finding out what other houses are for sale in the area and how much the sellers are asking. It also means finding out how much people paid for houses that have sold recently.

Ahmad: Oh, I see. Well, thanks a lot.

B. Discuss these questions with a partner.

1. What question did Ahmad use at the beginning to make sure that he understood the work of a real estate agent?

2. What questions did Ahmad ask to gather information about the effects of Hassan's job?

3. What did Ahmad say when he needed a minute to write some notes?

4. What did Ahmad say when he didn't understand something Hassan said?

C. Ahmad made these notes during the interview. Notice that he did not write complete sentences, except for the quotation. Compare Ahmad's notes with the parts of Hassan's answers that you underlined in the interview.

Notes on Hassan's Job

- Hassan, a real estate agent
- helps people buy, sell, and rent property
- 1.5 years
- less free time now: "I do most of my work on the weekends or during the evenings. That's when clients have time to talk to me, to see properties, to negotiate, or to fill out paperwork. That means that it is hard for me to spend time with my wife and children."
- no time for tennis
- learned how to listen well, pays attention to how people talk
- Client: "Yes, I like that house"—but didn't really like it
- feels good about work, proud of accomplishments
- Hassan: "I've done well in real estate, and that's because I've worked hard. You can't sell houses unless you research the market, advertise, and get out and meet people. I've done all those things, and, as a result, I've been very successful."

EXERCISE 6

To get ready for your writing assignment, follow the directions and interview a partner. If you have never had a job, choose a job and make up answers.

1. Make a list of interview questions. You can use some of the questions in the sample interview above.

2. Get ready to take notes during your interview. You can't depend on your memory to remember everything. If the person you are interviewing says something that you think you can use in your writing assignment, put the whole statement in quotation marks in your notes.

3. Interview your partner, and let your partner interview you.

4. After your interview, read over your notes. Make sure that they are clear. If they are not, ask your partner more questions to fill in the gaps. If you need more information to write a paragraph, ask your partner more questions.

The following steps will help you get ready to write an effect paragraph. As you read through the steps, you will see how Ahmad, a student from Iran, prepared to write a paragraph about the effects his neighbor Hassan has experienced from his work as a real estate agent.

Complete steps 1 to 3, and then write your first draft.

Ahmad's Steps

STEP 1   If you have had a job, make a **list** of the effects of that job. Think of all kinds of effects—physical, mental, social, and emotional.

If you are going to write about someone else's job, prepare for and conduct an **interview** with that person. Take careful notes. Then make a list of ways that job has affected the person you interviewed.

Ahmad listed these effects of Hassan's job, based on his interview notes.

> *Hassan has had to give up family time and personal time.*
>
> *Hassan has learned to be a good listener.*
>
> *Working as a real estate agent has given Hassan a sense of accomplishment.*

STEP 2   Look over your list of effects, and decide how to organize them. If you have more than three effects on your list, you should choose the three that you can develop best and cross out the others. Draft a topic sentence, and make a two-level **outline**, leaving space to fill in the third level later.

Ahmad made the following brief outline. Notice that he left space to develop the third level later.

> *Being a real estate agent has affected Hassan in three ways.*
>   I. Hassan has had to give up family time and personal time.
>   A. _____
>   B. _____
>   II. Hassan has learned to be a good listener.
>   A. _____
>   B. _____
>   III. Working as a real estate agent has given Hassan a sense of accomplishment.
>   A. _____
>   B. _____

STEP 3 To develop the third level, you need sensory details, examples, explanations, or quotations. Think about your work experience or review your interview notes, and then complete the third level.

Ahmad completed his outline this way.

> *Being a real estate agent has affected Hassan in three ways.*
>   I. Hassan has had to give up family time and personal time.
>   A. works on weekends and in the evenings when clients have time to talk, to see properties, to negotiate, or to fill out paperwork
>   B. hard to spend time with wife and children
>   C. no time for tennis
>   II. Hassan has learned to be a good listener.
>   A. pays close attention to what people say and how they say it
>   III. Working as a real estate agent has given Hassan a sense of accomplishment.
>   A. He has researched the market, advertised, and met people.
>   B. As a result, he has been very successful.

Write your first draft. If you need to define or explain the type of job that you are writing about, include a definition or explanation before your topic sentence.

Ahmad's First Draft

○	*My Neighbor Hassan, the Real Estate Agent*
	¹*My neighbor Hassan is a real estate agent.* ²*A real estate agent is someone who helps clients buy, sell, or rent property.* ³*Being a real estate agent has affected Hassan in three ways.* ⁴*First, he has given up a lot of his family and personal time.* ⁵*Hassan does most of his work on the weekends or in the evenings, so he has very little time for his family and no time for his favorite sport, tennis.* ⁶*Second, working as a real estate agent has made Hassan a good listener.* ⁷*He has learned to pay close attention to what people say and how they say it.* ⁸*Finally, working as a real estate agent has given Hassan a sense of accomplishment.* ⁹*He has researched the market, advertised, and met people.* ¹⁰*As a result, he has been very successful.*

As Ahmad worked through the rest of this chapter, he made various changes to his draft. Then he completed the assignment with this draft.

Ahmad's Final Draft

The Effects of Being a Real Estate Agent

[1]My neighbor Hassan is a real estate agent. [2]A real estate agent is someone who helps clients buy, sell, or rent property. [3]Being a real estate agent has had one negative and two positive effects on Hassan. [4]First, he has had to give up a lot of his family and personal time. [5]Hassan says, "I do most of my work on the weekends or during the evenings. [6]That's when clients have time to talk to me, to see properties, to negotiate, or to fill out paperwork." [7]As a result, it is hard for Hassan to spend time with his wife and children, and he has no time for tennis anymore. [8]However, working as a real estate agent has made Hassan a good listener. [9]He has learned to pay close attention to what people say and how they say it. [10]For example, a client may say to Hassan, "Yes, I like that house," but he can tell by her voice that she is not enthusiastic about it. [11]Finally, working as a real estate agent has given Hassan a sense of accomplishment. [12]Hassan says, "Real estate has been financially rewarding for me, and that's because I've worked hard. [13]You can't sell houses unless you research the market, advertise, and get out and meet people. [14]I've done all those things, and, as a result, I've been very successful."

With a partner, review Ahmad's final draft. Then do the activities and answer the questions.

1. Put brackets [ ] around the topic sentence in both the first and the final draft, and notice how Ahmad revised it.

2. What is the purpose of sentence 2 in Ahmad's drafts?

3. a. Find the three supporting points in Ahmad's final draft, and above the sentences write *I*, *II*, and *III*.

   b. What transition did Ahmad use to introduce the second supporting point in his final draft? Why did Ahmad use this transition?

4. a. Compare Ahmad's first and final drafts. Underline all the sentences that Ahmad added to his final draft.

   b. What part of the paragraph (first level, second level, or third level) do the added sentences belong to?

   c. What kind of development (sensory details, examples, explanations, quotations) do they represent? Write *sensory details*, *example*, *explanation*, or *quotation* next to each sentence you have underlined.

■ REVISING

As you study this section of the chapter, you will learn more about paragraphs and sentences. As you finish each exercise or section, review your draft, and use what you have learned to improve your writing. Follow the instructions in the Revision Checkpoint boxes to improve your work.

Composition Focus

The second and third levels: paragraph unity. A good paragraph has **unity**. That means it is about one topic only. Therefore, your paragraph for this chapter's assignment should only be about one job and its effects on one person. If you include information about a different person, a different job, or anything else that is not related to the topic, your paragraph will not have unity.

EXERCISE 8

The following paragraph has a problem with unity. Read the paragraph, underline the topic sentence, and circle the topic. Then cross out the sentence that is about a different topic.

My Brother's New Career

¹My brother Jiang has been an automobile mechanic for three years, and the work has affected him in several ways. ²First, he has developed the ability to analyze automotive problems efficiently, and he is proud of this skill. ³He says, "I can hear a 'klunk' or a 'ping' noise and usually figure out what is causing the problem right away." ⁴Second, he has become comfortable using computers. ⁵It seems that computers are used in almost every field these days, including medicine. ⁶Finally, Jiang has improved his communication skills. ⁷When customers pick up their cars, they want to know what was done to them. ⁸Jiang has learned to explain his repairs to customers clearly so that they can understand. ⁹He gives them a little technical information about how their vehicles work and advises them about future maintenance.

The second and third levels: paragraph focus. There are many ways to **focus** on a topic. For example, when writing about a job, you can explain the process of doing the job, describe the workers or the workplace, or tell why the job is a good one. However, the assignment for this chapter asks you to focus on how a particular job affects a particular person. Therefore, if you focus on any other aspect of the topic, your paragraph will have a focus problem.

EXERCISE 9

A. The following paragraph has a focus problem. Read the paragraph, underline the topic sentence, and circle the controlling idea. Then put brackets [ ] around the sentence that does not focus on the specific assignment for this chapter.

Being a Jewelry Store Clerk

¹I am a salesclerk in a jewelry shop, and this job has had three positive effects on me. ²First of all, the job has benefited me financially. ³My hourly salary is quite good, and, in addition, I get a 20 percent commission on all the jewelry I sell. ⁴Second, the shop is bright, clean, and shiny, and the diamonds, pearls, precious stones, and gold bands and chains are beautiful. ⁵Finally, this job has taught me about running a business. ⁶I have learned to keep good records, to maintain a clean, welcoming store, and to treat customers respectfully. ⁷I hope someday to have my own business, and I think that as a result of having this job, I will know how to make it succeed.

B. *Compare what you and your partner underlined. Together, fix the focus problem by revising the sentence(s) you have bracketed. Afterward, share your revisions with your teacher and classmates.*

Paragraph Unity and Focus
Reread your paragraph, and check it for unity and focus. If any part of your paragraph is about a different topic or does not focus on the effects of one job on a particular person, revise it now.

The third level: using quotations as support. In Chapter 3 you learned to use sensory details, examples, and explanations to develop the third level of a paragraph. (See page 71.) These three strategies are effective ways to develop the third level of your paragraph about the effects of a job. In addition, you can use **quotations**. That is, if you interviewed someone and you wrote down what he or she said, you can use those quotations to develop the supporting points of your paragraph.

EXERCISE 10

A. *Read the following interview notes, and underline the quotations.*

Notes on Brenda's Job

- flower shop
- self-employed
- creative—makes many different kinds of arrangements
- enjoys working with flowers
- Brenda: "It's more like play than work for me."
- likes her customers
- Customers usually buy flowers for someone they care about, so they are feeling kind toward others when they come to her shop.
- Brenda: "Because the flowers are always pretty, the customers are always satisfied. They never complain."
- likes being on her own
- Brenda: "I am my own boss. I decide on my own hours and holidays."
- "I don't want anyone looking over my shoulder."

B. Read the paragraph based on these notes, and pay attention to the quotations. Circle the commas and periods used with the quotations. What words do the commas follow? Are the periods inside or outside the quotation marks?

Owning a Flower Shop

[1]My friend Brenda has her own business, a flower shop. [2]Owning this business has had three positive effects on her. [3]First of all, Brenda is a very creative person, and she can make a wide variety of beautiful flower arrangements. [4]She gets pleasure from working with the flowers and greens of various colors and shapes. [5]She says, "It's more like play than work for me." [6]Second, Brenda says that her customers make her feel good. [7]She thinks that this is because when people buy flowers for someone, they have a kind and generous attitude toward others in general. [8]Brenda also thinks that the flowers make customers cheerful. [9]She says, "Because the flowers are always pretty, the customers are always satisfied. [10]They never complain." [11]Finally, being self-employed pleases Brenda because she likes her independence. [12]She says, "I am my own boss. [13]I decide on my own hours and holidays." [14]In addition, Brenda doesn't want anyone monitoring her behavior at work. [15]She often says, "I don't want anyone looking over my shoulder."

 For more on using correct punctuation with quotations, see Appendix IB, page 245.

EXERCISE 11

The following paragraph contains several quotations, but the quotations do not have correct punctuation. Read the paragraph, and supply periods and commas where they are needed.

The Effects of Being an RN

[1]My friend Luisa has been a registered nurse for one year. [2]Being an RN has had three effects on her. [3]First, she feels secure because she is earning a decent salary and she knows that she will always be able to find work. [4]She says, "There's always a shortage of nurses" [5]Second, Luisa's work schedule has required her to change her sleep schedule. [6]She works from midnight to 8:00 A.M. and finds it hard to be active at night and sleep during the day. [7]She says "Working nights has affected my social life as well. [8]When my friends are going out to a party, I'm getting ready for work " [9]Finally, Luisa says that the major effect on her of her work as an RN is the heavy responsibility she carries. [10]"I'm

taking care of several people who are very sick at the same time " Luisa commented recently. [11]"If two of them need me at once, that means that one of them will not be helped right away, and the consequences can be serious "

EXERCISE 12

Read the quotations in the box and the paragraph titled "The Effects of Being a Travel Agent." Then, on another piece of paper, rewrite the paragraph and add the quotations.

Quotations

"Because customers usually ask the same questions—about departure and arrival times, refund policies, and things like that—I've gotten good at responding. It has been very rewarding for me to know that I'm communicating well and helping people."

"I never thought I would see Rio de Janeiro, or Caracas, or Sydney. I love to travel."

The Effects of Being a Travel Agent

[1]My cousin Leo has been a travel agent for two years, and the job has affected him in two ways. [2]First of all, his English has improved significantly. [3]He spends almost eight hours a day talking on the phone, giving people advice about flight times, ticket prices, customs regulations, visas, and the weather in the places they are planning to visit. [4]Second, he has been able to get free airline tickets, and he has traveled to South America and Australia. [5]Leo's travel experiences have taught him a lot about cultural differences, and he plans to travel more and to learn as much as he can.

 **REVISION CHECKPOINT 2**

Paragraph Development and Using Quotations as Support
Put brackets [ ] around all the sentences on the third level of your paragraph. Make sure that the third level is fully developed. If it is not well developed, add sensory details, examples, explanations, or quotations to make the paragraph more effective as a whole.

Paragraph connections: Transitions, repeated words, and related words.
A good paragraph has more than unity, focus, and good development. The sentences in an effective paragraph must be clearly **connected** to one another so that readers can follow the ideas easily. To make sure that the sentences in your paragraph are connected, you can use **transitions**, **repeated words**, and **related words**.

Transitions: You have learned to use the transitions *first, second,* and *third / finally* to help the reader identify the supporting points in your paragraph. (See page 15.)

Repeated words: You can repeat certain key words throughout a paragraph to help readers focus on your topic. For example, in the paragraph above, "The Effects of Being a Travel Agent," the word *travel* appears five times.

Related words: To help readers follow your ideas, you can use words that are related to each other. For example, if you use the word *fashion*, readers might expect to find the words *designer*, *design*, and *style* in the text, too. In "The Effects of Being a Travel Agent," we see *flight times*, *ticket prices*, *customs regulations*, *visas*, and *airline tickets*, all of which are related to travel agents and travel agencies.

Exercise 13

A. *Look for connections in the following paragraph. Circle the transitions, underline the repeated words, and put brackets [ ] around the related words.*

Being a Computer Repair Technician

¹I have been a "computer doctor" for five years, and the job has had three effects on me. ²First of all, I have found that I enjoy traveling around and meeting people. ³I get calls from people who are having computer problems, and I go to their homes and offices. ⁴I meet new people every day, so I never get bored. ⁵Second, the job has been mentally stimulating. ⁶I often encounter new technical problems—things I've never seen or heard of before—and it is always a challenge to solve them. ⁷In addition, new software comes out all the time, so I have to attend seminars, take online classes, and read articles to stay on top of the developments. ⁸Finally, being a "computer doctor" has given me a sense of job security. ⁹More and more people are buying computers, and most of them will need a technician someday, so I don't think that I will ever be out of a job!

B. *Discuss these questions with your classmates and teacher.*

1. What are the transitions in the paragraph?
2. Which words are repeated?
3. Which words are related to each other?

REVISION CHECKPOINT 3

Paragraph Connections: Transitions, Repeated Words, and Related Words
Check your paragraph for connections: Make sure that you have used **transitions**. Check for **repeated** and **related words**. If you can improve the connections in your paragraph by adding transitions or changing the vocabulary, do it now.

Language Focus

Using the present perfect with the simple present and the simple past tenses. In many cases, when you are writing a paragraph, you need to use more than one verb tense. In fact, all the model paragraphs in this chapter contain two or three of the tenses in the chart.

Tenses	Examples	Uses
simple present	I **am** a baker. I **make** bread. I always* **work** at night.	Use the simple present to talk about an action or situation that is true now, was true in the past, and will be true in the future.
present perfect	My job as a baker **has made** me more careful. I **have been** a baker since** 2007.	1. Use the present perfect to talk about something that has happened at an indefinite time in the past. 2. Use the present perfect to talk about an action or situation that began in the past and has continued to the present.
simple past	I **started** my job as a baker in 2007.	Use the simple past to talk about an action or situation that began and ended in the past.

*Use the simple present with frequency adverbs (*always, usually, often sometimes, seldom, never,* etc.).

> Ana *usually works* on weekends.

**Use the present perfect with *since* + a time expression.

> Carlos *has worked* as an architect *since 2002.*

 For more on the English tense system, see Appendix IA, pages 214–216.

EXERCISE 14

The following paragraph contains three verb tenses. When the tense shifts, there is a vertical line (|). With a partner, read the paragraph and the note about the tenses in sentences 1–5. Then, on another piece of paper, identify and explain the tenses of the underlined verbs in sentences 6–11.

NOTE

Sentences 1 and 2 are in the simple present because they are about something that is true now, was true in the past, and will be true in the future.

Sentences 3 and 4 are in the present perfect because they describe things that have happened at an indefinite time in the past.

Sentence 5 is in the simple present because it describes something that happens now, happened in the past, and will happen in the future.

¹I am self-employed. ²I make wedding cakes in my home and deliver them to wedding receptions. | ³Doing this kind of work has had three effects on my life. ⁴For one thing, I have enjoyed the flexibility of self-employment. | ⁵If I want to have a weekend off to go to a party or to take a trip, I don't take an assignment then. | ⁶In addition, this job has allowed me to develop my creativity. | ⁷I often try out new cake recipes and new kinds of decoration. ⁸For example, I make different kinds of flowers out of sugar, and sometimes I combine handmade and real flowers on a cake. | ⁹Finally, this job has taught me how to succeed financially. | ¹⁰The first year I was in business, I undercharged customers because I didn't accurately estimate the cost of making cakes. | ¹¹Since then, I haven't lost any money, and I have had a lot of fun making wedding cakes.

Choosing and combining verb tenses. Because we use the simple present to talk about a situation or activity that exists now, a paragraph about a current job often begins with a statement in the simple present.

> I *am* self-employed. I *make* wedding cakes in my home and *deliver* them to wedding receptions.

However, when we want to describe effects, we change to the present perfect because that tense tells about something that has occurred at an indefinite time in the past or an action or situation that began in the past and has continued to the present.

> Doing this kind of work *has had* three effects on my life. For one thing, I *have enjoyed* the flexibility of self-employment.

When we add details about the job, we use the simple present because the characteristics of a job are usually unchanging—the same in the past, the present, and the future.

> If I *want* to have a weekend off to go to a party or to take a trip, I *don't take* an assignment at that time.

EXERCISE 15

The following paragraphs contain simple present, present perfect, and simple past verbs. All the verbs are underlined. Each paragraph contains <u>four</u> verb tense errors. Find and correct the errors.

1.   **The Effects of Being a Commercial Pilot**

¹My friend Rosa <u>is</u> a commercial airline pilot. ²Being a pilot <u>has had</u> two effects on her. ³First, she <u>feels</u> very responsible because people <u>depended</u> [*depend*] on her to keep them safe, so she <u>is</u> extremely diligent about her job. ⁴She always <u>arrives</u> at work a little early. ⁵Then she <u>goes over</u> her flight plan and <u>makes</u> sure it <u>was</u> accurate. ⁶Second, Rosa's self-esteem <u>increases</u> since she <u>became</u> a pilot. ⁷She <u>senses</u> that the crew members <u>respect</u> her because they <u>realize</u> that she <u>spends</u> many hours in flight school and <u>took</u> many exams before she <u>got</u> her pilot's license.

2.   **The Effects of Being an Industrial Chemist**

¹I <u>am</u> an industrial chemist, and I <u>do</u> research in the field of paper recycling. ²My job <u>has had</u> three positive effects on me. ³First of all, I <u>feel</u> satisfied because I <u>am</u> able to use my education to make my living. ⁴I <u>study</u> chemical engineering in college, and after graduation I <u>found</u> a position in a large research lab. ⁵I <u>was</u> in this lab since 2004. ⁶Second, my position <u>gives</u> me a lot of freedom. ⁷I <u>decide</u> what aspect of recycling I <u>want</u> to study, and then I <u>write</u> a proposal. ⁸If my proposal <u>gets</u> funded, I <u>design</u> and <u>have conducted</u> the research. ⁹Finally, my job <u>has given</u> me a sense of accomplishment because my research <u>has improved</u> the process of paper recycling. ¹⁰That <u>means</u> that now it <u>costs</u> less to recycle paper than it <u>does</u> in the past, so less paper <u>is wasted</u> today. ¹¹Recycling <u>saves</u> trees, and trees <u>are</u> important to the environment, so I <u>am</u> proud of the work I <u>have done</u>.

EXERCISE 16

Fill in the blanks in the paragraph with verbs in the present perfect, simple present, or simple past tense.

How Being a Medical Assistant Has Affected Thuyen

My older sister Thuyen (1) _____*is*_____ (be) a medical assistant in a pediatrician's office. Being a medical assistant (2) _____ (have) three effects on her. First of all, she enjoys the job because of its variety. Sometimes she (3) _____ (schedule) appointments, sometimes she (4) _____ (check) patients' blood pressure, pulse, temperature, height, and weight, and sometimes she (5) _____ (ask) parents questions about their children's medical histories. Second, she has developed an important skill on this job: She has learned how to calm crying babies and how to put nervous children and their parents at ease. She just (6) _____ (use) her pleasant voice to talk about something they are interested in. Finally, while working on this job, Thuyen made an important discovery. She found out that working in the field of children's health is her passion. She says, "I (7) _____ (love) working in pediatrics because I (8) _____ (love) being around kids. And I (9) _____ (believe) that children's health is very important because children (10) _____ (be) the future generation."

REVISION CHECKPOINT 4

The Present Perfect with the Simple Present and Simple Past Tenses
Underline all the verbs in your draft, and check your use of tenses. If you find any verb tense errors, correct them now. If you are unsure about the correct tense for a particular verb, write a question to your teacher in the margin of your paper.

Participial adjectives. In Chapter 3 you learned to use *-ing* adjectives to describe things that you have feelings about. (See pages 54–55.) Notice that in the following example, the *thing that causes the reaction or feeling* is the subject of each sentence.

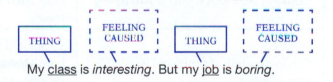

My <u>class</u> is *interesting*. But my <u>job</u> is *boring*.

In the following example, the subject of each sentence is the *person who experiences a reaction or feeling*. In this case, *-ed* adjectives are used.

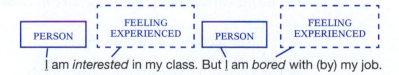

<u>I</u> am *interested* in my class. But <u>I</u> am *bored* with (by) my job.

English has a number of pairs of *-ed* and *-ing* adjectives. Some of them are shown in the chart. Notice that different prepositions follow the *-ed* forms.

-ing Form	*-ed* Form
boring Washing floors is **boring**.	bored (with, by) I am **bored with / by** washing floors.
challenging Cutting a child's hair is **challenging**.	challenged (by) I am **challenged by** cutting a child's hair.
frustrating Driving in heavy traffic is **frustrating**.	frustrated (with, by) I am **frustrated with / by** driving in heavy traffic.
fulfilling Making customers happy is **fulfilling**.	fulfilled (by) I am **fulfilled by** making customers happy.
interesting Meeting new people is **interesting**.	interested (in) I am **interested in** meeting new people.
motivating Receiving tips is **motivating**.	motivated (by) I am **motivated by** receiving tips.
rewarding Helping kids do math is **rewarding**.	rewarded (by) I am **rewarded by** helping kids do math.
satisfying Cooking delicious meals is **satisfying**.	satisfied (by) I am **satisfied by** cooking delicious meals.
stimulating Solving technical problems is **stimulating**.	stimulated (by) I am **stimulated by** solving technical problems.

EXERCISE 17

Underline the correct participial adjective in each statement.

1. My cousin Taesun is a city bus driver.

    a. His job is often (<u>frustrating</u> / frustrated).

    b. He is often (frustrating / <u>frustrated</u>) by his job.

2. Connie is a marketing analyst.

   a. Her job is (stimulating / stimulated).

   b. She is (stimulating / stimulated) by her job.

3. Ari is a dishwasher.

   a. He is often (boring / bored) at work.

   b. His job is (boring / bored).

4. Pedro is an aeronautical technician. He repairs aircraft.

   a. He is often (challenging / challenged) by his job.

   b. His job is often (challenging / challenged).

5. Nobu is a librarian.

   a. He says his job is (rewarding / rewarded).

   b. He says he is (rewarding / rewarded) by his job.

6. Michelle is a computer programmer.

   a. Her work is (motivating / motivated).

   b. She is (motivating / motivated) by her work.

EXERCISE 18

The following paragraph has <u>four</u> mistakes in participial adjectives. Read the paragraph, and underline all the participial adjectives. Find and correct the mistakes. The first two participial adjectives have been marked for you.

Being a Café Manager

[1]Working as a café manager has affected me positively and negatively. [2]This job has been <u>satisfying</u> for me because I enjoy being in the center of things. [3]As manager, my main responsibility is to coordinate between the owner and the staff. [4]I also order supplies and balance the cash register at the end of each day. [5]Although I enjoy the work, the job is ~~challenged~~ *challenging*. [6]For example, sometimes the waiters complain about the kitchen staff, or vice versa. [7]And sometimes the suppliers don't deliver what I have ordered. [8]In addition, I work six days a week, nights and weekends, eleven or twelve hours a day.

[9]I seldom see my kids because I come home late at night when they are asleep. [10]And, truthfully, I am always tiring and often stressed when I come home, especially when a problem comes up at work. [11]For example, last week the chef quit suddenly. [12]He was frustrating because his assistant didn't have enough experience. [13]Fortunately, I found a replacement for him quickly. [14]Being a café manager is always demanding but never bored.

For more on participial adjectives, see Appendix IA, page 225.

REVISION CHECKPOINT 5

Participial Adjectives

Review your draft, and see if you have used any participial adjectives. If you have used some, make sure that you have selected the correct ending, *-ing* or *-ed*, for each one. If you find a mistake, fix it now.

■ FINAL DRAFT

1. Before you write your final draft, look over your paragraph one last time to decide if you want to make any further changes.

2. Prepare a final draft of your composition. Make sure that you have used capital letters at the beginnings of your sentences and periods at the end, and check your spelling.

3. Exchange papers with one or two classmates. Read each other's papers carefully. Turn to page 250 in Appendix II, and fill out the Peer Review Form.

4. Check your paper again and make any necessary corrections. Turn in your paper to your teacher.

■ CHAPTER REVIEW

Look back at what you have accomplished in Chapter 4. Check off (✔) what you have learned and what you have used while writing and revising your composition.

Chapter 4 Topics	Learned	Used
using -ly adverbs (pages 89–90)		
using effect or affect in a topic sentence (page 93)		
conducting a prewriting interview and taking notes in order to gather information before writing (page 96)		
identifying effects and listing them in a brief (two-level) outline (pages 98–99)		
recognizing and correcting problems with paragraph unity and focus (pages 102–103)		
using quotations to develop the third level of a paragraph (page 104)		
using transitions and repeated and related words to create connections between ideas in a paragraph (pages 106–107)		
understanding the meaning of the simple present, the present perfect, and the simple past and combining these tenses in a paragraph (page 108)		
using -ed and -ing participial adjectives (pages 111–112)		

Growing Up in Different Cultures

Writing a Contrast Paragraph

Have you noticed cultural differences in the way people raise their children? Although societies have different approaches to child rearing, people in every society see the role of parenting as extremely important, and the reason is simple: Children are the future. In this chapter, you will write a contrast paragraph about raising children or growing up.

This chapter will help you

- write a topic sentence for a contrast paragraph.
- choose side-by-side or point-by-point organization for your paragraph.
- make parallel lists to gather information and ideas for writing.
- evaluate your paragraph for balanced development.
- use contrast signals.
- use a consistent point of view.

Before You Read

The following article was written by an anthropologist (a person who studies societies and cultures) and seven psychologists (people who study the human mind and behavior). These eight social scientists—who live in five different countries—study parenting styles around the world in order to understand how parents' ideas about parenting affect children, family life, and society.

Do your own "social science research." Complete the following activities on your own. Then share your answers with a partner or a small group.

1. List five beliefs that people in your culture have about raising children. Rank them from 1 (most important) to 5 (least important). For example, do people in your culture value cooperative behavior and politeness in their children?

2. In your opinion, what is the best way to put a baby to sleep?

Reading

**PUTTING THE BABY TO BED IN
FIVE CULTURES**

*by Sara Harkness, Charles M. Super, Jong-Hay Rha, Marjolijn Blom, Blanca Huitron,
Ughetta Moscardino, Saskia van Schaik, and Margreet de Looze*

1   We all sleep, but for a baby, learning how to coordinate sleep with the rest of the family is one of life's biggest challenges. Helping babies to achieve a more mature sleeping pattern is therefore a universal task for parents, but how parents do this varies widely across cultures.

phenomenon: *an event or thing that you can observe*

2   Putting the baby to bed is a relatively modern **phenomenon**. For babies in many traditional societies, sleep is something that just happens anywhere when the baby feels tired. In a rural Kipsigis community of Kenya that Harkness and Super studied in the 1970s, for example, mothers or older sisters carried babies on their backs for most of the day. At night, babies slept in skin-to-skin **contact**

contact: *touching*

with their mothers in a small hut where the other young children also slept. In this culture, mothers did not try to schedule their babies' sleep either during the day or the night—bedtime for babies was the same as for their mothers.

3   In modern societies, babies often have their own bed or even their own room. Even so, parents in modern cultures choose different strategies for putting the baby to bed (Harkness et al, 2007). A mother in a middle-class town in the Netherlands described her own approach as follows: "We put his pajamas on . . . a clean diaper, and then, ya, we tuck him

routine: *schedule or sequence of activities*

self-regulate: *to control oneself*

in, he gets his doll and music on. And a kiss. We just lay him down, walk away." This practice reflects the cultural beliefs of these mothers: An essential part of supporting the baby's health and development is a regular and restful daily **routine**. Babies are expected to learn early to **self-regulate**, including going to sleep by themselves.

4   In contrast, Korean mothers often expect to follow the baby's own schedule  for sleeping and eating, even if that is difficult. A middle-class Korean mother described putting her baby to bed as a long and sometimes difficult process. She said, "My baby does not fall asleep lying down. I have to walk around or sit in a chair holding her in my arms. When she goes into sleep, I always sleep next to her—that way she can sleep well." At some point, the baby will achieve a more regular schedule—but in the meantime, the mother or other caretaker will always be physically present and respond to the baby's needs.

5   Many cultures share the idea that small babies need support in falling asleep. For example, a Spanish mother in the city of Seville recounted, "When I put her to bed she's already completely asleep. If she wakes up when she's put down in her **cradle**, I rock it a little, I sing some more, or I pick her up so she'll fall asleep again." Similarly, Italian mothers in the city of Padua emphasized the importance of physical and emotional closeness for the baby to feel secure and relaxed. As one mother described, "In the evening, before putting her to bed I carry her, I rock her and sing her to sleep, because she likes to be **cuddled**, and I also enjoy this physical contact before we separate for the night."

cradle: *a baby's bed that can rock*

cuddled: *held lovingly*

conflicted: *confused because of opposing ideas*

6   Middle-class parents in the United States seem **conflicted** about how to put their babies to bed. Following the U.S. cultural idea of independence, they believe that babies should learn early to fall asleep on their own. At the same time, however, they worry that a baby may not feel secure without a loving parent in the room. Some parents choose to sleep with their babies, while others put a baby in his or her own bed and room from the very beginning. The two choices reflect two **contradictory** cultural ideas, one that emphasizes the importance of independence and the other that focuses on the creation of a close parent-child relationship.

✷contradictory: *referring to two opposing ideas that cannot both be true*

7   In summary, even simple routines like putting a baby to bed at night can help us understand cultural ideas that provide direction for the ways that people live their lives in different parts of the world. How parents put the baby to bed and what they say about it can open a window into the richly diverse cultural worlds of parenting.

Harkness, S., Super, C. M., Moscardino, U., Rha, J.-H., Blom, M. J. M., Huitrón, B., Johnston, C., Sutherland, M., Hyun, O.-K., Axia, G., & Palacios, J. (2007). Cultural models and developmental agendas: Implications for arousal and self-regulation in early infancy. *Journal of Developmental Processes,* 2(1), 5–39.

ABOUT the AUTHOR

Sara Harkness (an anthropologist) and Charles M. Super (a developmental psychologist) are professors at the University of Connecticut. Co-authors Jong-Hay Rha (Korea), Marjolijn Blom (the Netherlands), Blanca Huitron (Mexico), Ughetta Moscardino (Italy), Saskia van Schaik (the Netherlands), and Margreet de Looze (the Netherlands) are psychologists who have collaborated with Harkness and Super on the International Baby Study, which is the source of the quotations in this article.

Understanding the Reading

With a partner or a small group, discuss the following questions.

1. The first paragraph of "Putting the Baby to Bed in Five Cultures" gives the main ideas of the text. Reread the first paragraph. If you have questions about vocabulary, discuss the meanings of the words. Then, without looking back, restate the main ideas in your own words.

2. Harkness and her co-authors first describe the customs associated with babies' sleep in the Kipsigis community of Kenya in 1982. Why is it incorrect to say that Kipsigis mothers "put their babies to sleep"?

3. a. The mothers in the Netherlands, Korea, Spain, and Italy all described their babies' bedtime routines. They also indicated what they expect their babies to do at bedtime. Refer to the reading, and fill in details in the chart.

Points of Comparison	Netherlands	Korea	Spain	Italy
things the mother *does* when she puts her baby to bed	She puts pajamas and a clean diaper on her baby. She gives him his doll and plays music for him. Then she tucks him in and kisses him goodnight.			
things the mother *expects* when she puts her baby to bed	She expects the baby to go to sleep by himself.			

b. Tell your partners about the similarities and differences between the bedtime routines in the different countries. For example:

> Both the mother in Spain and the mother in Italy sing to their babies.

> The mother in the Netherlands expects her baby to follow the parents' routine and regulate his own sleep, but the mother in Korea does not expect her baby to fall asleep on her own.

> The baby in the Netherlands gets a kiss, but the baby in Italy gets cuddled.

4. What are the two contradictory views of U.S. parents about putting babies to sleep?

5. After reading this article, did you change your opinion about the best way to put a baby to sleep?

Vocabulary Building

Words used as more than one part of speech. In English, some words are used as more than one part of speech. For example, *influence* is used as both a verb and a noun.

VERB

Parents *influence* children.

NOUN

Parents' *influence* is important in their children's lives.

EXERCISE 1

*Underline the word that is used as both a noun and a verb in each pair of sentences below, and then write (**n.**) for noun or (**v.**) for verb after each sentence.*

1. a. The <u>play</u> of small children includes imitation of adult activities. __*n.*__.

   b. When children <u>play</u>, they often try out social roles such as "mother" or "father." __*v.*__.

2. a. Listening to the talk of preschoolers gives us clues about their knowledge of the world. _____

   b. U.S. mothers frequently talk to their children about safety. _____

3. a. Parents discipline children of different ages in different ways for bad behavior. _____

   b. Like parents, teachers must use discipline to control students' bad behavior. _____

4. a. U.S. culture values both competition and cooperation. _____

   b. Community values influence how people raise their children. _____

5. a. People usually parent their children in a way that is similar to the way they were raised themselves. _____

   b. First-time parents find that their new babies are the focus of their lives. _____

6. a. Preschool-age children cannot always control their own behavior. _____

   b. Some U.S. teenagers refuse to accept any parental control. _____

7. a. Separation from family and friends can cause children harm. _____

   b. Someone who has harmed another person should be punished. _____

8. a. As a child masters a new skill, he or she experiences a new feeling of pride. _____

   b. Children's early experiences have long-lasting effects on them. _____

📖 *For more on parts of speech and word order in sentences, see Appendix IA, page 190.*

Person nouns and concept nouns. Some word families have more than one noun. A word family may have both a noun that refers to a person and a noun that refers to a general idea or concept. Look at the examples below.

PERSON NOUN

An *adolescent* experiences many different emotions.

CONCEPT NOUN

Adolescence is a time of emotional change.

Words that belong to the Academic Word List are identified with a star (✳) symbol.

EXERCISE 2

A. Use your dictionary to fill in the blanks in the chart.

	Person Nouns	**Concept Nouns**
1.	adviser	*advice*
2.		caregiving
3.	child	
4.	companion	
5.		discipline
6.	friend	
7. ✳		individuality
8.	infant	
9.		parenthood, parenting

B. Underline either person nouns or concept nouns to complete the sentences.

1. The behavior of an (individuality / <u>individual</u>) is an expression of his or her values.

2. As any parent of a baby or toddler can tell you, (caregiver / caregiving) is a demanding job.

3. An only (child / childhood) does not have the (companion / companionship) of siblings.

4. (Infant / Infancy) is a period of rapid growth and development.

5. My father, who was the (disciplinarian / discipline) in our family, punished my brothers and me if we did not fulfill all our obligations.

6. When their relatives live far away, new mothers often seek (adviser / advice) about (parent / parenting) from a (friend / friendship).

Academic vocabulary that describes families and child rearing. As you read through this chapter, you will see model paragraphs about child development and child rearing in different cultures. Some of the words you will see are formal, academic terms that are used in the field of psychology.

NOTE
In this exercise, some words need to be made plural. (siblings, roles)

EXERCISE 3

Discuss the meanings of these academic terms with your teacher and classmates. Then, on another piece of paper, rewrite each sentence that follows, replacing the italicized word or phrase with a formal, academic term.

*attachment (to)	extended family	*role
behavior	*generation	role model
child rearing	imitate	separation anxiety
*conflict	*maturity	sibling
develop	nuclear family	

1. Teenagers need *people they can look up to* in their families.

   Teenagers need role models in their families.

2. Toddlers *copy* older children.

3. Sometimes *brothers and sisters* compete for their parents' attention.

4. Young children's *feeling of love and loyalty for* the people who care for them is necessary for their emotional health.

5. *The way people raise children* has changed since my grandparents' time.

6. In industrial countries, most children grow up within a *household that consists only of parents and their children*.

7. People who have grown up in *a household that consists of parents, grandparents, uncles, aunts, and their children* usually believe that an individual's wishes are less important than the needs of the whole group.

8. Children who grow up without one of their parents often show *adult-like ways of thinking and acting* at a young age.

9. Working women often have several *parts* to play in their lives—wife, mother, and employee.

10. In every society, people see the benefits of caring and helpful *ways to act*.

11. During the elementary school years, children *grow up* intellectually, emotionally, and socially.

12. Babysitters who take care of one-year-olds have to find ways to distract them when the children experience *fear when their mothers leave*.

13. Sometimes there is *disagreement* among family members about how to spend money.

14. The older *group of relatives born in the same period of time* in any family has more life experience than the younger *group of relatives born in the same period of time*.

TIP
You need to use new words more than once to make them part of your permanent vocabulary, so try to put some of the new vocabulary from this section of the chapter in your writing assignment.

■ WRITING

Assignment

After you study pages 124–136, you will do the following assignment.

Write a contrast paragraph about one of the following topics. For the topic you select, choose one of the four controlling ideas (a, b, c, or d). Your paragraph must have two or three supporting points.

Remember: Choose one topic. Then choose one controlling idea for your topic.

Topic 1. Compare two cultures with respect to the way they
CONTROLLING IDEAS: a. care for children, OR
   b. view children's role in the family, OR
   c. expect children to behave, OR
   d. teach children correct behavior.

Topic 2. Compare people of two age groups (adults, teenagers, children, toddlers, or babies) in one cultural setting with respect to how they
CONTROLLING IDEAS: a. contribute to family life, OR
   b. think about responsibility, OR
   c. express their individuality, OR
   d. amuse themselves.

Topic 3. Compare yourself now to yourself at a younger age with respect to
CONTROLLING IDEAS: a. your interests, OR
   b. your goals, OR
   c. your motivations, OR
   d. your role in your family.

Understanding Your Assignment

The topic sentence of a contrast paragraph. You can begin the topic sentence of a contrast paragraph with the noun *difference*, the adjective *different*, or the verb *differ*.

NOUN
There is a *difference* between newborns and one-year-olds.

ADJECTIVE
Newborns and one-year-olds are *different*.

VERB
Newborns and one-year-olds *differ*.

EXERCISE 4

Read the topic sentences. Then, on another piece of paper, rewrite each one in two ways by using **differences, different,** *or* **differ.**

1. The social skills of four-year-olds and eight-year-olds are different.

   The social skills of four-year-olds and eight-year-olds differ.

   There are differences between the social skills of four-year-olds and eight-year-olds.

2. The parenting styles of Thai and Italian mothers differ.

3. There are differences in parents' attitudes toward punishment.

4. The treatment of toddlers in Malaysian and U.S. cultures differs.

5. There are differences between three-year-olds' and seven-year-olds' understanding of cause and effect.

6. Team sports that are organized by adults and team sports that are organized by children are different.

The organization of a contrast paragraph. A contrast paragraph can be organized two ways: You can use *side-by-side* or *point-by-point* organization. Look at the model paragraphs and outlines.

Contrast Pattern 1: Side-by-Side Organization

With side-by-side organization, you first discuss one thing completely and then discuss the other thing.

Newborns and One-Year-Olds

[1]Newborns and one-year-olds are very different. [2]Newborns cannot move their bodies or control the movement of their arms and legs. [3]Their arms are usually folded close to their bodies, and their hands are tightly closed. [4]Newborns are only able to see people and things that move and that are about two feet away. [5]They have no memories, so they do not recognize anyone, and they have no attachments to people. [6]Newborns cry when they are uncomfortable or hungry. [7]On the other hand, one-year-olds can sit and stand, and some can even walk. [8]They use their fingers and thumbs to pick up small objects. [9]One-year-olds can see very well, and, because they can remember, they recognize people and things. [10]They have formed attachments to their family members, especially to their mothers. [11]One-year-olds whine, point, and talk when they want or need something. [12]They smile and laugh when they recognize friendly faces and show interest in things that are new and different. [13]They become shy when strangers appear and fearful when their mothers go away.

Newborns and one-year-olds are very different.

   I. newborns

       A. Newborns cannot move their bodies or control the movement of their arms and legs. Their arms are usually folded close to their bodies, and their hands are tightly closed.

       B. Newborns are only able to see people and things that move and that are about two feet away. They have no memories, so they do not recognize anyone, and they have no attachments to people.

       C. Newborns cry when they are uncomfortable or hungry.

  II. one-year-olds

       A. One-year-olds can sit and stand, and some can even walk. They use their fingers and thumbs to pick up small objects.

       B. One-year-olds can see very well, and, because they can remember, they recognize people and things. They have formed attachments to their family members, especially to their mothers.

       C. One-year-olds whine, point, and talk when they want or need something. They smile and laugh when they recognize friendly faces and show interest in things that are new and different. They become shy when strangers appear and fearful when their mothers go away.

Contrast Pattern 2: Point-by-Point Organization

With point-by-point organization, you move back and forth between the two things you are contrasting as you discuss each point of difference.

Newborns and One-Year-Olds

[1]Newborns and one-year-olds are very different. [2]<u>First</u>, they differ in terms of their physical development and muscle control. [3]Newborns cannot move their bodies or control the movement of their arms and legs. [4]Their arms are usually folded close to their bodies, and their hands are tightly closed. [5]<u>By comparison</u>, one-year-olds can sit and stand, and some can even walk. [6]They use their fingers and thumbs to pick up small objects. [7]<u>Second</u>, newborns and one-year-olds differ in terms of what they see and recognize and their attachment to caregivers. [8]Newborns are only able to see people and things that move and that are about two feet away. [9]They have no memories, so they do not recognize anyone, and they cannot form attachments to people. [10]<u>On the other hand</u>, one-year-olds can see very well, and, because they can remember, they recognize people and things. [11]They have formed attachments to their family members, especially to their mothers. [12]<u>Finally</u>, newborns and one-year-olds differ in terms of their emotions and their communication with others. [13]Newborns cry when they are uncomfortable or hungry. [14]<u>In contrast</u>, one-year-olds whine, point, and talk when they want or need something. [15]They smile and laugh when they recognize friendly faces and show interest in things that are new and different. [16]They become shy when strangers appear and fearful when their mothers go away.

Newborns and one-year-olds are very different.

   I. physical development and muscle control
      A. Newborns cannot move their bodies or control the movement of their arms and legs. Their arms are usually folded close to their bodies, and their hands are tightly closed.
      B. One-year-olds can sit and stand, and some can even walk. They use their fingers and thumbs to pick up small objects.
  II. what they see and recognize and their attachment to caregivers
      A. Newborns are only able to see people and things that move and are about two feet away. Newborns have no memories, so they do not recognize anyone, and they cannot form attachments to people.
      B. One-year-olds can see very well, and, because they can remember, they recognize people and things. They have formed attachments to their family members, especially to their mothers.
 III. emotions and their communication with others
      A. Newborns cry when they are uncomfortable or hungry.
      B. One-year-olds whine, point, and talk when they want or need something. They smile and laugh when they recognize friendly faces and show interest in things that are new and different. They become shy when strangers appear and fearful when their mothers go away.

EXERCISE 5

With a partner, complete the activities and answer the questions.

1. Count the transitions in the two paragraphs about newborns and one-year-olds. How many transitions are in the paragraph with side-by-side organization? _____ How many are in the paragraph with point-by-point organization? _____ Why does one paragraph need more transitions than the other?

2. Notice that the paragraph with point-by-point organization has more sentences than the paragraph with side-by-side organization. Find the three sentences that appear only in the paragraph with point-by-point organization, and underline them. What is the purpose of these sentences?

3. Compare the two outlines. How is the second level (major supporting points) of the side-by-side outline different from the second level of the point-by-point outline?

TIP
The paragraphs about newborns and one-year-olds contain three transitions that signal contrast: *on the other hand*, *by comparison*, and *in contrast*. These transitions have the same meaning as *however* or *but*. For more on transitions that signal contrast, see pages 140–141 in the Language Focus section of this chapter.

EXERCISE 6

The following sample outlines do not have topic sentences. Read each outline, and decide whether it has side-by-side *or* point-by-point *organization. Then write (1) the name of the pattern of organization and (2) an appropriate topic sentence for the paragraph.*

1.

Zimbabwean and U.S. Teenagers

TOPIC SENTENCE: _____

_____

  I. how teenagers see adults

    A. In Zimbabwe, teenagers see all adults as role models and disciplinarians.

    B. In the United States, teenagers see only their parents, teachers, and coaches as role models and disciplinarians.

  II. who teenagers feel close to

    A. In Zimbabwe, teenagers feel closer to their family members and teachers than their friends.

    B. In the United States, teenagers feel closer to their friends than to their family members.

  III. who teenagers have conflict with

    A. In Zimbabwe, teenagers tend to have more conflict with their friends than with their parents.

    B. In the United States, teenagers tend to have more conflict with their parents than with their friends.

Pattern of organization: _____

2.

The Meaning of Maturity in U.S. and Arab Cultures

TOPIC SENTENCE: _____

_____

  I. maturity in U.S. culture

    A. In the United States, parents expect their children to "leave the nest," usually between the ages of eighteen and twenty-one.

    B. When young people leave home, they see themselves as separate from their families. They spend very little free time with their families, and they make decisions on their own.

    C. After they leave their family homes, young people do not see themselves as having important roles in their families or as being responsible for their families.

II. maturity in Arab culture

    A. Children are not expected to move away from their parents' home unless they need to leave for education, employment, or marriage.

    B. Young people remain psychologically connected to their families, and their identities incorporate their roles as members of their families. They ask their parents for advice when necessary, and parents expect them to follow the advice they give. At this time of their lives, young people spend their leisure time with their parents and siblings.

    C. Young people see their roles in their families becoming more important in the future as they mature and can handle more responsibility.

Pattern of organization: _____

TIP
Do not include definitions or transition words in an outline.

EXERCISE 7

On another piece of paper, make an outline of each of the following paragraphs. After each outline, write the name of the pattern of organization.

1.   **Adolescent Friendships in Canada and Cuba**

[1]Friendships between adolescents in Canada and adolescents in Cuba differ in two ways. [2]First, Canadian and Cuban teens see friendships differently. [3]In Cuba, friendships are long-lasting relationships that involve obligations such as helping each other with schoolwork. [4]Canadian teens, on the other hand, do not usually expect friendships to be long lasting or to include obligations. [5]They see friendships as simply offering opportunities to have fun with peers. [6]Second, Cuban teens choose their friends differently from the way Canadian teens do. [7]Cuban teens often choose neighbors as their friends because there is a tradition of strong neighborhood ties in Cuba. [8]Canadian teens, on the other hand, do not always choose neighbors as their close friends. [9]Instead, they seek out other teens who share their particular interests.

2.   **Motor Skill Development at Ages One and Five**

[1]Motor skills are physical movements that babies and children must learn as they grow. [2]Because the development of bones, muscles, and the nervous system takes place gradually over the first few years of life, children's motor skills are very different at ages one and five. [3]At a year old, babies have developed some, but not all, of the motor skills they will master later on. [4]One-year-olds can pull themselves up on their feet by grabbing a piece of furniture, and if their leg muscles have developed enough, they begin to walk. [5]One-year-olds can feed themselves and pick up a cup and drink from it. [6]At five, children have mastered almost all the motor skills that they will ever learn. [7]Five-year-olds are able to skip, hop on one foot, jump rope, and run or dance on their toes. [8]They can write with a pencil, cut in a straight line with a pair of scissors, fasten buttons, and perhaps even tie their shoelaces.

The Writing Process

Developing parallel lists. When you write a contrast paragraph, you need parallel (similar) pieces of information for the two things you are contrasting. To choose parallel pieces of information for your paragraph, you can develop two lists, as you see here. A writer developed these lists before writing a paragraph contrasting Chinese and British teenagers. Notice that the writer drew lines connecting parallel pieces of information and crossed out pieces of information that were not parallel.

Chinese Teenagers	**British Teenagers**
• are very close to their families	• do not share all of their parents' values
• share all or most of their parents' values	• are not as close to their families
• argue with their parents very seldom or never	• see academic success as a personal achievement that is the result of individual effort
• see academic success as something one must do in order to be a good person	• argue with their parents occasionally or frequently
• ~~have learned not to display negative emotions~~	• study hard to prepare for their own futures
• study hard to honor their parents and to prepare for their own futures	• ~~have several ways to distinguish themselves from others: as successful students, as athletes, or as socially active young people~~
• see remaining *inter*dependent with their families as a goal for their futures	• see becoming *in*dependent from their families as a goal for their futures
• achieve their identities through relationships with their families	• achieve their identities through separation from their families

EXERCISE 8

Look at the parallel lists. Draw lines connecting parallel pieces of information, and cross out pieces of information that are not parallel.

The Language Skills of Two-Year-Olds	The Language Skills of Four-Year-Olds
• know how to say 50 words and understand 150–300 words	• understand nearly 1,000 words
• use two-word sentences to talk about immediate experiences such as "See kitty" and "Have ball"	• can carry on an extended conversation
• are not able to carry on an extended conversation but can answer simple questions such as "Is Daddy home?" with brief answers such as "No"	• use simple, compound, and complex sentences with few grammatical mistakes to talk about events in the present, past, and future and to describe ideas and feelings
• use two pronouns, *I* and *me*, although not correctly	• Even non-family members can understand almost all of what four-year-olds say.
• Even family members cannot understand much of what a two-year-old says.	• can tell stories
• like listening to simple stories	• know their first and last names and the name of the street on which they live
• refer to themselves by first name	• are beginning to understand when to speak and when to remain silent and know how to simplify their speech when talking to younger children
• do not understand when to speak and when to remain silent or how to adjust speech	• understand comparisons such as *longer* or *larger*

The following steps will help you get ready to write a contrast paragraph. As you read through the steps, you will see how Denise, a student who has lived in both Polynesia and France, prepared to write a paragraph contrasting family relationships and child rearing in these two places.

Complete steps 1 and 2, and then write your first draft.

Denise's Steps

STEP 1 From page 124, select one of the three topics and one of the four points of comparison listed in that topic. Then make **parallel lists**. If you are unable to find at least two points of comparison (two parallel items on your lists), then select a different topic and make new parallel lists.

Denise decided to compare two cultures—the culture of Polynesia and the culture of France—with respect to how people care for children. She made the following parallel lists.

Polynesia	France
• large extended families	• Most families are small with two parents and one or two children.
• Children are always with grandparents, aunts, uncles, cousins, and siblings of all ages.	• Grandparents usually do not live with their grandchildren but often take care of them if the children's mother works.
• Family members take turns feeding, entertaining, and soothing babies, so babies are used to many different people holding them and never feel separation anxiety.	• Children feel closest to their mothers, who give them everything they need, so most French babies experience separation anxiety between the ages of seven and twelve months.
• Three- and four-year-old siblings often watch toddlers, and toddlers become close to their siblings as well as to their mothers.	• ~~Many toddlers and preschoolers attend some kind of day care or preschool.~~
• ~~By copying their older siblings, toddlers learn to feed and dress themselves.~~	• Siblings under ten do not watch toddlers.

STEP 2 Draft a topic sentence for your paper. Then look over your parallel lists, and think about how to organize them. You can make outlines for both side-by-side and point-by-point organization in order to compare the two and decide which you prefer.

Denise decided to use side-by-side organization. She made the outline you see here.

TIP
In general, if you want to focus on the points of comparison, point-by-point organization will work better. If you want to focus on the two parts of the topic, use side-by-side organization.

The care of children in Polynesia and in France differs in several ways.

I. Polynesia

   A. Families are large and extended; children are always with grandparents, aunts, uncles, cousins, and siblings of all ages.

   B. Family members take turns feeding, entertaining, and soothing babies; babies are used to this and never feel separation anxiety.

   C. Three- and four-year-old siblings often watch toddlers, so toddlers become close to these older siblings as well as to their mothers.

II. France

   A. Most families are small; there are two parents and one or two children in a household, and grandparents usually do not live with grandchildren but often take care of them if the children's mother works.

   B. Mothers give their babies everything they need, so their babies feel closest to them; most French babies experience separation anxiety between the ages of seven and twelve months.

   C. Siblings under ten do not watch toddlers.

STEP 3   Write your first draft.

Denise wrote the following draft paragraph.

Denise's First Draft

> *Differences between the Care of Children in Polynesia and France*
>
> [1]The care of children in Polynesia and in France differs in several ways. [2]In Polynesia, families are large and extended, so children are always with grandparents, aunts, uncles, cousins, and siblings. [3]Family members take turns feeding and soothing babies, so babies are used to being with many different people and never feel separation anxiety. [4]Three- and four-year-old siblings often watch toddlers, so toddlers become close to these older siblings as well as to their mothers. [5]In France, on the other hand, most families are small. [6]The average family has two parents and one or two children. [7]Grandparents usually do not live with their grandchildren but often take care of them if the children's mother works. [8]Mothers give their babies everything they need, so the babies feel closest to their mothers. [9]Most French babies experience separation anxiety between the ages of seven and twelve months. [10]Siblings under ten do not watch toddlers.

STEP 4   Evaluate how well the pattern of organization you have chosen works. Sometimes it is not possible to know whether side-by-side or point-by-point organization will produce a better paragraph without trying both patterns and comparing them. If you are not happy with your first draft, rewrite it with the other pattern of organization, and then select the better of the two.

Denise concluded that side-by-side organization worked well in her composition. Later, as she worked through the rest of this chapter, she made various changes to her draft and then finally wrote this draft.

Denise's Final Draft

Differences between the Care of Children in Polynesia and France

[1]The care of children in Polynesia and in France differs in several ways because the family structures are different. [2]In Polynesia, families are large and extended, so children are always with grandparents, aunts, uncles, cousins, and siblings. [3]Polynesians hold babies facing the people around them, so babies feel that they are part of the group. [4]Family members take turns feeding, entertaining, and soothing babies, so babies are used to being with many different people and never feel separation anxiety. [5]Three- and four-year-old siblings often watch toddlers, so toddlers become attached to these older siblings as well as to their mothers. [6]In France, on the other hand, most families are small. [7]The average family consists of two parents and one or two children. [8]Grandparents usually do not live with their grandchildren but often take care of them if the children's mother works. [9]French mothers fulfill all their babies' physical, intellectual, and emotional needs. [10]They usually hold their babies facing them and talk to them one-on-one, and they play with and read to their toddlers often. [11]As a result, French children's primary attachment is to their mothers. [12]Most French babies experience separation anxiety between the ages of seven and twelve months. [13]Siblings under ten do not watch toddlers, but brothers and sisters play together increasingly as they grow older. [14]Overall, the experience of growing up in a Polynesian family is quite different from that of growing up in a French family.

With a partner, review Denise's first and final drafts, and then do the activities and discuss the questions.

1. Put brackets [ ] around the topic sentences in both drafts, and notice that Denise added information to the topic sentence when she revised. How does the added information help you understand the topic better?

2. Denise used the side-by-side pattern in this contrast paragraph. Circle the transition she used to introduce the second part of the paragraph.

3. Compare Denise's first and final drafts. Underline all the words, phrases, and sentences that are different in the final draft. Notice the kinds of changes Denise made. In the margin next to each change, write *V* if she changed the vocabulary and *I* if she added information. Explain how both of these kinds of changes affect the final draft.

4. What is the purpose of the last sentence in Denise's final draft?

■ REVISING

As you study this section of the chapter, you will learn more about paragraphs and sentences. After you finish each section, review your draft. Follow the instructions in the Revision Checkpoint boxes to check and revise your work.

Composition Focus

Developing the third level. As you learned in Chapters 3 and 4, you can develop the third level of a paragraph with sensory details, examples, explanations, and quotations. You can use the same strategies for the third level in a contrast paragraph.

EXERCISE 10

*Read the paragraph, and put brackets [ ] around the sentences in the third level. Then, in the margin, label the strategies (**sensory details, examples, explanations,** or **quotations**) that the writer used.*

Japanese and U.S. Mothers

[1]The parenting styles of Japanese and U.S. mothers differ in three ways. [2]First of all, the treatment of infants (the way mothers handle and care for babies) is different. [[3]Japanese mothers carry their infants on their backs while they do their housework, and they sing or hum to them. [4]U.S. mothers, in contrast, leave their babies in a bed or a playpen and talk to them as they do their chores.] [5]Second, the treatment of toddlers

examples, sensory details

is different. [6]Japanese mothers try to make sure that their youngsters do not experience anger or frustration, and they try to avoid conflict with their children. [7]For example, if a child does not like a particular vegetable, the Japanese mother will say, "It's OK. You don't need to eat that." [8]By comparison, many U.S. mothers will encourage their child to eat it by saying, "You need to eat vegetables to grow up big and strong." [9]Finally, the treatment of older children differs. [10]Japanese mothers often teach their children the concept of "losing to win." [11]For example, if a child is arguing with his friend over a toy, his mother tells him that he can become a winner by giving the toy to his friend. [12]This way, she teaches him a lesson in social harmony (peaceful relations). [13]In order to get their children to behave, U.S. mothers use either rewards such as candy or toys or threats of a "time out" punishment (time the child must spend alone away from family members and friends).

REVISION CHECKPOINT 1

Development of the Third Level
Reread your paragraph, and focus on the third level. Ask yourself if you have used all the strategies available to you (sensory details, examples, explanations, and quotations). If you can improve the development of the third level of your paragraph, do it now.

Balanced development. Contrast paragraphs discuss two things, and writers must pay equal attention to both. When you make parallel lists during your prewriting step, you begin to see how well you will be able to develop each part of your paper. Then, after your first draft, review your writing to make sure that you discussed both parts of your topic in a balanced way.

The following paragraph is not developed in a balanced way. As you read it, look for an information gap. Following the paragraph, you will see an outline. Notice that the questions in the outline identify the information that is missing from the paragraph.

How Three-Year-Olds and Eight-Year-Olds Understand Time

[1]Three-year-olds and eight-year-olds differ in their understanding of time. [2]First, they differ in their ability to understand clocks and calendars. [3]Three-year-olds cannot read clocks, and they do not know what calendars are. [4]By comparison, eight-year-olds use clocks and calendars to find out the time or date. [5]Second, three-year-olds and eight-year-olds differ in terms of how they talk about time. [6]Generally, three-year-olds seldom talk about the past or the future unless they have experienced or are going to experience an important event, such as a friend's birthday.

Outline

Three-year-olds and eight-year-olds differ in their understanding of time.

    I. clocks and calendars

        A. Three-year-olds cannot read clocks and do not know what calendars are.

        B. Eight-year-olds use clocks and calendars to find out the time or date.

    II. how children at these ages talk about time

        A. Three-year-olds seldom talk about the past or the future unless they have experienced or are going to experience an important event, such as a friend's birthday.

        B. *How often do eight-year-olds talk about time? When or how do they talk about the past or future?*

Exercise 11

The following paragraphs do not have balanced development. Read each paragraph, and make an outline of it on another piece of paper. Where you find that there is an information gap, write one or more questions in your outline, and underline them.

1.   **Children's Chores in Mixtecan and U.S. Cultures**

    [1]There are major differences between the Mixtecan culture of southern Mexico and U.S. culture regarding children's chores. [2]First, Mixtecan children are assigned many more chores at an earlier age. [3]At about age six or seven, Mixtecan boys may be required to find food and water for a goat or burro. [4]Girls are often charged with looking after younger siblings, cooking, and washing dishes. [5]Second, Mixtecan and U.S. children have different attitudes, or opinions, about chores. [6]Mixtecan children usually think it is an honor to be assigned chores because it means that they are valued members of their communities. [7]By comparison, U.S. children tend to resent doing chores.

2.   **Javanese Children's Lives before and after Eighteen Months**

    [1]At around eighteen months, Javanese children experience a change in their lives as their siblings begin to replace their mothers as their primary caregivers. [2]Before eighteen months, a Javanese child spends all his time with his mother. [3]His mother responds to him every time he cries or whines. [4]She often plays quietly with him with small toys such as human and animal figures. [5]While playing, his mother might direct him to put the "family" of little human figures together. [6]Her play usually reflects the activities of the household—parents taking care of children, families eating together, and children going to school. [7]However, at about eighteen months, the toddler's life changes when an older sibling begins to take care of him. [8]His older sibling takes him out of the house, and together they join a mixed-age group of neighborhood children.

Balanced Development

Exchange drafts with a partner, and, on a separate piece of paper, make an outline of your partner's paragraph. If your partner's paper is not developed in a balanced way and there are information gaps in the paper, write questions in your outline, and underline them. Give the outline you made to your partner along with his or her paper.

Finally, study your partner's outline of your paper. If the outline contains questions, consider revising your draft to include answers to those questions. If you are unsure about whether or not the development of your paragraph is balanced, write a question to your teacher in the margin of your paper.

Concluding sentences. Some paragraphs need a concluding sentence. A paragraph should have a concluding sentence if it seems too short or somehow incomplete without one. A concluding sentence can do two things: It can repeat the main idea of the paragraph, or it can give a general opinion about the information in the paragraph. Here are two possible concluding sentences for two paragraphs in this chapter.

A conclusion that repeats the main idea of the paragraph, from "Japanese and U.S. Mothers" (pages 136–137):

> Differences in Japanese and U.S. parenting styles are evident at each stage of a child's development.

A conclusion that gives a general opinion about the information in the paragraph, from "Motor Skill Development at Ages One and Five" (page 129):

> An amazing amount of motor skill development takes place between ages one and five.

EXERCISE 12

TIP In your concluding sentences, try not to introduce any new ideas.

Write a concluding sentence on the lines for one of the following paragraphs.

"Newborns and One-Year-Olds" (page 125 or page 126)

_____

_____

"Adolescent Friendships in Canada and Cuba" (page 129)

_____

_____

Concluding Sentence
Reread your paragraph, and decide whether or not it needs a concluding sentence. If you think it needs a conclusion, write a sentence that either repeats the main idea of the paragraph or gives a general opinion about the information in the paragraph.

Language Focus

Signals of contrast: coordinating and subordinating conjunctions and transitions. English has a variety of contrast signals, as you can see in the chart.

Kinds of Signals	Examples	Explanations and Rules of Punctuation
coordinating conjunction: *but*	Spanish families usually have two children, *but* Ukrainian families often have one.	Use *but* to join two clauses that contain contrasting ideas. The clauses joined by *but* are both independent. Put a comma before *but*.
subordinating conjunctions: *while* and *whereas*	*While / Whereas* Spanish families usually have two children, Ukrainian families often have one. Spanish families usually have two children, *while / whereas* Ukrainian families often have one.	Use *while* and *whereas* to join two clauses that contain contrasting ideas. The clause that begins with *while* or *whereas* is the dependent clause. Put a comma between the two clauses.

Note. Use *but* to join clauses that have any kind of contrasting information. Use *while* and *whereas* only to join clauses that directly compare two people, two groups of people, two places, or two things.

A three-year-old can play with a ball, *but* she can't catch one. (not *while* or *whereas*)

A three-year-old can't catch a ball, *but / while / whereas* a five-year-old can catch one.

(continued)

Kinds of Signal	Examples	Explanations and Rules of Punctuation
transitions: *by comparison,* *however,* *in contrast,* *on the other hand*	Spanish families usually have two children. **By comparison**, Ukrainian families often have one. Spanish families usually have two children. Ukrainian families, **by comparison**, often have one. Spanish families usually have two children. **However**, Ukrainian families often have one. Spanish families usually have two children. Ukrainian families, **however**, often have one. Spanish families usually have two children. **In contrast**, Ukrainian families often have one. Spanish families usually have two children. Ukrainian families, **in contrast**, often have one. Spanish families usually have two children. **On the other hand**, Ukrainian families often have one. Spanish families usually have two children. Ukrainian families, **on the other hand**, often have one.	Use *by comparison, however, in contrast,* and *on the other hand* to show a logical relationship between two sentences. A transition cannot join clauses. A transition usually comes at the beginning of the second sentence, following the period, but sometimes the transition is placed after the subject of the second sentence. When the transition is at the beginning of the sentence, put a comma after it. When the transition follows the subject, put commas before and after it.

Note. Use *however* between clauses that have any kind of contrasting information. Use *by comparison, in contrast,* and *on the other hand* only between clauses that directly compare two people, two groups of people, two places, or two things.

Three-year-olds try to run. *However,* they can't move very fast. (not *by comparison, in contrast,* or *on the other hand*)

Two-year-olds usually learn by imitating others. *However / By comparison / In contrast / On the other hand,* five-year-olds usually learn by asking questions.

For more on coordinating conjunctions, see Appendix IA, page 196; for more on subordinating conjunctions, see Appendix IA, pages 198–199; and for more on transitions, see Appendix IA, pages 233–234.

EXERCISE 13

Underline the contrast signal in each sentence, and notice whether it is a coordinating conjunction, subordinating conjunction, or transition. Then, on another piece of paper, rewrite each sentence two times, using the two other types of contrast signals. Be sure to use correct punctuation.

1. Infants sleep about twenty hours a day, <u>while</u> ten-year-olds sleep nine or ten hours a day.

    Infants sleep about twenty hours a day, but ten-year-olds sleep nine or ten hours a day.

    Infants sleep about twenty hours a day. By comparison, ten-year-olds sleep nine or ten hours a day.

2. A one-year-old does not know the difference between correct and incorrect behavior, but a two-year-old does.

3. Japanese babies usually sleep with their mothers, while U.S. babies usually sleep alone.

4. Twelve-month-olds like to play with one toy at a time, but eighteen-month-olds enjoy playing with several toys at once.

5. Urban Polish families have one or two children, whereas rural Polish families have three or four.

6. U.S. children often misbehave in order to get attention. Mayan children, by comparison, do not act out to obtain attention.

7. Five-year-olds tend to describe people in terms of their appearance, whereas teenagers describe people in terms of their personalities.

EXERCISE 14

Fill in the blanks in the two paragraphs with contrast signals (coordinating conjunctions, subordinating conjunctions, or transitions). The punctuation of the sentences will help you decide which kind of signal to use.

1. **Families in Pakistan and Germany**

    Families in Pakistan and Germany are different in three ways. First, the size of Pakistani and German families differs. Most Pakistanis live in extended families, with three generations and a large number of children under one roof, (a) _____*while*_____ most Germans live in nuclear families with one or two children. Second, family decision making differs. In Pakistan, the oldest male member is the head of a family, and the other family members follow his decisions. In Germany, (b) _____, there are two kinds of families: In some German families, the father makes decisions for the whole family, (c) _____ in other families men and women share decision making. Finally, Pakistani and German families differ in terms of values. Pakistani families value obedience in children and loyalty in all family members. In Germany, (d) _____, family values vary. For example, some German families value obedience to the father, (e) _____ other families value equality among family members.

2. **Parental Attitudes and Responses to Conflict and Anger**

   Parents among the Tamang of Nepal and parents in the United States respond to children's social conflicts and emotions differently. First, Tamang and U.S. parents have different attitudes about anger. Tamang parents think that being angry is bad and children who show anger are misbehaving. U.S. parents, (a) _____, think it is normal for children to get angry sometimes. Second, Tamang and U.S. parents treat angry children differently. Tamang parents always scold and punish angry children, (b) _____ U.S. parents will scold and punish their children only if the children's anger leads to aggression (angry words and actions that can start a fight). Usually they just try to calm angry children by saying, "Settle down. Getting angry does not make a bad situation better." Finally, Tamang and U.S. parents view their children's responsibility in conflicts differently. For example, if a classmate spills a drink on her child's homework, a Tamang mother says that her child is at fault. She says that her child carelessly left the homework in the wrong place. A U.S. mother, (c) _____, may sympathize with her child by saying, "That's too bad," or may try to get the child to accept the misfortune by saying, "Accidents happen sometimes." The differences in Tamang and U.S. parents' attitudes and responses to their children's social difficulties reflect the different values of the two cultures.

REVISION CHECKPOINT 4

Signals of Contrast
Review your draft, and underline all the contrast signals you have used. (If you used side-by-side-style organization, you will have only one contrast signal in your paper. If you used point-by-point organization, you should have one contrast signal for every point of comparison.)

   Check the punctuation of your sentences. If you find any punctuation errors, correct them now. If you are unsure about the correct punctuation of a sentence, write a question to your teacher in the margin of your paper.

Using consistent pronoun point of view to keep paragraph focus. When
you write a paragraph, you have to choose a subject for each sentence.
As you move from sentence to sentence, you should try to repeat subjects
or choose related subjects so that readers can follow your ideas. To help
readers focus, you should avoid changing subjects for no reason. For
example, if you start the paragraph with *I* and then change to *he* and later to
you, readers might get lost because the paragraph does not have a *consistent
point of view*. *Point of view* refers to the subjects of most of the sentences in
a paragraph. There are five points of view that you can use.

EXERCISE 15

*Fill in the chart with the correct subject pronouns or possessive
adjectives. Notice that the third person singular has three subject
pronouns and three possessive adjectives.*

Points of View	Subject Pronouns	Possessive Adjectives
1. first person singular	I	*my*
2. second person singular or plural		your
3. third person singular	he, she, it	
4. first person plural		our
5. third person plural	they	

 For more on pronouns, see Appendix IA, page 228.

Third person point of view. Choosing third person pronouns can be tricky.
Look at these examples, and decide which sounds best to you.

> A parent must care for *his* child.
>
> A parent must care for *her* child.
>
> A parent must care for *his or her* child.

All three of the choices above are correct, but sometimes one pronoun is
better than another. For example, when you are writing for an audience of
men, use *his*, and when you are writing for women, use *her*. When you are
writing for both men and women, you can use *his or her*. However, a better
choice is to write in the third person *plural* point of view.

> *Parents* must care for *their* children.

In this book, most model paragraphs are in the third person plural point of
view. That is, most paragraphs use plural nouns and the third person plural
pronoun *they*.

NOTE

The first sentence in "Newborns and One-Year-Olds" has a compound subject. (*X* and *Y* are . . .) Other sentences have more than one subject. (*X* does something, and *Y* does something else. *X* does something when *Y* does something else.)

EXERCISE 16

A. *Turn to page 125, and reread "Newborns and One-Year-Olds." Underline all the subject nouns and pronouns in the paragraph.*

B. *What point of view is used in "Newborns and One-Year-Olds"? Why is this point of view the best choice for this paragraph?*

_____

_____

The writer of "Newborns and One-Year-Olds" used just one point of view—third person plural—throughout the paragraph. This strategy works well in this paragraph, but it is not always possible to stay with one point of view. In many paragraphs, the point of view changes when the level changes. For example, a paragraph may start in the third person plural and shift to the third person singular in the second or third level.

EXERCISE 17

A. *Read the topic sentence of the following paragraph, and write the name of its point of view here.*

_____

B. *Read the rest of the paragraph, and draw a line | at each place where the point of view changes. Write the name of the point of view of each section in the margin.*

Conversations with Two- and Three-Year-Old Children

[1]The talk of two-year-olds is quite different from the talk of three-year-olds. [2]Two-year-olds do not take turns in conversation and are not good listeners. | [3]A two-year-old tends to make announcements about what he is doing and how he is doing it, such as "I'm making the car go fast." [4]A two-year-old wants his mother to be his audience, but he does not pay much attention to her responses. [5]When she asks him a question like "Where is the car going?" he either ignores the question or repeats, "The car is going." [6]Three-year-olds, by comparison, listen to what their mothers say, take turns, and contribute new information to the conversation. [7]For example, when a three-year-old's mother says, "I see you are dressing your dolly," the three-year-old may reply, "Yes. Dolly's going to the park with her daddy. Today is her daddy's day off." [8]Because of their more advanced language and greater understanding of others' thoughts and feelings, three-year-olds can have real conversations, whereas two-year-olds cannot.

third person plural

The writer changed from the third person plural *they* to the third person singular *he* and *she* in the explanations and examples in this paragraph. This change is a signal to the reader that the writer is moving from the second to the third level in the paragraph.

> ### Using Point of View
> Review your draft, and notice if you used one point of view or changed your point of view. If you changed point of view, ask yourself if you did so for a good reason, such as to highlight an example. If you have questions about the best point of view to use in any of the sentences in your paper, write a question for your teacher in the margin of your paper.

■FINAL DRAFT

1. Before you write your final draft, look over your paragraph one last time to decide if you want to make any further changes.

2. Prepare a final draft of your composition. Make sure that you have used capital letters, periods, and commas where they are needed, and check your spelling.

3. Exchange papers with one or two classmates. Read each other's papers carefully. Turn to page 251 in Appendix II, and answer the questions on the Peer Review Form.

4. Check your paper again and make any necessary corrections. Turn in your paper to your teacher.

■ CHAPTER REVIEW

Look back at what you have accomplished in Chapter 5. Check off (✔) what you have learned and what you have used while writing and revising your composition.

Chapter 5 Topics	Learned	Used
understanding that some words are used as more than one part of speech (page 120)		
understanding that there are both person nouns and concept nouns (page 121)		
writing a topic sentence for a contrast paragraph (page 124)		
choosing side-by-side or point-by-point organization and making an outline (page 133)		
using parallel lists to gather information and ideas for a contrast paragraph (page 130)		
using sensory details, examples, explanations, and quotations to develop the third level of a contrast paragraph (page 136)		
checking a contrast paragraph for balanced development and addressing information gaps (page 137)		
writing a concluding sentence (page 139)		
using contrast signals (coordinating and subordinating conjunctions and transitions) and punctuating them correctly (pages 140–141)		
checking pronoun point of view in a paragraph (pages 144–145)		

Making Communities Better

Writing an Opinion Paragraph and Essay

What does *quality of life* mean to you? People have different opinions about what they need in order to live a good life. For many people, a good quality of life means having a clean, safe place to live; a good job; and access to health care and education. It also means living in a society in which citizens respect each other and the government treats citizens fairly. In this chapter we will look at problems that affect quality of life and suggest ways to solve them.

This chapter will help you

- write a topic sentence for an opinion paragraph.
- find and develop supporting points for an opinion paragraph.
- use a survey to gather ideas and information before writing.
- expand a paragraph to a complete essay.
- write real future and unreal present or future conditional sentences to support an opinion.
- use modal verbs to express necessity, suggestion, and possibility.

■ READING FOR WRITING

Before You Read

Look at the photos on page 148, and complete the activities. Then share your answers with a partner or small group.

1. Over half the people in the world now live in cities. What are some of the problems that city dwellers face? List five problems, and rank them from least serious to most serious.

least serious   a. _____

      ↑   b. _____

             c. _____

      ↓   d. _____

most serious   e. _____

2. Do you have ideas about how to solve any of the problems you listed above? If so, what solutions would you recommend?

3. The following reading is on the topic of crime and violence in cities. Read the text all the way through one time for understanding. Then read it a second time, and put a star (*) next to any idea that seems important and a question mark (?) next to any sentence that you don't understand.

Reading

FROM VIOLENCE TO JUSTICE AND SECURITY IN CITIES

Adapted from the original article by Franz Vanderschueren

dweller: *a person who lives in a place*

rate: *how often something happens*

lack: *to not have something that you need*

target: *something that people want to reach or have*

1   Worldwide, 60 percent of city **dwellers** become crime victims within a five-year period. Crime **rates** vary from country to country, but in general, crime in cities is increasing, and life there is becoming more difficult and less pleasant. There is no single cause for increasing crime, but a number of reasons:

- In some parts of the world, the number of city dwellers living in extreme poverty has grown greatly. Very poor people who **lack** everything— good housing, opportunities to study, and regular employment—live alongside people who have much more, and they feel marginalized, or left out. Poverty does not always lead to criminal behavior, but it can contribute to it.
- At the same time, advertising encourages people to want things, and people in modern societies value material possessions.
- In cities, homes, cars, and other kinds of property are left unguarded while people work, making easy **targets** for thieves. In the past, community members kept a watchful eye on their neighborhoods, but in modern cities, neighbors seldom know or look out for one another.

social classes: *groups divided according to wealth and power*

self-esteem: *a feeling of being worthy of respect*

law-abiding: *following the law*

overwhelmed: *having too much to handle*

convict: *to prove in a court that someone is guilty*

revenue: *money that a government receives*

juvenile: *younger than an adult*

offender: *someone who breaks the law*

make restitution: *to pay for harm one has caused*

- Families of all **social classes** are under stress and sometimes do not provide positive social experiences for their children. Negative social experiences at home can make young people lose **self-esteem** and motivation. If young people cannot find rewards as regular, **law-abiding** citizens, they may turn to crime.

- Children and young people see thousands of acts of violence on television and in movies, and research shows that viewing so many acts of violence increases violent behavior.

- Finally, the criminal justice systems of countries around the world are not able to stop crime. In poorer countries, police departments are **overwhelmed** by the number of reported crimes, and the court systems are slow. In richer countries, those who commit violent crimes are **convicted** and put in prison, and the prison populations are growing. However, putting people in crowded prisons does not change their behavior or reduce crime.

2   Crime affects individuals, families, and communities. City dwellers today feel less safe and use public space less. As a result, businesses suffer, and **tax revenues** drop. At the same time, governments must spend more to increase police protection for citizens. As people around the world have faced this problem of rising crime, they have tried a variety of solutions:

- In some cities and neighborhoods within cities, citizens have responded to crime on their own. In a neighborhood watch program, people take turns looking for possibly illegal activities in their area. A neighborhood watch system has been used in Tanzania, where family groups organize to protect their own communities.

- Some countries have organized crime prevention programs at both the local and national level. For example, Japan has a large number of very small police stations throughout the country. The officers in these stations are required to visit each family and business in their neighborhoods at least twice a year. In addition, the neighborhood police officers deal with **juvenile offenders** in a special way. They allow those who commit less serious offenses to sign a letter of apology instead of going to court. This makes the public feel more positive about the police.

- Some countries do not use their traditional court systems for less serious offenses. In Uganda, for example, local councils handle less serious crimes quickly, free of charge, in a way that residents can understand. In France, under a system called *penal mediation*, offenders face their victims and, through discussion, find a way to **make restitution.**

3   These examples show that people everywhere can develop solutions to the problems of crime and violence. While solutions vary from place to place and culture to culture, they share common characteristics. Good solutions are accessible to people—that is, they are inexpensive, fast, and located conveniently in their city neighborhoods. Finally, good solutions do not rely only on punishment, but they do require cooperation among neighbors, the police, and government.

 **AUTHOR** Franz Vanderschueren is a professor of sociology at Hurtado University in Santiago, Chile. He was director of the United Nations Safer Cities Program from 1996 to 2001.

Understanding the Reading

A. Compare your marking of the text with a partner or a small group. Discuss the meaning of any sentence that you put a question mark next to with your classmates and teacher.

B. Complete the following activities, and then discuss them with a partner or small group.

1. Vanderschueren lists six causes of urban crime in the article. Which ones do you think are the most important? Rank the causes from most important (6) to least important (1) by writing numbers next to them.

2. Which paragraph discusses the effects of urban crime? How many effects does it mention? What are they?

3. Look at the list of solutions to the problem of crime that have been developed in different countries. Which of these solutions appeals to you most? Why?

4. According to Vanderschueren, what are the characteristics of good solutions to the problem of crime? Do you agree? Why or why not?

Vocabulary Building

Synonyms. English, like other languages, has both *synonyms* and *related words*. **Synonyms** are words that have the same meaning. Synonyms can replace each other in sentences. **Related words** have similar, but not exactly the same, meanings. Related words can sometimes replace each other in a sentence.

Synonyms

toxic (adj.) ⟷ poisonous (adj.)

Automobile exhaust is *toxic / poisonous*.

increase (n.) ⟷ rise (n.)

The *increase / rise* in crime is bad for tourism.

Related Words

- crime (n.): illegal activities

  Unlocked cars and houses can be an invitation for people to commit *crime*.

- violence (n.): behavior that is intended to hurt other people

  Movies that show fighting, shooting, or bombing can encourage people to commit acts of *violence*.

- unequal (adj.): not the same everywhere or for everyone

  The amount of rain in the two cities is *unequal*.

- unfair (adj.): not following the belief that all people should receive the same treatment

  The difference in the amount of police protection in the two communities is *unfair*.

Knowing about synonyms and related words is helpful when you write. With this knowledge, you can avoid repeating words and choose the most appropriate words to express your meaning.

Words that belong to the Academic Word List are identified with a star (✶) symbol.

EXERCISE 1

*With a partner, write **S** next to the pairs of words that are synonyms and **R** next to the pairs of words that are related but are not synonyms. Refer to your dictionary if you need to.*

1. __R__ resident   citizen
2. _____ rapid   fast
3. _____ prosperous   wealthy
4. _____ district   neighborhood
5. _____ transit   transportation
6. _____ effect   ✶consequence
7. _____ protected   peaceful
8. _____ lead to   cause
9. _____ suspicious   ✶illegal
10. _____ deal with   handle
11. _____ smoke   smog
12. _____ lack (n.)   need (n.)

Nouns that are both countable and uncountable. Many nouns have both countable and uncountable forms. The two forms have related but different meanings: The countable sense is always more specific, and the uncountable sense is more general. Look at these examples.

COUNTABLE, SPECIFIC:	He owns two *businesses*. (separate commercial operations)
UNCOUNTABLE, GENERAL:	*Business* has been good this year. (the amount of profit from all sales of goods and services)
COUNTABLE, SPECIFIC:	Lee has traveled a lot, and he has observed various *societies*. (separate national or cultural groups)
UNCOUNTABLE, GENERAL:	We must follow the rules of *society*. (the people we live among and the traditions and laws that organize our lives together)

 For more on countable and uncountable nouns, see Appendix IA, page 221.

EXERCISE 2

*Each noun below has a countable and an uncountable form. Choose the correct forms to complete each pair of sentences. Then write **C** or **U** at the end of each sentence to show whether the noun is countable or uncountable.*

1. culture
   a. _____Culture_____ influences how we think. (*U*)
   b. Criminal justice systems differ across _____cultures_____.
      (*C*)

2. *community
   a. Street festivals give my city a sense of _____.
      (   )
   b. Some _____ have developed neighborhood watch systems. (   )

3. punishment
   a. The _____ for theft and burglary range from one month to several years in prison. (   )
   b. In some cultures, shame is a form of _____.
      (   )

4. property
   a. Parks are public _____. (   )
   b. _____ in the center of town are more valuable than those on the margins. (   )

5. activity

   a. There isn't much _____ in the streets in this district. (   )

   b. The community center offers different _____ for young people. (   )

6. organization

   a. Bringing infrastructure to neighborhoods that lack it requires planning and _____. (   )

   b. International aid _____ offer financial help to cities and national governments. (   )

■WRITING

Assignment

After you study pages 155–164, you will do the following assignment.

Write a one-paragraph composition that gives an opinion about improving the quality of life in your city, town, rural area, state, province, or country. You may want to suggest a solution to one of the problems or issues in the list.

- discrimination
- education
- employment
- garbage or waste
- housing
- lack of parks and open space

- natural disasters
- pollution
- poverty
- public health
- transportation
- violence or crime
- water or food safety

Your first draft will be a paragraph. The topic sentence of your paragraph will make a suggestion or give an opinion, and the body of your paragraph will include two or three supporting points.

Then, on pages 165–176, you will learn how to expand your paragraph to a four- or five-paragraph essay. Your final draft will be an essay.

Understanding Your Assignment

The topic sentence of an opinion paragraph. The topic sentence of an opinion paragraph offers an opinion or a suggestion. The topic sentence usually contains *should* or *should not*.

> The downtown area of my city *should have* more parking.

> Our city *should not allow* smoking in restaurants.

The supporting points of an opinion paragraph. Writers must support their suggestions or opinions. A supporting point in an opinion paragraph answers the question *Why?*

TOPIC SENTENCE: My town lacks a place to watch professional sports, so it should build a sports arena.

SUPPORTING POINT 1: The residents love sports.

SUPPORTING POINT 2: A new arena will attract new businesses to our town.

Why?

SUPPORTING POINT 3: Our town has a large empty area in a good location. An arena will be the best use of that space.

TOPIC SENTENCE: My city should plant more trees.

SUPPORTING POINT 1: Trees are beautiful.

Why?

SUPPORTING POINT 2: The streets are hot in the summer, and trees provide shade.

SUPPORTING POINT 3: When it rains, tree roots take in water. That prevents flooding.

Identifying the problem. Writers compose opinion paragraphs about quality-of-life issues because they have ideas about how to solve problems. Writers present problems in their paragraphs in various ways. In the first example above, the writer mentioned the problem in the topic sentence: *My town lacks a place to watch professional sports*. In the second example, the writer mentioned two problems as supporting reasons: *The streets are hot in the summer*, and *There is flooding when it rains*.

Read the following opinion paragraphs. Put brackets [ ] around the suggestion or opinion, and underline the supporting points (the second level of the paragraph). Then answer the questions.

1. **Housing for Homeless Families**

[¹The state of Texas should provide free or low-cost housing for homeless families for two reasons.] ²<u>First, if parents have permanent or long-term housing, they will be more likely to find and keep well-paying jobs and be able to provide for their children</u>. ³People without a home have difficulty keeping clean, and they also find it extremely hard to maintain a schedule. ⁴For these reasons, employers may not want to hire homeless people. ⁵Second, homelessness has negative effects on children. ⁶Children need stability in their lives. ⁷Homeless children often do not know where they will sleep next. ⁸They do not feel secure anywhere because they may be asked to leave at any time. ⁹In my daughter's elementary school class, there is a girl who is homeless. ¹⁰This girl is quiet, and she lacks confidence. ¹¹She never does her homework because she has no place to do it. ¹²If this girl had a place to live, she would probably be more successful in school. ¹³Having a home should be the right of all families.

a. How many problems does the paragraph mention? _____

b. Write the problems described in the paragraph in your own words.

_____

_____

_____

_____

c. Does the paragraph say who should solve the problem? If so, where?

_____

2. **Expand Weekend Library Hours**

¹The public library in our town should be open on Sunday for two reasons. ²First, students need a quiet place to study. ³Many students live in small apartments with several family members, including younger brothers and sisters, so they don't have a quiet place to read and write without interruptions at home. ⁴Therefore, they need the library to complete their homework assignments successfully. ⁵If the library were open

on Sundays, students would have many more hours when they could use it. ⁶Second, many other people need expanded access to library services, too. ⁷Some people go to the library when they need information about products, businesses, or local laws. ⁸Others like to go to the library to borrow some music or a movie or to find a good novel to read. ⁹However, people who work full-time usually can't use the library on weekdays, and with only one weekend day—Saturday—when the library is open, they can rarely take advantage of its services. ¹⁰Therefore, for the benefit of students and working people, the public library should be open on Sundays.

a. How many problems does the paragraph mention? _____

b. Write the problems below in your own words.

_____

c. Does the paragraph say who should solve the problem? If so, where?

_____

Problems, benefits, and imagined situations. The supporting points of an opinion paragraph can refer to problems, benefits, or both. In addition, in a supporting point, a writer may ask readers to imagine what it would be like if things were different. Look at this example.

The town of Apple Creek should have a history museum.

a. The children of Apple Creek have little appreciation for history because there are no monuments or exhibits in their town. (problem)

b. Children learn school subjects best when they have experiences outside of the classroom that relate to their academic lessons. (benefit)

c. If Apple Creek had a history museum, grandparents could take their grandchildren there and show them what the world was like when they were young. (imagined situation)

EXERCISE 4

Here are some topic sentences for opinion paragraphs. Each one is followed by four sentences. All but one of the four sentences are good supporting points for the topic sentence. In each item, cross out the sentence that does not support the opinion expressed in the topic sentence.

1. It should be illegal to carry a gun in the United States.

a. If carrying guns were illegal, there would be fewer murders, robberies, muggings, and other types of violent crime.

b. ~~Guns are expensive.~~

c. There are many accidental gun deaths in the United States.

d. If guns were illegal, citizens would feel safer.

2. The city of Cairo, Egypt, should create pedestrian-only zones in the city center.

    a. The older streets are narrow and were not designed for cars.

    b. There is too much traffic in the downtown area.

    c. If there were pedestrian-only zones, there would be fewer cars and less pollution.

    d. Trees planted on the streets would provide shade from the hot sun.

3. The city of Moscow, Russia, should not allow smoking on the street.

    a. A law banning smoking on the street would reduce teenage smoking because teenagers are more likely to smoke in public places than at home.

    b. Russia has a very low cigarette tax compared to other countries.

    c. If a law banned smoking on the street, many people would develop a negative attitude toward smoking.

    d. If people smoked less, there would be less suffering from illnesses caused by smoking, such as heart disease and lung cancer.

4. The government of Uganda should take steps to stop the spread of malaria.

    a. Malaria affects many citizens in Uganda, and it is the leading cause of death of children under five.

    b. The symptoms of malaria are fever, chills, sweating, and headaches.

    c. If people do not lose workdays because they are ill or need to take care of sick children, the country's economy will be stronger.

    d. With government support, local businesses can make inexpensive bed nets that protect people from the mosquitoes that spread the disease.

5. The Brazilian state of São Paulo should take steps to increase public transit in order to reduce air pollution in the São Paulo Metropolitan Region.

    a. Cars produce most of the air pollution in the São Paulo Metropolitan Region.

    b. Air pollution particularly affects children, who may develop lung problems later in life as a result of growing up in a polluted environment.

    c. The population of the São Paulo Metropolitan Region includes many different ethnic groups.

    d. Another Brazilian city, Curitiba, has a very efficient and affordable public transportation system, which has reduced air pollution.

TIP

Choice d. in number 5 compares the city of São Paulo to another Brazilian city, Curitiba. A comparison of two similar things can be an effective supporting point in an opinion paragraph when the comparison shows that the change you are recommending is possible. The Curitiba example shows that another Brazilian city has successfully created a public transportation system, so it is an effective supporting point.

The third level of an opinion paragraph. In prior chapters you used sensory details, examples, quotations, and explanation to develop supporting points in paragraphs. These strategies can all be used in opinion paragraphs. However, explanations that include cause-and-effect reasoning are the most common—and often the most effective—kind of development. Cause-and-effect explanations include problems, benefits, and imagined situations.

EXERCISE 5

Put brackets [ ] around the sentences that make up the third level in the opinion paragraph below. Next to each pair of brackets, identify the strategy (or strategies) of development by writing **sensory details**, **example**, **quotation**, *or* **cause-and-effect reasoning**.

Urban Gardens for Washington, D.C.

¹The city government in Washington, D.C., should encourage its residents to start fruit and vegetable gardens in their backyards, on their rooftops, and in empty lots. ²First, parts of Washington do not have convenient supermarkets.

example, quotation, cause and effect reasoning

[³My friend Mirna, who lives in a part of Washington called Anacostia, says, "I don't have a car, and the nearest market is ten long blocks from my house. ⁴It's very hard to carry fruits and vegetables home."] ⁵Second, many people in Washington do not have healthy eating habits. ⁶They go to fast-food restaurants and consume greasy, salty burgers and fries, which make them gain weight and increase their risk of hypertension, heart attacks, and cancer. ⁷If they grew their own food, they would eat more raw fruit and fresh vegetables and become healthier as a result. ⁸Finally, gardening benefits people psychologically in several ways. ⁹City people have a lot of stress in their lives, and getting outside and working in a garden can help them relax. ¹⁰Gardeners can enjoy the sight of delicate pink peach blossoms, the hum of bees in squash blossoms, or the taste of a juicy, sweet melon. ¹¹These simple pleasures lift their spirits. ¹²In addition, gardeners meet and talk to their neighbors more often than people who don't garden. ¹³If the city helped residents set up community gardens in empty lots, neighbors would have a chance to meet and plan gardens together. ¹⁴This would broaden people's social lives, provide a healthier diet, and beautify the city.

The Writing Process

Using a survey to gather ideas and information for an opinion paragraph. A **survey** is a way of collecting information about a topic or an issue (problem) from other people. To conduct a survey, you make a list of questions, ask several people (respondents) the questions, and write down their answers. Doing a survey before writing will help you understand your topic better. A survey will tell you if other people think the problem you have identified is important, what ideas they have for solving it, and what reasons they give to support their solutions. Here is a sample survey with questions and answers from five respondents.

RESPONDENT 1	RESPONDENT 2	RESPONDENT 3	RESPONDENT 4	RESPONDENT 5
1. Do you think automobiles are a problem in the Greater Los Angeles area?				
No. I like cars.	*Yes, and pollution is a serious problem.*	*Yes, because during rush hours people waste time in traffic.*	*Maybe, but we need them.*	*Yes, there are too many cars.*
2. Why are automobiles a problem?				
	Air pollution causes health problems like asthma, bronchitis, and probably cancer.	*Everybody has to go to work and go home at the same time, and most commuters drive because it is faster than public transportation.*	*The smog is bad, especially in the summer.*	*Air pollution affects health, especially the health of children and elderly people who live near freeways.*
3. Who should solve the problems that automobiles cause?				
	The city should solve them.	*Employers can help solve them.*	*not sure*	*The government should.*
4. What action(s) should be taken? Why?				
	If the city provides more trains and buses, people will use them because gasoline is expensive.	*Employers should let people set their own work schedules when possible. Then everyone would not have to commute at the same time.*	*not sure*	*"In Commerce City, where I live, public transit is free. The buses are fast because drivers do not have to spend time waiting for people to pay fares. Many Commerce residents choose to ride public transit."*

Using survey results in an opinion paragraph. You will conduct a survey as part of your prewriting. Before you conduct your survey, you will probably have some ideas about your topic. However, as you do the survey, you may find that other people see the problem differently, and their comments may make you reconsider your opinion. On the other hand, your survey results may give you new ideas that support your opinion.

You can use the ideas and information from the survey in your writing. Look at Respondent 5's final answer in the survey. It is in quotation marks because the writer wanted to remember the exact words the respondent used. If a respondent gives you an original idea or an interesting statement, write down his or her exact words in quotation marks so you can use a quotation as support in your paper.

The steps that follow will help you get ready to write an opinion paragraph. As you read through the steps, you will see how Tran, a student from Vietnam who lives in the Greater Los Angeles area, prepared to write a paragraph about transportation.

Complete steps 1 to 4, and then write your first draft.

Tran's Steps

STEP 1 To select a topic, make a **list** of ideas about how to improve the quality of life in your area. If you like, you can make a list of problems first and then write a solution for each problem. Then circle the solution you think you might be able to write an opinion paragraph about.

Tran made the following lists about the Greater Los Angeles area.

Problems		Solutions
crime	⟶	more police on the streets
traffic	⟶	(better public transit)
poverty	⟶	more jobs
some high school students are not prepared for college	⟶	year-round schools

After you choose a topic, draft a **topic sentence** for your opinion paragraph. Next, list all the supporting points that you can think of. Put a check (✔) next to the supporting points that you think you will be able to explain or illustrate most effectively. (Because you will need to develop each supporting point more when you write an essay, select only supporting points that you can develop well.)

Tran drafted the following topic sentence and supporting points.

The Greater Los Angeles area should improve its public transportation.

    ✔ *The L.A. area has too much pollution, and public transit reduces pollution.*

    ✔ *Public transit is very important to low-income people who don't own cars.*

    There would be fewer automobile accidents if more people took public transit.

STEP 3 Write a list of **survey questions** like the questions in the sample survey on page 160, and conduct your survey. After you finish, review the results of your survey. Did the survey results change your opinion? Did they give you new ideas about how to support your original point of view? Revise your topic sentence and supporting points if necessary.

Tran conducted a survey and obtained the results you saw on page 160. Respondent 5's last comment made Tran reconsider the opinion he had expressed in his draft topic sentence, so he rewrote his topic sentence, as you see here.

The Greater Los Angeles area should provide free public transportation.

STEP 4 Before you write your first draft, make a **three-level outline**. For the third level, use explanations (cause-and-effect reasoning) as well as examples, quotations, and description.

Tran made the following outline.

> The Greater Los Angeles area should provide free public transportation.
>
> I. The L.A. area has too much traffic and too much air pollution.
>
>   A. If people can ride buses and trains for free, they will drive less, and the traffic and smog will decrease. That will be better for everyone's health, but especially for people who live near the freeways.
>
> II. If public transportation is free, life will be a little easier for people.
>
>   A. People working in minimum-wage jobs find it hard to survive in today's economy.
>
>   B. The cost of rent, food, medicine, and other necessities is high.
>
> III. Free public transit is faster than paid public transit.
>
>   A. The city of Commerce, which is in the Los Angeles area, offers free public transit. My cousin Ly, who lives in Commerce, says, "The buses are fast because drivers do not have to spend time waiting for people to pay fares."

Write your first draft.

Tran's First Draft

A Solution for Los Angeles

¹The Greater Los Angeles area should provide free public transportation. ²First, the L.A. area has too much traffic and too much air pollution. ³If people can ride buses and trains for free, they will drive less, and the traffic and smog will decrease. ⁴That will be better for everyone's health, but especially for people who live near the freeways and on busy streets. ⁵Second, if public transportation is free, life will be a little easier for people. ⁶Many people working in minimum-wage jobs find it hard to survive in today's economy. ⁷The cost of rent, food, medicine, and other necessities is high. ⁸Third, free public transit is faster than paid public transit. ⁹The city of Commerce, which is in the Los Angeles area, offers free public transit. ¹⁰My cousin Ly, who lives in Commerce, says, "The buses are fast because drivers do not have to spend time waiting for people to pay fares."

As Tran worked through the rest of this chapter, he expanded his paragraph to an essay. You will see how he did this on pages 166–167 and 170–172.

EXERCISE 6

With a partner, review Tran's first draft paragraph. Answer the questions, and follow the directions to mark the text.

1. Where is the topic sentence in Tran's paragraph? Put brackets [ ] around it.

2. What transitions did Tran use to identify his supporting points?

3. Underline the supporting points in Tran's paragraph.

4. Circle one supporting idea that Tran took from his survey.

■ EXPANDING YOUR FIRST DRAFT TO AN ESSAY

As you study this section of the chapter, you will learn how to expand your paragraph to an essay. When you expand a paragraph to an essay, you keep the basic parts of the paragraph—the main idea statement (topic sentence), the second level (supporting points), and the third level (development)—and add to them.

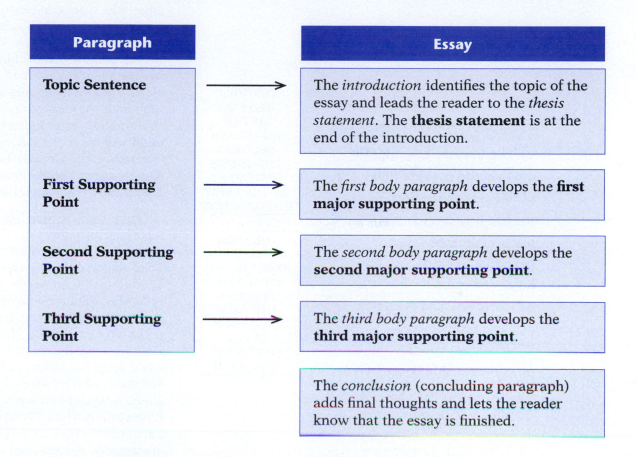

Paragraph	Essay
Topic Sentence	The *introduction* identifies the topic of the essay and leads the reader to the *thesis statement*. The **thesis statement** is at the end of the introduction.
First Supporting Point	The *first body paragraph* develops the **first major supporting point**.
Second Supporting Point	The *second body paragraph* develops the **second major supporting point**.
Third Supporting Point	The *third body paragraph* develops the **third major supporting point**.
	The *conclusion* (concluding paragraph) adds final thoughts and lets the reader know that the essay is finished.

On pages 166–167, you can see how Tran expanded his paragraph to an essay. Notice that the topic sentence of Tran's paragraph becomes the **thesis statement** (main idea statement) of his essay. Where does the thesis statement appear in the essay? Where do the major supporting points from Tran's paragraph appear in his essay?

EXPANSION OF TRAN'S PARAGRAPH TO AN ESSAY:
A SOLUTION FOR LOS ANGELES

Essay

[1]The Greater Los Angeles area includes over eighty cities which are connected by numerous freeways. [2]Each city has many wide streets as well. [3]Noisy, polluting traffic fills the freeways and streets at all hours of the day and night, and at rush hour the cars barely move. [4]Automobiles are ruining the quality of life in the L.A. area. [5]Therefore, **the Greater Los Angeles area should provide free public transportation**.

INTRODUCTION

Paragraph

[1]**The Greater Los Angeles area should provide free public transportation.** [2]First, the L.A. area has too much traffic and too much air pollution. [3]If people can ride buses and trains for free, they will drive less, and the traffic and smog will decrease. [4]That will be better for everyone's health, but especially for people who live near the freeways and on busy streets.

THE TOPIC SENTENCE OF THE PARAGRAPH BECOMES THE THESIS STATEMENT OF THE ESSAY INTRODUCTION.

THE FIRST SUPPORTING POINT IN THE PARAGRAPH BECOMES THE TOPIC SENTENCE OF THE FIRST BODY PARAGRAPH.

[6]First, the L.A. area has too much air pollution. [7]Automobiles cause most of the pollution, and there are about 12 million of them on the roads every day. [8]Mountains surround the urban area and trap the pollution over the city. [9]There isn't much wind to blow the smog away, but there is a lot of sunshine, which causes chemical changes in air pollution, making it more dangerous. [10]Possible harmful effects of air pollution are asthma, emphysema, and cancer. [11]Air pollution affects children and elderly people most, especially if they live near a freeway. [12]If public buses and trains are free, people will drive less, and the smog will decrease. [13]That will be better for everyone's health.

BODY PARAGRAPH 1

Paragraph (continued)

⁵<u>Second, if public transportation is free, life will be a little easier for people.</u> ⁶Many people working in minimum-wage jobs find it hard to survive in today's economy. ⁷The cost of rent, food, medicine, and other necessities is high. ⁸<u>Third, free public transit is faster than paid public transit.</u> ⁹The city of Commerce, which is in the Los Angeles area, offers free public transit. ¹⁰My cousin Ly, who lives in Commerce, says, "The buses are fast because drivers do not have to spend time waiting for people to pay fares."

THE SECOND SUPPORTING POINT IN THE PARAGRAPH BECOMES THE TOPIC SENTENCE OF THE SECOND BODY PARAGRAPH.

THE THIRD SUPPORTING POINT IN THE PARAGRAPH BECOMES THE TOPIC SENTENCE OF THE THIRD BODY PARAGRAPH.

THE CONCLUDING PARAGRAPH IS ADDED TO THE ESSAY.

Essay (continued)

BODY PARAGRAPH 2

¹⁴<u>Second, if public transportation is free, life will be a little easier for people.</u> ¹⁵Many people working in minimum-wage jobs find it hard to survive in today's economy. ¹⁶The cost of rent, food, medicine, and other necessities is high. ¹⁷People earning the minimum wage live on the margin; that means if they have an emergency, they may not be able to eat three meals a day for a while. ¹⁸A friend of mine who works as a dishwasher pays $5.00 a day to ride public transit to his job in downtown L.A. ¹⁹This amounts to more than 12 percent of his take-home pay. ²⁰If there is free public transportation, life will be a little less stressful for him.

BODY PARAGRAPH 3

²¹<u>Third, free public transit is faster than paid public transit.</u> ²²The city of Commerce, which is in the Los Angeles area, offers free public transit. ²³My cousin Ly, who lives in Commerce, says, "The buses are fast because drivers do not have to spend time waiting for people to pay fares." ²⁴The residents of Commerce seem very satisfied. ²⁵Ly explains, "Many Commerce residents choose to ride public transit, which reduces traffic congestion." ²⁶Commerce has set a good example for the whole Los Angeles area.

CONCLUSION

²⁷Offering free public transit in the Los Angeles area would give several benefits. ²⁸It would reduce smog, help residents working on low-wage jobs, and make public transit quicker. ²⁹Therefore, the Greater L.A. area ought to give citizens free public transportation.

EXERCISE 7

A. *With a partner, put brackets [ ] around all the sentences that Tran added to the body paragraphs of his essay.*

B. *What questions do you think Tran asked himself as he expanded each supporting point in his paragraph? Write some of these questions on another piece of paper.*

Example:

Paragraph	Essay	Questions
[2]First, the L.A. area has too much traffic and too much air pollution. [3]If people can ride buses and trains for free, they will drive less, and the traffic and smog will decrease. [4]That will be better for everyone's health. . . .	[6]First, the L.A. area has too much air pollution. [[7]Automobiles cause most of the pollution, and there are about 12 million of them on the roads every day. [8]Mountains surround the urban area and trap the pollution over the city. [9]There isn't much wind to blow the smog away, but there is a lot of sunshine, which causes chemical changes in air pollution. . . .	*What causes most of the air pollution?* *How many cars are there in the Los Angeles area?* *Do the mountains affect the air quality?* *How does LA's weather affect the air pollution?*

The Process of Changing Your Paragraph to an Essay

Expand your paragraph to an essay now. Study Tran's body paragraph development on pages 166–167, and follow the steps below. You will need several pieces of paper to complete the steps.

First, you will write the *thesis statement*. Then you will write the *body paragraphs*, the *introduction*, and finally the *conclusion*. This is the best sequence to follow because, if you wrote the introduction first, you might put information in it that should be in the body of the essay.

Writing the Thesis Statement and the Body of the Essay

STEP 1   **To begin, copy your topic sentence on the top of one piece of paper, and write "thesis statement" next to it.** The thesis statement is the main idea statement of your essay. It will be at the end of your introduction. The controlling idea of your thesis statement will tell the reader what will come in your body paragraphs.

STEP 2   **Find the supporting points (second level) in your paragraph, and underline them. Copy each supporting point at the top of a separate piece of paper.** Each supporting point will become the topic sentence of a body paragraph. (See how Tran did this step on pages 170–172.)

STEP 3   **Reread your first-draft paragraph, and notice how you developed your first supporting point. On the paper with the first supporting point, write as many questions as possible to get ready to further develop the supporting point. Use the question words** *Who, What, Where, When, Why,* **and** *How.* This step is very important because good body paragraphs are the heart of a successful essay. They show the development of your ideas. (See how Tran did this step on pages 170–172.)

STEP 4   **Think about your questions, and plan how you will answer them. If you want, you can make an outline of each body paragraph before you begin to write.** (See how Tran did this step on pages 170–172.)

STEP 5   **Write a draft of each body paragraph.** (See how Tran did this step on pages 170–172.)

STEP 6   **Organize your papers by putting the body paragraphs in the order in which you want them to appear in your essay.**

Tran's Body Paragraph Development: Topic sentence, development questions, outline

BODY PARAGRAPH 1

Topic Sentence: First, the L.A. area has too much traffic and too much air pollution.

Questions:

What causes most of the air pollution?

How many cars are there in the Los Angeles area?

Do the mountains affect the air quality?

How does L.A.'s weather affect the air pollution?

How does air pollution affect human health?

Who does the pollution affect?

Outline:

The Los Angeles area has too much air pollution.

I. the causes of air pollution in the L.A. area

II. the effects of air pollution in the L.A area

III. the effects of free public transportation on smog

Paragraph:

First, the L.A. area has too much air pollution. Automobiles cause most of the pollution, and there are about 12 million of them on the roads every day. Mountains surround the urban area and trap the pollution over the city. There isn't much wind to blow the smog away, but there is a lot of sunshine, which causes chemical changes in air pollution, making it more dangerous. Possible harmful effects of air pollution are asthma, emphysema, and cancer. Air pollution affects children and elderly people most, especially if they live near a freeway. If public buses and trains are free, people will drive less, and the smog will decrease. That will be better for everyone's health.

BODY PARAGRAPH 2

Topic Sentence: Second, if public transportation is free, life will be a little easier for people.

Questions:

Why is it hard for people working in minimum-wage jobs to survive in today's economy?

What happens to people in minimum-wage jobs when they have an emergency?

Do I know anyone earning minimum wage who could serve as an example?

What percent of my friend's take-home pay does he spend on transportation?

Outline:

If public transportation is free, life will be a little easier for people.

I. people working in minimum-wage jobs find it hard to survive
   A. high cost of living
   B. living on the margin
   C. my friend's transportation costs

Paragraph:

Second, if public transportation is free, life will be a little easier for people. Many people working in minimum-wage jobs find it hard to survive in today's economy. The cost of rent, food, medicine, and other necessities is high. People earning the minimum wage live on the margin; that means if they have an emergency, they may not be able to eat three meals a day for a while. A friend of mine who works as a dishwasher pays $5.00 a day to ride public transit to his job in downtown L.A. This amounts to more than 12 percent of his take-home pay. If there is free public transportation, life will be a little less stressful for him.

BODY PARAGRAPH 3

Topic Sentence: Third, free public transit is faster than paid public transit.

Questions:

How do the residents of Commerce feel about their free public
transit?

Do people in Commerce choose public transit over driving?

Outline:

Free public transit is faster than paid public transit.

I. Commerce offers free public transit.

A. The buses are fast because drivers do not have to wait.

B. The residents seem satisfied.

C. The residents choose to ride public transit,
which reduces traffic congestion.

Paragraph:

Third, free public transit is faster than paid public transit. The city of
Commerce, which is in the Los Angeles area, offers free
public transit. My cousin Ly, who lives in Commerce, says, "The buses
are fast because drivers do not have to spend time waiting for people
to pay fares." The residents of Commerce seem very satisfied. Ly
explains, "Many Commerce residents choose to ride public transit,
which reduces traffic congestion." Commerce has set a good example
for the whole Los Angeles area.

Body Paragraphs

Show your partner the **thesis statement** for your paper, and let him or her read all your draft body **paragraphs**. Ask your partner to look for information gaps and write questions in the margin if more information is needed.

When you get your papers back from your partner, make changes to your body paragraphs as necessary.

Writing the Introduction of the Essay

The **introduction** of an opinion essay
- names the topic of the essay.
- leads readers to the thesis statement, which is the last sentence in the introduction.

The introduction may also
- give background information (general information or facts about the place you are writing about or what has happened there in the past).
- explain the problem and / or give a solution.

Look at the introduction to Tran's essay again.

BACKGROUND AND
EXPLANATION

IDENTIFYING
THE PROBLEM

THESIS
STATEMENT

[1]The Greater Los Angeles area includes over eighty cities which are connected by numerous freeways. [2]Each city has many wide streets as well. [3] Noisy, polluting traffic fills the freeways and streets at all hours of the day and night, and at rush hour the cars barely move. [4]Automobiles are ruining the quality of life in the L.A. area. [5]Therefore, the Greater Los Angeles area should provide free public transportation.

Look at another essay introduction.

IDENTIFYING
THE PROBLEM

BACKGROUND AND
EXPLANATION

THESIS
STATEMENT

[1]Cities are expensive places to live, and the lowest-paid workers in cities often live in poverty. [2]National minimum wages do not provide enough money for workers who live in cities to afford rent, food, and other necessities such as child care. [3]Therefore, cities across North America have passed a living wage law. [4]A living wage is always higher than the national minimum wage and is based on the cost of supporting a family of four above the poverty line in a particular city. [5]Montreal, Canada, should have a minimum wage law.

EXERCISE 8

Read the following essay introductions, and notice what their various parts do. Label the parts as **identifying the problem**, **background**, **explanation**, *and* **thesis statement**.

background and
explanation

1.   [1]Some of my friends have complained to me that landlords did not rent apartments to them. [2]One friend was very depressed because three different landlords refused to rent to her. [3]The apartments all seemed to be available. [4]Local landlords seem to discriminate against some potential renters because of their skin color or their accents. [5]Cities should enforce the laws that ban discrimination in housing for two important reasons.

2. [1]Phoenix, Arizona, is in a hot and dry region where there is almost no rain. [2]People in Phoenix get their water from two rivers that gather and transport rainwater and melting snow from a vast area. [3]The residents of Phoenix waste this fresh, clean water by using it to irrigate their lawns. [4]To avoid this waste, the city of Phoenix should require new homes to have plumbing systems that recycle water for outdoor landscaping.

To write an introduction for your essay, follow these steps.

 **STEP 1**   **Review your thesis statement and your body paragraphs.**

 **STEP 2**   **On the piece of paper that has your thesis statement at the top, write one to three sentences in paragraph form that identify the topic, define or explain it if necessary, and lead readers to your thesis statement. At the end of the introduction, rewrite your thesis statement.**

REVISION CHECKPOINT 2

Introduction
Review your introduction and make sure that the sentences fit together smoothly. If the sentences do not fit together well, try changing their order.

The introduction should answer any questions readers may have, such as *What is the problem? Where does it exist? Who should fix it?* and *How should it be fixed?* If your introduction requires more information, make any necessary additions to it now.

Writing the Conclusion and Completing Your Essay

The **conclusion**—the last paragraph in an essay—tells readers that the essay is finished by reminding them of the main idea and supporting points. To write a good conclusion,

*   write a summary of the main idea and supporting points. You can begin your conclusion with the supporting points and end with the main idea.
*   use synonyms to avoid repeating words.
*   do not introduce new information that will make readers ask questions.

EXERCISE 9

Reread the thesis statement and the topic sentences of the body paragraphs of Tran's essay on pages 166–167. Then read Tran's conclusion, and notice that the ideas are the same but the vocabulary is different. On the lines, write the synonyms that Tran used. The thesis statement has been done for you.

Synonyms Used in the Conclusion

should = ought to, provide = give,

transportation = transit

THESIS: The Greater Los Angeles area should provide free public transportation.

TOPIC SENTENCES OF BODY PARAGRAPHS:

First, the L.A. area has too much air pollution.

_____

_____

Second, if public transportation is free, life will be a little easier for people.

_____

_____

Third, free public transit is faster than paid public transit.

_____

_____

EXERCISE 10

Read the following thesis statement and topic sentences of body paragraphs for an essay about parks in Seoul, South Korea. Using as many synonyms as possible, write a one- to two-sentence conclusion that summarizes the main points of this essay.

THESIS: Seoul, South Korea, should create more playgrounds and parks.

TOPIC SENTENCES OF BODY PARAGRAPHS:

First, parks give children a place to move their bodies and to release tension.

Second, communal play spaces near residential areas give children a place to find same-age companions and to engage in cooperative play.

Third, if children lack convenient public spaces for recreation, they will amuse themselves in busy city streets or in empty lots where they can get injured.

CONCLUSION: _____

_____

_____

_____

To complete your essay and write a conclusion, follow these steps.

STEP 1 Get a new piece of paper, and write the title of your essay on top.

STEP 2 Copy your introduction and your body paragraphs as you have written them, or, if you notice ways to improve them, make changes as you rewrite them. Add a transition (*First, Second, Third / Finally*) at the beginning of each body paragraph.

STEP 3 At the end of the essay, add a short concluding paragraph that summarizes the thesis statement and the topic sentences of the body paragraphs. Use some synonyms to avoid repetition.

REVISION CHECKPOINT 3

The Conclusion
Review your conclusion. Make sure that it does not repeat too much of the vocabulary in your thesis statement or in the topic sentences of your body paragraphs. Also, make sure that it does not introduce any new information.
   If you have questions about any part of your essay, write them in the margin of your paper.

Language Focus

Conditional sentences: real future and unreal present or future. As mentioned earlier in this chapter, writers of opinion paragraphs and essays often ask readers to imagine future events or possibilities. To do this, they use conditional sentences like the following.

> If public transportation *is* free, life *will be* a little easier for people. (real future)

> If public transportation *were* free, life *would be* a little easier for people. (unreal present or future)

1. The **real future conditional** is about a future event that the writer thinks is possible and, therefore, *real*.

   REAL FUTURE: If New York *builds* new parking structures, more people *will drive* into the city. (New York can do this. It is a real possibility.)

2. The **unreal conditional** is about an event that the writer thinks probably *will not* or *cannot* happen and is, therefore, *unreal*. This kind of conditional sentence can refer to the present or the future.

   UNREAL PRESENT OR FUTURE: If parking places in New York *were* cheap, more people *would drive*. (Parking places in New York will never be cheap; almost everything is expensive in New York.)

Notice that the unreal sentence has a past tense verb form, *were*, but it is not a past tense sentence. The past tense form after *if* is a signal that the sentence is unreal.

To understand the tense of a conditional sentence, you must look at the verbs in both clauses.

- In a *real future conditional sentence*, what tense is used in the *if* clause? _____

  What tense is used in the main clause? _____

- In an *unreal present or future conditional sentence*, what tense is used in the *if* clause? _____

  What modal verb is used in the main clause? _____

Unreal conditional sentences do not use was in the *if* clause. In other words, when you use the *be* verb in the dependent clause in an unreal conditional sentence, you must use *were*, even if the subject is singular. Look at the following examples.

were
If parking in New York ~~was~~ cheap, more people would drive.

were
If crime ~~was~~ not a problem in my city, I would go out at night.

EXERCISE 11

Reread "Housing for Homeless Families" on page 156 and "Expand Weekend Library Hours" on pages 156–157, and circle all the conditional sentences. In the margin next to each sentence you circle, write **real future** *or* **unreal present** *or* **future.**

EXERCISE 12

A. *Fill in the blanks in the following sentences with the correct forms of the verbs in parentheses.*

1. In recent years, most of the new houses built across the United States have been built in suburbs. When people live in suburbs, they need cars to get to work, to go shopping, and to visit their friends. If there weren't so many people living in suburbs and using cars, there _____ *would be* _____ (be) less air pollution.

2. Honeybees pollinate most kinds of fruits and vegetables. Recently, honeybee populations have been getting smaller, and scientists don't know why. If scientists don't find out how to save the honeybees, we _____ (have, *negative*) strawberries, apples, cucumbers, or squash.

3. Farmers around the world use fertilizers to make their crops productive. When fertilized crops are watered, the fertilizer runs off into rivers and then into the ocean, where it changes the natural balance and kills fish. If farmers _____ (reduce, *negative*) the amount of fertilizer they use, there will not be many fish left in parts of the ocean.

4. People in the United States have always liked big cars. Big cars burn more fuel and produce more pollution than small cars. If the U.S. government _____ (make) laws limiting the size of passenger vehicles, there would be less air pollution.

5. When diesel fuel—the type of fuel most large trucks use—is burned, sulfur dioxide and tiny particles of various kinds are released into the atmosphere. Both sulfur dioxide and tiny particles are harmful to human health. If people live next to a truck route for a long time, they _____ (have) a greater risk of getting lung disease.

6. Many slums (poor neighborhoods) lack running water, sanitation, and garbage collection. This makes residents' lives difficult and threatens their health. If children _____ (grow up) in difficult, unsafe conditions, they will not be able to achieve as much in their lives as children who grow up in comfortable, safe conditions.

7. Individual families usually build slums one house at a time without any overall plan. If people build slums without planning, it _____ (be) difficult to bring infrastructure (roads, water, sanitation, electricity) there later.

8. Some governments do not think the residents of illegal slums have rights to services. If the governments _____ (think) these people had legal rights, they would make more efforts to provide services to them.

B. *Check your answers with a partner, and as you check, discuss the meaning of each sentence. Tell whether the statement is* real future *or* unreal present *or* future.

For more on conditional sentences, see Appendix IA, pages 231–232.

Conditional Sentences
Review your essay to see if you have used any conditional sentences. If you have any conditional sentences, decide whether they are *real future* or *unreal present* or *future* sentences. Make sure that the verbs are correct. If you find any mistakes, fix them now.

Modal verbs. Modal verbs add meaning to sentences.

> Poverty does not always lead to criminal behavior, but it *can* contribute to it. (possibility)

> Governments *must* spend more to increase police protection for citizens. (necessity)

Each modal has its own meaning, so writers need to choose modals carefully. Statements of advice, opinion, necessity, and possibility are common in opinion paragraphs and essays, so writers often use the modal verbs *should*, *must*, and *can*. The verb *need to* (which is not a true modal) is used as well.

Note: Modal verbs do not have the third person singular *-s*. However, *need to*, which is not a true modal, has *-s* (*needs to*) after *he*, *she*, or *it*.

MODAL	EXAMPLE	MEANING
Advice or Opinion		
should	I think the government **should** provide job training.	This is the best thing to do.
ought to	I think the government **ought to** provide job training.	almost the same as *should*, but more formal
Necessity		
must	A property owner **must** pay taxes.	strong necessity; a situation demands a certain action or response
need to*	A property owner **needs to** take care of his or her building.	necessity

(continued)

Possibility		
may	When the river floods, people **may** lose their homes. When electric cars become more efficient, people **may** buy them.	Something is possible now or in the future.
Possibility or Ability		
can	The mayor **can** hire more police. Discrimination **can** have harmful effects.	Someone has the possibility or ability (knowledge, intelligence, physical strength, influence, etc.) to do something. Something is possible.
Note. "Discrimination *can* have harmful effects" expresses stronger possibility than "Discrimination *may* have harmful effects."		

 For more on modals, see Appendix IA, pages 217–218.

EXERCISE 13

*Read the paragraph, and underline the modal verbs. In the margin next to each modal, write its meaning (**advice or opinion**, **necessity**, *or* **possibility**).*

Healthy Cities

advice or opinion

[1]City governments <u>should</u> take responsibility for the health of their citizens by creating separate industrial and residential zones. [2]Each zone needs to have an effective waste management system. [3]Solid waste from industrial production can be toxic, so industries must dispose of it far from people's homes. [4]Industries can also reduce air and water pollution in cities by using equipment to trap and contain waste. [5]In residential zones, cities should provide sanitation systems for human waste, which can spread disease. [6]Individual citizens ought to cooperate with government to solve health-related problems, and city governments must use planning and regulation (laws) to make sure cities are healthy places for citizens to live.

EXERCISE 14

A. *Read the following essay and fill in modals of advice or opinion* (**should, ought to**), *necessity* (**must, need to**), *and possibility* (**may, can**).

Clean Water—A Human Right

One-sixth of the world's people lack access to clean water. Many of these people live in rapidly growing cities. In my opinion, city governments (1) _____*should*_____ provide their citizens with safe drinking water.

Water and sanitation are closely related. Lack of sanitation (2) _____ lead to contamination of drinking water (making drinking water dirty or unsafe), and contaminated drinking water causes disease. Each year over 5 million children under five die of water-related diseases. These diseases (3) _____ be prevented if cities provide sanitation.

People who do not have running water in or near their homes spend a great deal of time, effort, and money obtaining it. They (4) _____ buy drinking water from a private vendor (seller) and collect water for washing from a river or lake. If a family of four uses 150 liters a day, a family member, usually the mother, (5) _____ carry the water home in bottles or buckets. This means that she (6) _____ make about ten trips, carrying 15 kilograms (33 pounds) per trip. In addition, because in many places water is shut off for periods of time during the day, she (7) _____ need to wait in line for an hour or more to fill her containers. Finally, water vendors often charge from five to fifty times more than city water systems do, so families who don't have running water in their houses pay much more than those who have it.

When city governments and local residents cooperate, public access to clean water is possible. Residents (8) _____ contribute to water and sanitation projects by collecting small amounts of money for pipes or tools and donating their own labor. Governments (9) _____ provide the professionals who (10) _____ plan and oversee the project. Sometimes governments (11) _____ also need to work with international aid organizations, banks, landowners, and private companies in order to give citizens access to water and sanitation.

People's livelihoods (their ways of earning money to support themselves) are affected by their living conditions. If people have clean water, they will lead more productive lives. And if a country has a healthy workforce, it (12) _____ grow economically. Therefore, city governments (13) _____ make providing clean water a top priority.

B. *Compare your answers with a partner's. If you have different answers in a particular sentence, discuss the meaning of the modal (suggestion, necessity, possibility).*

You can use the modal *may* in real future conditional sentences if you want to say that a result is possible but does not always occur. Look at these examples.

REAL FUTURE CONDITIONAL:

may

If people live near a freeway, they ~~will~~ get lung cancer.

may

If residents live near a noisy airport, they ~~will~~ experience extra stress in their lives.

Modal Verbs

Review your essay and identify the modal verbs that you have used. Check each one and make sure it communicates the meaning you want to express in that sentence. Make changes if necessary.

You can also check to see if you have repeated any modal too often. You may be able to replace the repeated modal with another modal of the same meaning.

■ FINAL DRAFT

1. Before you write your final draft, look over your essay one last time to decide if you want to make any further changes.

2. Prepare a final draft of your essay. Make sure that you have used capital letters, periods, and commas where they are needed, and check your spelling.

3. Exchange papers with one or two classmates. Read each other's papers carefully. Turn to page 252 in Appendix II, and fill out the Peer Review Form.

4. Check your paper again and make any necessary corrections. Turn in your paper to your teacher.

■ CHAPTER REVIEW

Look back at what you have accomplished in Chapter 6. Check off (✓) what you have learned and what you have used while writing and revising your paragraph and essay.

Chapter 6 Topics	Learned	Used
Using a dictionary to find synonyms (page 151)		
Using a dictionary to find out the meanings of nouns that are both countable and uncountable (page 153)		
Writing an opinion statement that can be either the topic sentence of a paragraph or the thesis statement of an essay (page 155)		
Using cause-and-effect reasoning to write and develop supporting points for an opinion statement (page 155)		
Expanding a paragraph to an essay by writing an introduction, body paragraphs, and a conclusion (pages 165–174)		
Using real future or unreal present and future conditional statements (pages 176–177)		
Using modals to express advice or opinion, necessity, and possibility (pages 179–180)		

Appendix IA: Grammar

This grammar appendix will help you understand how English works. It starts with basic definitions of parts of speech and parts of sentences. It then continues with more specific information about sentences that you will need to know to write English correctly.

■ 1. Parts of Speech

1a. Nouns

Nouns refer to persons, places, and things. Examples of nouns are *doctor*, *park*, and *textbook*. Some nouns name abstract things, things that we cannot see, hear, or touch, such as *idea*, *honesty*, and *importance*.

> While he was sitting in a comfortable **chair** in his **office**, the **professor** talked to me about the **meaning** of **democracy**.

1b. Verbs

There are various kinds of **verbs**. Some verbs refer to actions, such as *talk* and *dance*.

> Doug and Ginger **were talking** for an hour. They **are dancing** now.

Some verbs refer to the activities of the senses and the mind.

> The engine **looks** and **sounds** fine. I **believe** it runs perfectly. I **think** I will buy the car.

Some verbs refer to ownership of things or possession of characteristics.

> Jorge **owns** an apartment. The apartment **has** a lot of space.

The verbs *be* and *exist* refer to the existence of things.

> Indonesia **is** an island nation. This giant flower **exists** only on one island in Indonesia.

Other verbs refer to a change.

> I **get** sleepy at about 10:00 P.M.

> Ana **became** a doctor in 2007.

1c. Adjectives

Adjectives describe persons, places, and things.

> In his **fresh white** coat, Dr. Morgan entered his **modern** laboratory and greeted his **new** assistants.

1d. Adverbs

Adverbs modify the verb in a sentence. They tell *where*, *how*, and *when*.

> Please send your application **here**. (*Where?*)
>
> The children sat **quietly**. (*How?*)
>
> Diego will enter law school **soon**. (*When?*)

Adverbs can also modify an entire sentence.

> **Sadly**, Marie died before her grandchild was born.
>
> **Unexpectedly**, the economy improved.

1e. Prepositions

Prepositions are small connecting words or phrases. Here are some common prepositions.

about	by	in	to
at	for	next to	with
between	from	on	

Prepositions are followed by nouns called **objects of prepositions**.

> I wrote my name *on my* **paper**, and then I gave it *to my* **teacher**.

Most prepositions add information about time or place.

> I will come back **on** *Sunday.* (*When?*)
>
> Salif Keita was performing **in** *a large theater.* (*Where?*)

A preposition together with the noun object that follows it, and any words that modify that noun, is called a **prepositional phrase**. Prepositional phrases can follow nouns and modify them, or they can come at the beginning or end of a sentence and modify the verb or the whole sentence.

> This novel **by** *Sandra Cisneros* is very interesting.
>
> **In** *my reading class*, I learned to make predictions.
>
> I learned to make predictions **in** *my reading class*.

1f. Pronouns

Most **pronouns** refer to nouns that have been mentioned already.

> I sent the letter to Olga, and **she** received **it**.

> Laura presented her ideas to Mike. **He** thought **they** were wonderful.

Some pronouns are **indefinite**. They refer to someone or something that is unknown.

> I want a perfect job. I want to work for **someone** who is kind and to do **something** that is interesting.

1g. Articles

English has two **articles**, *a* (or *an*) and *the*. Articles come before nouns and give information about whether or not the nouns are specific. The article *a* (or *an*) is not specific. It means "one" or "any." (*An* is used before a word that begins with a vowel sound, and *a* is used before other words.)

> I want to buy **a** banana and **an** orange.

The means the "specific thing you (the reader or listener) already know about."

> **The** moon was full last night.

Use *a* or *an* to introduce a noun that gives new information. Afterward, use *the* to refer to that noun.

> I saw **a** bird. **The** bird was black and white.

> My dad caught **a** fish. Later, we ate **the** fish.

1h. Conjunctions

Conjunctions join sentence parts and entire sentences. They add various meanings to sentences, such as *addition*, *contrast*, and *reason*.

> Ozier has a brother **and** a sister. (*addition*)

> Carolina is a citizen of Panama, **but** her brother is a citizen of the United States. (*contrast*)

> Marcus travels a lot **because** he is a musician. (*reason*)

EXERCISE 1
*Identify the parts of speech of the underlined words in the following paragraph. Mark nouns (**n.**), verbs (**v.**), adjectives (**adj.**), adverbs (**adv.**), prepositions (**prep.**), pronouns (**pron.**), articles (**art.**), and conjunctions (**conj.**).*

(1. *n.*)
The giant panda—the only black and white <u>bear</u>—lives in the
(2.____)
mountains <u>in</u> China. An adult panda's diet consists mainly of bamboo.
(3.____)   (4.____)
<u>The</u> panda has large teeth and <u>strong</u> jaw muscles for crushing bamboo
(5.____)
stalks, <u>and</u> it needs to eat huge amounts every day to maintain its weight
(6.____)   (7.____)
of over 95 kilograms (209 pounds). Baby pandas <u>begin</u> to eat bamboo <u>at</u> six
(8.____) (9.____)
months, <u>but</u> <u>they</u> need their mothers' milk to survive until near the end of

(10._____)   (11._____)

their first year. <u>A</u> newborn panda looks like a <u>tiny</u> pink rat and weighs about
                                        (12._____)

110 grams (4 ounces). By the time <u>it</u> leaves its mother at eighteen months

to two years old, it weighs about 45 kilograms (99 pounds). It is not certain
                (13._____) (14._____)   (15._____)

how many pandas <u>still</u> <u>exist</u> in the wild. <u>Unfortunately</u>, there may be only
                                        (16._____)

two to three thousand. The Chinese <u>government</u> has created more than

forty panda reserves to protect this much-loved endangered species.

■ 2. The Basic Sentence Parts

2a. Subjects

The **subject** of a sentence is the person, place, or thing that the sentence is
about. If the verb of the sentence is an action verb, the subject is the doer of
the action. Subjects can be nouns, pronouns, and -*ing* words (gerunds).

SUBJECT
Sandy is a nurse.

SUBJECT
She works for a hospital.

SUBJECT
Nursing requires knowledge and skill.

You can identify the subject of a sentence as either a single word or a group
of words, whichever one is clearer.

SUBJECT
The friendly **woman** in the information booth gave me directions to the hotel.

SUBJECT
The friendly woman in the information booth gave me directions to the hotel.

2b. Verbs

An action **verb** in a sentence tells what the subject does. Verbs of sensory
and mental activity, ownership, existence, and change give other kinds of
information about the subject. (See Appendix IA, page 185.)

ACTION VERB   MENTAL ACTIVITY VERB
Mario **jogs** on the beach after work. He **thinks** about his girlfriend.

VERB OF POSSESSION   VERB OF CHANGE
His girlfriend **has** a degree in physiology. She **is becoming** a doctor.

2c. Objects

Many verbs are followed by nouns or pronouns called **objects**. The object of a verb answers the question *What?* or *Who?*

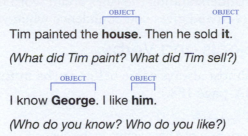

Tim painted the **house**. Then he sold **it**.

(What did Tim paint? What did Tim sell?)

I know **George**. I like **him**.

(Who do you know? Who do you like?)

2d. Complements

Verbs of existence, the senses, or change are followed by **complements**. Complements, which can be nouns, adjectives, or prepositional phrases, give information about the subject of the sentence.

Jassem is an **engineer**. He looks **intelligent** and seems **young**. He is

from Kuwait.

EXERCISE 2

*Identify the subjects, verbs, objects, and complements in the following sentences. Write **S** above the subjects, **V** above the verbs, **O** above the objects, and **C** above the complements. You may find more than one subject, verb, object, or complement in a sentence, and some sentences have more than one subject-verb combination.*

1. All spiders have eight legs and produce silk.

2. Usually female spiders make webs.

3. Sticky webs trap insects.

4. In order to produce eggs, females need the protein from insects.

5. Spider webs can be very large and take different forms.

6. Spiders may seem frightening, but they are beneficial to humans.

7. Spiders eat mosquitoes, flies, and other insect pests.

8. Four hundred million years ago, spiders were among the first creatures on land.

9. As a species, spiders have been extremely successful.

■ 3. Word Order in Sentences

In English, word order is important because it affects the meanings of sentences. Understanding the rules about word order helps you understand parts of speech and gives you confidence when you compose sentences.

3a. Subjects and Verbs

Subjects almost always come before **verbs** in English sentences. (See Appendix IA, page 188.)

SUBJECT | VERB

Barbara brought her camera to the concert.

There are exceptions to this rule. In sentences that begin with *there*, the subject follows the *be* verb.

VERB | SUBJECT

There **was** a big **storm** last night.

In commands, the subject (you) is not included. It is understood.

VERB | VERB

Get up. Come here.

In questions, the verb, or part of the verb, comes before the subject.

SUBJ.

VERB | SUBJECT   V. | V.

Is Mauricio tired? What time **did he go** to bed last night?

3b. Objects and Complements of Verbs

Verbs can be followed by either **objects** or **complements.** (See Appendix IA, page 189).

Action verbs can be followed by **objects** that can be either nouns or pronouns.

VERB | OBJECT   V. OBJ.

I **baked** the **bread**. Then I **ate it**.

Some verbs can be followed by two objects—an **indirect object** and a **direct object**.

INDIR.
VERB OBJ. | DIR. OBJECT

The salesman *sold* **me** the **jacket**.

You can make this sentence another way. The indirect object can follow a preposition.

DIRECT   INDIR.
VERB | OBJECT | OBJECT

The salesman *sold* the **jacket** *to* **me**.

Here are some verbs frequently followed by both direct and indirect objects.

Verb + Indirect Object + Direct Object OR Verb + Direct Object + *to* + Indirect Object	Verb + Indirect Object + Direct Object OR Verb + Direct Object + *for* + Indirect Object
give, hand, lend, mail, pass, sell, send, show, tell, write	buy, find, fix, get, make
Please give **me** the **ticket**. I.O. D.O. Please give the **ticket** to **me**. D.O. I.O. I'll hand **you** a **pen**. I.O. D.O. I'll hand a **pen** to **you**. D.O. I.O. Joe lent **Simon** a **bicycle**. I.O. D.O. Joe lent a **bicycle** to **Simon**. D.O. I.O.	I am buying the **kids drinks**. I.O. D.O. I am buying **drinks** for the **kids**. D.O. I.O. Fred found **me** an **apartment**. I.O. D.O. Fred found an **apartment** for **me**. D.O. I.O. Robin fixed **us breakfast**. I.O. D.O. Robin fixed **breakfast** for **us**. D.O. I.O.

Note. To find out what kind(s) of objects and which preposition(s) may follow any verb, look in your dictionary.

EXERCISE 3

Each sentence contains both a direct and an indirect object. Underline each direct object, and mark it **D.O.** *Underline each indirect object, and mark it* **I.O.** *On another piece of paper, rewrite the sentences using the other word order.*

1. Marcus sent the <u>photographs</u> to <u>us</u>.
   D.O. I.O.

   Marcus sent us the photographs.

2. Sasha bought <u>Peter's family</u> <u>tickets</u>.
   I.O. D.O.

   Sasha bought tickets for Peter's family.

3. I will mail the receipt to you.

4. Amanda sold Reyna her used car.

5. Yuko got the homework assignment for you.

6. Mr. Nolan has shown Charlie the map.

7. I won't be able to lend them my car.

8. My mother has fixed a snack for us.

The *be* verb, as well as verbs of the senses and change (linking verbs), are followed by **complements**, not objects. Complements can be nouns, adjectives, or prepositional phrases.

That tree *is* a **maple**.

It *looks* very **old**.

It *is* **next to my apartment building**.

3c. Adjectives

Adjectives have three positions in English sentences.

- Adjectives often come before nouns.

  a **long** conversation

  some **refreshing** lemonade

- They follow the *be* verb and linking verbs.

  Otto *is* **polite**. He *seems* **responsible**.

- They also follow indefinite pronouns.

Tuyen wants to take her wedding photographs in *someplace* **special**.

The managers haven't found *anyone* **qualified** for the job.

3d. Adverbs

English has two kinds of **adverbs**: adverbs that modify the verb or the entire sentence and adverbs that modify adjectives or other adverbs. The majority of adverbs modify the verb or the entire sentence.

1. **Adverbs that modify the verb or the entire sentence.** These adverbs come in the beginning, middle, or end of a sentence. Some have only one possible position, while others have more than one.

   - **Beginning-of-sentence adverbs.** An adverb that modifies an entire sentence usually comes at the beginning.

     Luckily, the rain stopped.

The frequency adverb *sometimes* usually comes at the beginning of a sentence.

Sometimes Rodolfo takes the subway.

- **Middle-of-sentence adverbs**. Other frequency adverbs (*always, usually, often, seldom, never*) generally come in the middle of a sentence. These adverbs follow the *be* verb but come before other verbs. If a verb has two or more parts, the adverb follows the first part.

  Paula *is* **always** cheerful. She **frequently** *smiles*. Her friends *have* **often** *praised* her for her positive attitude.

  The adverb *also* usually comes in the middle of a sentence, but it can come at the beginning or the end.

  Serge likes to ski. He **also** plays tennis.
  (**Also**, he plays tennis. / He plays tennis **also**.)

- **End-of-sentence adverbs**. Adverbs of *place (Where?)*, *manner (How?)*, and *time (When?)* come at the ends of sentences. (See Appendix IA, page 186.)

  I saw the yellow cat **here**. *(place)*

  The cat moved **quickly** and **silently**. *(manner)*

  I hope to see the cat again **today**. *(time)*

2. **Adverbs that modify adjectives or other adverbs.** These adverbs come immediately before the adjectives or adverbs they modify.

   ADVERB ADJECTIVE

   Piri took a **very** *advanced* math class.

   ADVERB ADVERB

   He worked **extremely** *hard* to pass the class.

Examples of other adverbs that modify adjectives or other adverbs are *quite* (*quite* good, *quite* well) and *really* (*really* good, *really* well).

3e. Prepositional Phrases

Prepositional phrases have three different positions in sentences. (See Appendix IA, page 186.)

- Prepositional phrases that modify nouns come after the nouns they modify.

  The woman **with** *two small children* bought a sack **of** *cookies*.

- Prepositional phrases that modify verbs come at the ends of sentences.

  Tomorrow Harry will travel **to** another city. He will stay **in** a hotel. He

  will meet **with** his client.

- Prepositional phrases that modify entire sentences come at the beginnings of sentences.

  In the early morning, you can hear lots of birds singing in the woods.

  For me, driving is relaxing.

EXERCISE 4

Each of the sentences contains one word order error. Find and correct each error.

1. Taking pictures animals of requires preparation and patience.

2. First, I choose interesting something to photograph.

3. When I find an interesting animal, I think about its characteristics special.

4. For example, monkeys are social animals, so I photograph them in groups always.

5. I like to show animals in their natural also environment, but I don't want the environment to dominate the picture.

6. For instance, I took a picture of horse a with a barn in the distance.

7. Second, I animals photograph at eye level.

8. For example, I took a great picture of my neighbor's cat as sat it on the fence.

9. I third consider the animal's response to me.

10. If an animal shy is, I approach it carefully.

11. For instance, once rabbit there was a in the park.

12. Amazingly, I managed to photograph from only a meter away it.

13. How I did do it?

14. I waited quietly very until it hopped toward me.

15. I can take fortunately hundreds of shots with a digital camera and then select the best ones.

16. Then I e-mail my animal pictures my friends.

■ 4. Sentence Combining and Sentence Types

Sentence combining is a very important writing skill. The conjunctions that combine sentences show connections between ideas. Therefore, sentence combining allows you to show your thinking.

4a. Clauses

A **clause** is a group of words that contains both a subject and a verb. Every complete sentence—even a short, simple one—is also a clause because it contains both a subject and a verb. (See Appendix IA, page 188.)

SUBJECT VERB

Mei laughed.

A long sentence that contains only one subject-verb combination is also a clause.

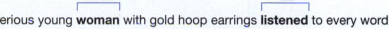

SUBJECT   VERB

The tall, serious young **woman** with gold hoop earrings **listened** to every word of the professor's lecture on the effects of modernization in China.

A clause may contain two or more subjects. This is called a **compound subject**. It may also contain two or more verbs. This is called a **compound verb**.

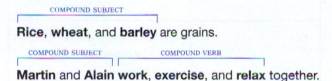

COMPOUND SUBJECT

Rice, wheat, and **barley** are grains.

COMPOUND SUBJECT   COMPOUND VERB

Martin and **Alain work**, **exercise**, and **relax** together.

4b. Coordinating Conjunctions and Independent Clauses

English has seven **coordinating conjunctions**. Each coordinating conjunction can join two or more clauses, and each coordinating conjunction has a different meaning.

Coordinating Conjunctions		
Coordinating Conjunctions	**Meaning**	**Examples**
and	addition	I watched the movie, **and** I liked it.
but	contrast	I watched the movie, **but** I didn't like it.
so	result	I wanted to watch the movie, **so** I went to the theater.
yet	contrast or surprising result	I had wanted to watch the movie, **yet** I didn't like it.
for*	reason or cause	I went to the theater, **for** I wanted to watch a movie.
or	a choice; only one of the two statements is true or possible	I watch movies at home, **or** I go to the theater. Every new movie appears first in a theater, **or** it first plays on TV.
nor**	both parts of the statement are negative	I don't like war movies, **nor** do I like horror movies.

*The coordinating conjunction *for* is formal. A more common way to express this idea is *I went to the theater* because *I wanted to watch a movie.* (Note that *because* is a subordinating conjunction.)

**After *nor*, a verb or a part of a verb comes before the subject.

Coordinating conjunctions join **independent clauses**. An independent clause is a clause that can be a complete sentence. The following sentence has three independent clauses.

INDEPENDENT CLAUSE   INDEPENDENT CLAUSE

Beijing is the capital of China, it was the location of the 2008 Olympic Games,

INDEPENDENT CLAUSE

and it has about sixty colleges and universities.

EXERCISE 5

Put brackets [ ] around the independent clauses in the following sentences.

1. [The blue whale is the largest animal living on Earth], but [it is not very well understood].

2. Scientists cannot easily study blue whales, for they are too big to approach safely.

3. The Pacific, Atlantic, and Indian Oceans are home to blue whales.

4. Blue whales were hunted for a hundred years, yet they survived.

5. According to scientists, a mature blue whale weighs about 181 metric tons (200 tons), and a newborn calf weighs 1,814 kilograms (4,000 pounds).

6. A blue whale eats tiny creatures called krill, and its mouth can hold 90 metric tons (100 tons) of food and water.

7. Blue whales dive more than 100 meters (330 feet), stay under water for up to 20 minutes, and send spouts up to 12 meters (40 feet) high in the air.

8. Blue whales produce sounds in their foreheads.

9. We humans cannot hear these very low sounds, nor do we know their purpose.

10. The sounds may help whales navigate, or they may help them find mates.

11. The noises of ships and military activities may disturb whales, so it is important to understand these sea giants better and to protect them.

EXERCISE 6

On another piece of paper, combine the following sentences using coordinating conjunctions. Do not use any conjunction more than once.

1. Few people have seen a wild elephant. They don't *, nor do they* know that elephants are threatened.

2. Wild elephants live in Africa and Asia. They are the largest land animals.

3. Female elephants spend their lives in groups called herds. Male elephants spend their lives alone.

4. The oldest female in the herd has experience and knowledge. She helps the herd survive.

5. In order to communicate, elephants make noises. They touch each other with their trunks.

6. People have hunted the elephant for decades. Its ivory tusks are valuable.

7. Various countries have created parks and reserves to protect elephants. Many elephants are still dying.

4c. Subordinating Conjunctions and Dependent Clauses

Like coordinating conjunctions, **subordinating conjunctions** join clauses and have different meanings.

Subordinating Conjunctions of Time		
Conjunction	**Meaning**	**Example**
after	sequence	I got a license **after** I passed the driving test. (2 ... 1)
as	happening at the same time	It started to rain **as** I was driving down the street.
before	sequence	I passed the driving test **before** I got a license. (1 ... 2)
by the time	completion before another event	The rain had stopped **by the time** I finished the driving test. (2 ... 1)
since	beginning at a point in time and continuing to the present	I have had a driver's license **since** I passed the driving test.
until	a period of time before an event	My brother waited **until** my driving test was finished. (1 ... 2)
when	sequence; two events happening at the same time	I smiled **when** I passed the test. (2 ... 1) My brother was waiting **when** I was taking the test.
while	happening at the same time	My brother was waiting **while** I was taking the test.

Subordinating Conjunctions of Reason	
as	I wanted to get a driver's license **as** my job was far from my home.
because	I wanted to get a driver's license **because** my job was far from my home.
since	I wanted to get a driver's license **since** my job was far from my home.

Subordinating Conjunction of Purpose	
so that	I wanted to get a driver's license **so that** I could drive to work.

Subordinating Conjunction of Condition (See Appendix IA, page 232.)	
if	I will be able to work in another city **if** I have a car. I would be able to work in another city **if** I had a car.

Subordinating Conjunctions of Contrast	
whereas	Walking to work is slow, **whereas** driving is fast.
while	Walking to work is slow, **while** driving is fast.

Subordinating Conjunction of Surprising Result	
although	I prefer to walk, **although** walking is slow.

Note. A subordinating conjunction and the dependent clause connected to it can come at the beginning or the end of a sentence with no change in meaning.

> I prefer to walk, **although** walking is slow.

> **Although** walking is slow, I prefer to walk.

A subordinating conjunction makes a clause **dependent** so that it cannot stand on its own and therefore must join an independent clause. The following sentence has one independent clause and two dependent clauses that are joined by the subordinating conjunctions *if* and *when*.

DEPENDENT CLAUSE   INDEPENDENT CLAUSE   DEPENDENT CLAUSE

If the river floods, people will have to leave their homes *when* the water rises.

EXERCISE 7

Underline the dependent clauses in the sentences. (Note that not every sentence has a dependent clause.)

1. Hurricanes (also known as typhoons and tropical cyclones) form over the sea <u>when warm, moist air rises</u>.

2. As the air cools, it forms clouds and rain.

3. Energy is released, and a low-pressure area is created, while the rotation of Earth causes the spiral effect.

4. If the conditions are right, the hurricane increases in intensity and moves northward north of the equator or southward south of the equator.

5. The hurricane creates a storm surge, or hill of water, on the surface of the sea.

6. The hurricane weakens after it reaches land, but by the time the hurricane loses force, the storm surge may have already caused flooding.

7. Although satellite pictures show scientists the size of hurricanes and their direction of movement, hurricane prediction is an imperfect science.

8. Some hurricanes suddenly become stronger, while others suddenly grow weaker, and scientists cannot explain these changes.

9. Scientists are doing research so that they can predict hurricanes more accurately and save lives.

EXERCISE 8

Read each pair of clauses, and select the subordinating conjunction that can join them logically. Then, on another piece of paper, combine the two clauses using that conjunction.

1. Hurricanes form over the ocean / tornados form over land. (if, whereas)

   Hurricanes form over the ocean, whereas tornados form over land.

2. Most tornados occur in the United States / the country's geography creates the right conditions for them. (although, since)

3. Tornados form / there are changes in air temperature and pressure in the atmosphere. (when, although)

4. Studying tornados is challenging / tornados can appear suddenly and disappear just as quickly. (as, until)

5. The average tornado warning gives people only thirteen minutes to prepare / the tornado arrives. (before, after)

6. People receive a hurricane warning / they don't have much time to find a safe place to go. (as, by the time)

7. Tornado winds range from 64 to 177 kilometers per hour (40 to 110 miles per hour) / people often hide in basements or cellars. (because, although)

8. Most tornados occur in the late afternoon / there are thunderstorms. (so that, when)

9. A tornado starts as a wide funnel and becomes narrower / it weakens. (as, whereas)

10. Frequently, a few houses in a town have disappeared and a few are still standing / a tornado has passed through. (until, after)

11. Scientists get a better understanding of tornados / we may be able to protect people's lives and property. (if, until)

4d. Types of Sentences

English has four types of sentences: **simple sentences**, **compound sentences**, **complex sentences**, and **compound-complex sentences**.

A **simple sentence** contains one independent clause.

INDEPENDENT CLAUSE

The plane arrived.

A **compound sentence** contains two (or more) independent clauses joined by one coordinating conjunction.

INDEPENDENT CLAUSE   INDEPENDENT CLAUSE

The plane arrived, *and* the passengers got off.

A **complex sentence** contains one independent clause and one (or more) dependent clauses.

DEPENDENT CLAUSE   INDEPENDENT CLAUSE

When the plane arrived, the passengers got off.

A **compound-complex sentence** contains two or more independent clauses and one or more dependent clauses.

DEPENDENT CLAUSE   INDEPENDENT CLAUSE   INDEPENDENT CLAUSE

When the plane arrived, the passengers got off, *and* the flight attendants cleaned the cabin.

EXERCISE 9

Identify the type of each sentence. Next to each sentence, write **S** *for simple,* **C** *for compound,* **CX** *for complex, or* **CCX** *for compound-complex.*

_S_   1. Reference librarians help people find books, magazines, and electronic resources.

_____   2. Technology is constantly changing, and the resources available on the Internet are limitless.

_____   3. Reference librarians cannot know everything about the Internet, but they must be familiar with the databases on their libraries' Web sites.

_____   4. Library databases include newspaper and magazine articles, encyclopedias, and special collections of articles about science, literature, or government.

_____   5. When a library user asks a reference librarian for help, the librarian must analyze the person's needs and skills so that he or she can lead the user to appropriate sources.

_____   6. Children's librarians must be aware of differences in reading ability and computer knowledge between older and younger children.

_____   7. As librarians give assistance, they often teach library users how to find information for themselves.

_____   8. Assisting library users is interesting work because librarians deal with many different people and various research topics, but it is also demanding work because librarians have to solve research problems, read quickly from a computer screen, and deliver information clearly and politely.

4e. Sentence Structure Problem: Run-on Sentences

If two clauses are together in one sentence *without* a coordinating or subordinating conjunction to join them, this is an error called a **run-on sentence**. To correct the error, you can put a period between the clauses, or you can add a coordinating or subordinating conjunction to join them.

RUN ON: The morning was cold ~~t~~ there was ice on the street. *. T*

RUN ON: Carla got up, she took a shower. *and*

RUN ON: ~~S~~he was late, she hurried. *Because s*

Note. A run-on sentence with a comma is sometimes called a **comma splice**.

A comma cannot replace a period or a conjunction.

RUN ON: The bus arrived Carla got to the station.

RUN ON: The bus arrived, Carla got to the station.

CORRECT: The bus arrived **when** Carla got to the station.

EXERCISE 10
*Read the following examples, and identify the run-on sentences. Next to each item, write **RO** if it is a run-on or **C** if the sentence is correct.*

__RO__ 1. Olympic athletes must have the right kind of body runners must be tall and thin.

_____ 2. Gymnasts need to be light, and they must have powerful muscles.

_____ 3. Swimmers must be tall and thin basketball players need speed and agility.

_____ 4. Olympic athletes are people with above-average ambition.

_____ 5. Being number one is very important to them.

_____ 6. Psychological strength is also important, an athlete must have the ability to commit to long-term goals.

_____ 7. Athletes need patience preparing for the Olympics takes a long time, and sometimes improvement comes slowly.

_____ 8. Olympic athletes have to be able to manage their emotions when they win and when they lose.

_____ 9. An Olympic athlete must be able to deal with hardships because athletes endure pain when they are training, and they also get injured.

_____ 10. Concentration is essential when an athlete performs before a crowd.

EXERCISE 11

The following examples are run-on sentences. On another piece of paper, rewrite each one, correcting the errors. Use coordinating and subordinating conjunctions as well as periods.

1. Nadaam is an annual event in Mongolia it has been an important part of Mongolian culture for over 800 years.

   > *Nadaam is an annual event in Mongolia, and it has been an important part of Mongolian culture for over 800 years.*

2. Nadaam celebrates the skills of warriors, hunters, and herders these skills have been important to the survival of Mongolian society.

   > *Nadaam celebrates the skills of warriors, hunters, and herders because these skills have been important to the survival of Mongolian society.*

3. The Nadaam games take place in the summer they include three sports, wrestling (hand-to-hand fighting), archery (shooting at a target with a bow and arrow), and horse racing.

4. Only males wrestle, females participate in the archery and horse racing.

5. In a Nadaam competition, a big, heavy wrestler can compete against a small, light wrestler that almost never happens in wrestling competitions in other countries.

6. A wrestler touches the ground with any part of his body except his hands or feet he has lost the competition.

7. Singing is an important part of Nadaam there are special songs for the archery competition and the horse races.

8. An archer shoots an arrow, a singer tells him in song how close to the target the arrow landed.

9. Both the spectators and the jockeys sing the horse race begins.

10. The jockeys in the horse races are children children don't weigh much the horses can run faster.

11. The races are over the winning horses receive as much praise as the winning jockeys sometimes people sing songs to the winning horses.

12. During Nadaam, there is plenty of barbecued meat, fruit, and ice cream for everyone it is a happy time for all.

4f. Sentence Structure Problem: Fragments

Writing a dependent clause as if it were a complete sentence is an error called a **fragment**. To correct the error, you can remove the subordinating conjunction, or add an independent clause.

FRAGMENT: ~~Since~~ I moved to the United States.

FRAGMENT: Since I moved to the United States~~.~~, I have been studying English.

Exercise 12

Read the following examples, and identify the ones that are fragments.
*Next to each item, write **F** for fragment or **C** if the sentence is correct. Then*
correct the fragments using the two methods described above.

___F___   1. Before engines and motors were invented.

   Before engines and motors were invented, horses did many kinds
   of work for people.

_____   2. Horses carried soldiers and travelers, pulled wagons, plowed fields, and herded cows.

_____   3. Humans first domesticated horses three or four thousand years ago.

_____   4. Today the only truly wild horse lives in Mongolia.

_____   5. Because the Mongolian Wild Horse has never been successfully domesticated.

_____   6. It is also called Przewalski's Horse.

_____   7. Between 1969 and 1992, all Mongolian Wild Horses were in zoos.

_____   8. After a Dutch couple saw Mongolian Wild Horses in the Prague Zoo.

_____   9. The couple decided to start an organization.

_____ 10. So that the horses would survive.

_____ 11. In 1992, the zoo-raised Mongolian Wild Horses were released into the wild.

_____ 12. Now there are about 250 Mongolian Wild Horses in Khustain Nuruu National Park in Mongolia.

_____ 13. Although these animals are all descendants of twelve to fifteen zoo animals.

_____ 14. If the Mongolian Wild Horses are protected.

■ 5. Three Types of Dependent Clauses

English has three types of dependent clauses: **adverb clauses**, **adjective clauses**, and **noun clauses**. All three kinds of dependent clauses allow you to show connections between ideas or pieces of information and to write longer, more sophisticated sentences.

5a. Adverb Clauses

Adverb clauses are joined to sentences by subordinating conjunctions of time, reason, purpose, condition, contrast, and surprising result. (The most common subordinating conjunctions are shown in Appendix IA, page 198.) An adverb clause can come before or after the main clause in a sentence.

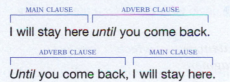

I will stay here *until* you come back.

Until you come back, I will stay here.

Note. When an adverb clause comes at the beginning of a sentence, it is followed by a comma. (See Appendix IB, page 243.)

EXERCISE 13

On another piece of paper, combine the following pairs of clauses using subordinating conjunctions. Refer to the list of subordinating conjunctions on page 198. Use commas when necessary.

1. Yuri Gagarin became the first person in space in 1961 / scientists have learned a lot about space travel.

> *Since Yuri Gagarin became the first person in space in 1961, scientists have learned a lot about space travel.*

2. Spacecraft have become more comfortable places for astronauts to be / they do their work.

3. Space suits offer more protection / astronauts do not suffer from extreme heat or cold during spacewalks.

4. Astronauts are in space / they do not experience the pull of Earth's gravity.

5. They float freely around the spacecraft / they are weightless.

6. Nearly half of all astronauts experience some motion sickness in the first one or two days / they adjust to being in space.

7. Weightlessness can make routine activities such as drinking a cup of water difficult / astronauts consume food and beverages from sealed plastic containers.

8. Astronauts exercise about two hours a day in space / weightlessness also makes people lose muscle and bone mass.

9. In addition to exercising, astronauts perform scientific experiments / they are traveling in space.

10. Nearly 500 people have flown aboard spacecraft on more than 250 space flights / there is still a great deal to learn about space travel.

5b. Adjective Clauses

An **adjective clause** is a dependent clause that follows a noun and modifies, or describes, that noun. By using adjective clauses, you can put more information in your sentences. An adjective clause begins with a **relative pronoun** (*who*, *which*, or *that*). The relative pronoun refers back to the noun that the clause modifies. For example, in the sentence that follows, ***who** works for a tire company* refers to *uncle*.

I have an uncle **who** *works for a tire company.*

Sara has a computer **which** *is very fast.*

You can create a sentence with an adjective clause by combining two sentences that refer to the same person or thing. In one of the sentences, change the noun or pronoun referring to that person or thing to a relative pronoun.

The relative pronouns **who** and **that** refer to people, and the relative pronouns **which** and **that** refer to things.

who/that

I read a novel by an *author. The author* is from Istanbul. →

I read a novel by an author **who/that** *is from Istanbul.*

which/that

I am going to read a *nonfiction book. It* is about Turkish history. →

I am going to read a nonfiction book **which/that** *is about Turkish history.*

EXERCISE 14

On another piece of paper, combine the following pairs of sentences using adjective clauses.

1. Hubble is a satellite. The satellite orbits Earth every 97 minutes.

   Hubble is a satellite that orbits Earth every 97 minutes.

   OR

   Hubble is a satellite which orbits Earth every 97 minutes.

2. Hubble gets its power from panels. The panels collect energy from the sun.

3. Hubble contains a powerful telescope and cameras. The cameras have taken photos of the planets, stars, and galaxies.

4. Telescopes on Earth cannot show as much as a telescope. This telescope is outside of Earth's atmosphere.

5. Hubble sends its photographs back to scientists. Scientists have learned about the birth and death of stars from these images.

6. The information provided by Hubble raises many questions. The questions remain to be answered.

7. Hubble has provided remarkable views of stellar events for people. These people have visited the Hubble website on the Internet.

In the previous examples, the relative pronoun is the subject of the adjective clause. A relative pronoun can also be the object of an adjective clause verb. In this case, the word order in the adjective clause is RELATIVE PRONOUN + SUBJECT + VERB.

who/that

You talked to the *man*. I know *him*. → You talked to the *man.* I know *him*.

You talked about the *movie*. I saw *it*. → You talked about the *movie.*

which/that
I saw *it*.

When the relative pronoun is the object of the verb, you can delete it.

You talked to the man ~~who~~ I know.

You talked about the movie ~~that~~ I saw.

EXERCISE 15

On another piece of paper, combine the following pairs of sentences. Change the second sentence in each pair into an adjective clause.

Note: In the example, the symbol **Ø** means the pronoun has been deleted.

1. The newspaper articles give me information about nutrition and health. I read the articles.

    The newspaper articles that I read give me information about nutrition and health.

    OR

    The newspaper articles which I read give me information about nutrition and health.

    OR

    The newspaper articles Ø I read give me information about nutrition and health.

2. When I go to the refrigerator, I try to remember the things. I have learned the things.

3. The natural sugar is better for you than processed sugar. Fruit contains natural sugar.

4. The kind of fat is better for you than the kind in red meat. Fish has this kind of fat.

5. Potatoes contain many of the vitamins. People need these vitamins.

6. Research suggests that the antioxidants help prevent cancer. People can get these antioxidants from beans, berries, and apples.

7. High blood pressure, heart disease, diabetes, osteoporosis, and depression are diseases. People can probably prevent these diseases with diet and exercise.

To sum up, when the relative pronoun is the subject of the adjective clause, there are two ways to make an adjective clause.

$$\overset{s \quad\quad v}{}$$

This is the store **which** *sells CDs*.

This is the store **that** *sells CDs*.

When the relative pronoun is the object of the adjective clause, you have three ways to make an adjective clause.

This is the store **which** I like.

This is the store **that** I like.

This is the store (**Ø**) I like.

EXERCISE 16

On another piece of paper, combine the following pairs of sentences, making the second sentence an adjective clause. Write all possible pronoun (or Ø pronoun) choices.

1. A shipwreck is a damaged ship. The ship sank to the ocean floor or washed up on the shore.

   A shipwreck is a damaged ship that sank to the ocean floor or washed up on the shore.

   OR

   A shipwreck is a damaged ship which sank to the ocean floor or washed up on the shore.

2. Historians are interested in the information. Shipwrecks reveal information about the past.

3. In 1998, near the island of Belitung, some Indonesian fishermen discovered a shipwreck. The shipwreck has provided information about trade between China and other countries in the ninth century.

4. Divers discovered a large number of Chinese bowls. Divers investigated the shipwreck.

5. Researchers say the ship was built by Arabian, Persian, or Indian shipbuilders. Researchers studied the design of the ship.

6. The discovery is important to historians. Historians want to know more about trade between Asian countries in past centuries.

5c. Noun Clauses

A **noun clause** occupies the place of a noun in a sentence—that is, it is in the place of a subject or an object. The direct object position is common.

SUBJECT
That fish live in water is well known.

OBJECT
Everyone knows **that fish live in water**.

You can omit *that* when the noun clause is in the object position.

Everyone knows ~~that~~ **fish live in water**.

Both statements and questions can become noun clauses. When a statement becomes a noun clause, *that* can introduce the clause.

The best things in life are free. → I think (***that***) *the best things in life are free.*

When a *Wh-* question becomes a noun clause, the question word introduces the clause.

Who discovered electricity? → I want to know ***who*** *discovered electricity.*

When a *Yes/No* question becomes a noun clause, **if** or **whether** introduces the clause.

Do animals communicate? → I wonder ***if/whether*** *animals communicate.*

EXERCISE 17

The following examples show statements and questions that become noun clauses. Write **that, Ø,** *a question word (***who, when, why, how much, how long,** *etc.),* **if,** *or* **whether** *before each noun clause.*

1. The amount of oil the Earth contains is limited. → I understand
   that or Ø _____ the amount of oil Earth contains is limited.

2. When will oil run out? → I don't know _____ oil will run out.

3. How high will the price of oil go? → Nobody knows _____ the price of oil will go.

4. Can solar and wind energy replace oil? → I wonder _____ solar and wind energy can replace oil.

5. Is it possible to burn coal without causing global warming? → Do you know _____ it is possible to burn coal without causing global warming?

6. How much of the energy used in transportation is from oil? → I'm not sure _____ of the energy used in transportation is from oil.

7. Every calorie of energy we eat takes ten times as much energy to produce in fossil fuels. → I wasn't aware _____ every calorie of energy we eat requires ten times as much energy to produce in fossil fuels.

8. One barrel of oil contains as much energy as that produced by twelve men working for a year. → That's amazing. I had no idea _____ one barrel of oil contains as much energy as that produced by twelve men working for a year.

- Noun Clauses Based on Questions
  When a question becomes a noun clause, it changes in three ways.

  1. Auxiliary verbs like *do* and *does* are omitted. When *does* is omitted, the third person singular verb is used.

     Do they work? → I am not sure **if they work**.

     Does Manuel work? I am not sure **if he works**.

  2. The word order usually changes. The word order of a noun clause is sentence word order, SUBJECT + VERB.

     V   S   S   V
     Where is Detroit? → I wonder **where Detroit is**.

  3. The final punctuation (period or question mark) is determined by the main clause, not the noun clause.

     I want to find out how often the bus comes.

     Can you tell me how often the bus comes?

EXERCISE 18

On another piece of paper, change the following statements and questions to noun clauses.

1. There are 120,000 varieties of rice. (Did you know . . .)

   Did you know (that) there are 120,000 varieties of rice?

2. White rice and brown rice come from the same plant. (Do you think . . .)

3. Should we wash rice before cooking it? (I wonder . . .)

4. China grows and eats one-third of the world's rice. (Is it true . . .)

5. Does rice contain protein? (Can you tell me . . .)

6. Can rice grow all over the world? (Do you know . . .)

7. How much water does rice cultivation require? (I am not sure . . .)

8. How long does it take a rice plant to mature? (Do you have any idea . . .)

9. Growing rice requires either lots of human labor or lots of oil. (Is it true . . .)

10. Rice seeds are planted by airplanes in California. (Did you know . . .)

11. How much did world rice production increase between the 1960s and 1990s as a result of plant breeding and the use of fertilizers? (I would like to find out . . .)

- Reported Speech
  Writers often need to report what someone wrote or said. To do this, they can use reporting verbs like *write* and *say* and either direct quotations or **reported speech** (noun clauses). When a statement or a question is reported in a noun clause, it can change in two ways.

  1. The subject (and object) of the noun clause changes when the point of view changes.

     > Lee writes, "I wanted to be a doctor." → Lee writes (*that*) **he** *wanted to be a doctor.*

     > My mother always says, "I love you." → My mother always says (*that*) **she** *loves* **me***.*

  2. When the reporting verb is past tense (*wrote* or *said*), the verb in the noun clause usually changes to past tense also.

     > George Bernard Shaw wrote, "Animals are my friends, and I don't eat my friends." → George Bernard Shaw wrote (*that*) *animals* **were** *his friends, and he* **didn't eat** *his friends.*

  When the reported statement is about something that is continuing or is always true, the verb in the noun clause does not change to past tense.

  > Someone said, "The dog is man's best friend." → Someone said (*that*) *the dog* **is** *man's best friend.*

EXERCISE 19

On another piece of paper, change the following quotations to reported speech. (You can combine sentences and omit unnecessary words. You can change the vocabulary, too, if you keep the same meaning.)

1. Martin Luther King said, "I am not interested in power for power's sake. . . ."

   Martin Luther King said (that) he was not interested in power for power's sake.

2. Albert Einstein wrote, "Life is like riding a bicycle. To keep your balance you must keep moving."

3. President John F. Kennedy said, ". . . our most basic human link is that we all inhabit this small planet, we all breathe the same air, we all cherish our children's futures, and we all are mortal."

4. Eleanor Roosevelt said, "Friendship with oneself is all-important because without it one cannot be friends with anyone else in the world."

5. Dr. Robert Schuller, a U.S. pastor, asked, "What would you attempt to do if you knew you could not fail?"

6. Television screenwriter Jeff Malvoin asked, "Is love supposed to last throughout all time, or is it like trains changing at random stops?"

7. Mark Twain wrote, "No man or woman really knows what perfect love is until they have been married a quarter of a century."

8. Confucius said, "Love is like a spice. It can sweeten your life—however, it can spoil it, too."

■ 6. More about Verbs

6a. Transitive, Intransitive, and Linking Verbs

English has three kinds of verbs: **transitive**, **intransitive**, and **linking** verbs.

Transitive verbs must have a direct object.

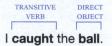

TRANSITIVE   DIRECT
VERB   OBJECT

I **caught** the **ball**.

Intransitive verbs cannot have a direct object.

INTRANSITIVE
VERB

The rain **fell**.

Linking verbs are followed by complements, not objects. Linking verbs include verbs of existence (*be, exist*), verbs of the senses (*look, appear, smell*), and verbs of change (*become, get*) and non-change (*stay, remain*). (Non-change verbs are often called *stative* verbs.)

LINKING   PREPOSITIONAL PHRASE
VERB   COMPLEMENT

This fruit *is* **from California**.

LINKING   ADJECTIVE
VERB   COMPLEMENT

Strawberry ice cream *tastes* **delicious**.

LINKING   NOUN
VERB   COMPLEMENT

The old warehouse *became* an apartment **building**.

LINKING   ADJECTIVE
VERB   COMPLEMENT

You *have stayed* **slender**.

(For more on objects and complements, see Appendix IA, page 189.)

Exercise 20

*Identify the three kinds of verbs in the following sentences. Underline all the verbs. Then write **T** before each sentence that has a transitive verb, **I** before each sentence that has an intransitive verb, and **L** before each sentence that has a linking verb.*

___L___ 1. Olive oil <u>appears</u> greenish or golden.

_____ 2. Olive trees grow around the Mediterranean Sea.

_____ 3. Virgin olive oil has no chemical additives.

_____ 4. Extra-virgin olive oil is the purest and highest quality.

_____ 5. Olive oil contains vitamin E.

_____ 6. Olive oil tastes fruity.

_____ 7. Olive trees live for hundreds of years.

_____ 8. Hundreds of olive varieties exist.

_____ 9. To make olive oil, growers grind and squeeze olives.

_____ 10. The manufacturers of cosmetics and soap sometimes use olive oil.

6b. Phrasal Verbs

Phrasal verbs consist of a verb and another word which together have a meaning that is different from the meaning of the verb alone. For example, the phrasal verb *get up* has a different meaning from the verb *get*. Some phrasal verbs are transitive (require an object), while others are intransitive (do not take an object). Here are some examples of common phrasal verbs.

Transitive Phrasal Verbs	**Intransitive Phrasal Verbs**
find out	come over
look up	eat out
pick up	go ahead
put on	grow up
set up	run away

Most transitive phrasal verbs allow the direct object to move. The direct object can be either between the two parts of the verb or after the verb.

DIRECT OBJECT

I *put* **my clothes** *on*.

DIRECT OBJECT

I *put on* **my clothes**.

6c. Verb Tense

The twelve English **verb tenses** tell about the time and length of actions, events, and situations. Four are **present tense verbs**, four are **past tense verbs**, and four are **future tense verbs**. Six of the twelve tenses are **progressive tenses**, which refer to continuing or repeating activities.

When you write about present-time events and situations, you are writing in the **present time frame** and you use some or all of the four present tenses. If you change to the **past time frame**, you use some or all of the four past tenses. If you change to the **future time frame**, you use some or all of the four future tenses. As you write, try to keep in mind the time frame you are in, and ask yourself how many of the tenses that belong to that time frame you need to use.

The Present Tenses for Writing in the Present Time Frame		
Tense	**Example**	**Use**
simple present	I **listen** to music.	a habitual action; an action or situation that is true now, was true in the past, and will be true in the future
present progressive	I **am listening** to music.	an action that is in progress now
present perfect	I **have listened** to music. I **have listened** to music for many years. I **have listened** to music since age three.	an action that has happened one or more times in the past at an indefinite time / indefinite times OR an action or situation that began at a point in time in the past and has continued or repeated until the present
present perfect progressive	I **have been listening** to music.	an action that has been in progress recently or has been repeated in the recent past

Note. *Listen* is a regular verb. That means that the past tense form and the past participle form that you see in the present perfect (have *listened*) both end in -*ed*.

If a verb is irregular, the past tense and the past participle might not be the same. For example, the past tense of *write* is *wrote*, and the past participle is *written*. English has many irregular verbs. (For a list of irregular verbs, see Appendix IA, pages 238–239.)

EXERCISE 21

Fill in the blanks with the correct present tenses from the chart on page 214. (In some cases, more than one tense is possible.) Use the verbs in parentheses.

Loja, Ecuador, a city of about 118,500, (1) _____is_____ an environmentally healthy city. Loja (2) _____ (have) strict land-use policies. In Loja, developers (3) _____ (need) to leave 20 percent of their land undeveloped for parks, and the city (4) _____ (require) citizens to donate time to the construction and maintenance of the parks. In addition, the city (5) _____ (enforce) strict water quality standards so that the water in the rivers is drinkable. Finally, Loja (6) _____ (allow) gas stations to sell only unleaded gasoline. Loja's air quality (7) _____ (improve) since this rule was made.

In the late 1990s, Loja began its recycling program. Since then, the city (8) _____ (recycle) all of its organic waste and 50 percent of its inorganic waste. Ninety-five percent of Loja's citizens (9) _____ (participate). Now Loja (10) _____ (serve) as a model of environmental planning for other cities.

The Past Tenses for Writing in the Past Time Frame		
Tense	**Example**	**Use**
simple past	I **listened** to music.	an action that began and ended in the past
past progressive	I **was listening** to music at nine o'clock last night.	an action that was in progress at a point in time in the past
past perfect	I **had listened** to that song three times before I understood it.	an action that happened before another event in the past
past perfect progressive	I **had been listening** to music for two hours before I fell asleep.	an action that had been in progress before another event in the past

EXERCISE 22

Fill in the blanks with the correct past tenses from the chart above. (In some cases, more than one tense is possible.)

In 1978, a woman (1) ___was reading___ (read) a newspaper article about a chemical waste dump near her home in the neighborhood of Love Canal in the City of Niagara Falls in New York State. She (2) ___realized___ (realize) that her son's school (3) _____ (be) near the old waste dump. She (4) _____ (go) to all her neighbors and (5) _____ (ask) them to sign a petition to close the school. Then the residents (6) _____ (begin) to notice that there (7) _____ (be) a lot of health problems in the area. For example, babies were born with birth defects, and children (8) _____ (suffer) from asthma and epilepsy.

The problem (9) _____ (start) in the 1940s. A chemical company (10) _____ (occupy) the site and (11) _____ (bury) 21,000 tons of toxic waste there. The chemical company (12) _____ (sell) the land in the 1950s, and other people (13) _____ (build) the homes and the school.

After the news media (14) _____ (tell) the story of the health problems in Love Canal in 1978, the government (15) _____ (decide) to move people out of the area, and Love Canal (16) _____ (become) a reminder of the need for environmental responsibility.

The Future Tenses for Writing in the Future Time Frame		
Tense	**Example**	**Use**
simple future	I **am going to listen** to music tonight. I **will listen** to music tonight.	a personal plan or intention OR a prediction about the future
future progressive	I **will be listening** to music at 9:30 P.M.	an action that will be in progress at a point in time in the future
future perfect	I **will have listened** to music for one hour by 10:00 P.M.	an action that will have been completed by a point in time in the future
future perfect progressive	I **will have been listening** to music for one hour by 10:00 P.M.	an action that will have been in progress for a period of time before a point in time in the future

EXERCISE 23

Fill in the blanks with the correct future tenses from the chart above. (In some cases, more than one tense is possible.) Use the verbs in parentheses.

China is developing an experimental city, Dongtan, on an island near Shanghai. Dongtan (1) _____*will be*_____ (be) a model city. There (2) _____ (be) no private cars. Instead, people (3) _____ (get around) by foot, bicycle, and electric or hydrogen-fueled public transportation. Dongtan (4) _____ (produce) its own energy from windmills and solar collectors. It (5) _____ (also use) organic waste to supply heat and electric power. Dongtan (6) _____ (recycle) 80 percent of its solid waste.

According to the master plan, the first inhabitants (7) _____ (move) to Dongtan in 2010. By 2020, Dongtan (8) _____ (become) a fully functioning city, and at least 100,000 people (9) _____ (work) and (10) _____ (live) there. By 2040, Dongtan (11) _____ (set) an example for other cities around the world. From the example of Dongtan, other cities (12) _____ (learn) how to design an urban environment in a way that provides for efficient energy use, waste management, and protection of the environment.

6d. Modal Verbs

Modal verbs come before other verbs and add meaning to sentences. True modals (*may, might, must, should, can,* and *would*) form questions and negatives differently from other verbs and do not agree with third person singular subjects. But there are some verb phrases with meanings like modals (*have to, need to, be supposed to, be able to*) that form questions and negatives like other verbs. Compare these examples.

Must he **sit** down?	***Does*** he **have to** sit down?
He **must sit** down.	He **needs to sit** down.

Some modals and modal-like verbs have more than one meaning. In addition, some have different meanings in the affirmative and the negative. Here are some of the most common modals and their meanings.

Modals and Modal-like Verbs	Affirmative	Negative (If Different in Meaning)
should, ought to	ADVICE OR OPINION You **should** / **ought to** study English if you want a better job.	
be supposed to	EXPECTATION The store opens at 10:00 a.m., and the salespeople **are supposed to** be there at 9:30.	WEAK PROHIBITION You **are not (aren't) supposed to** talk in the library, but many people do.
must	STRONG NECESSITY You **must** have a license in order to drive a car.	PROHIBITION Smoking is not allowed in gas stations. You **must not** smoke there.
have to	NECESSITY I **have to** wear a coat in winter.	LACK OF NECESSITY You **don't have to** take vitamins, but you might feel better if you do.
may, might	PRESENT OR FUTURE POSSIBILITY Lisa **may/might** be in Italy now, but I am not sure. I **may/might** change jobs next year, but I haven't decided yet.	
can	ABILITY OR POSSIBILITY Shoppers **can** buy books online now.	PROHIBITION OR IMPOSSIBILITY When buying online, shoppers **cannot (can't)** pay by check.
be able to	ABILITY OR POSSIBILITY Shoppers **are able** to buy books online now.	
would	UNREAL CONDITIONAL Harry **would** go visit his family if he had money and time.	

EXERCISE 24

Copy the following statements on another piece of paper, and add to each one a sentence of your own that contains a modal or modal-like verb. Use at least six different modals or modal-like verbs.

1. Heavy rain or snow and icy road conditions make driving dangerous.

> *If I had a choice, I would stay home in bad weather. / Drivers may not see other vehicles in stormy weather.*

2. Automobile accidents cause more serious injuries when cars are traveling at high speed.

3. Driver error and alcohol consumption are responsible for most traffic accidents.

4. Careless drivers are a threat to pedestrians and other drivers.

5. Crosswalks are for pedestrian safety.

6. Seat belts protect drivers.

7. New tires and brakes help prevent accidents.

8. Cell phones are sometimes used to call for help after accidents have occurred, and they have also been used to take pictures of accidents.

6e. Subject-Verb Agreement

Subjects and verbs must agree in English. To avoid errors with subject-verb agreement, you must pay attention to certain tenses, verbs, and sentence patterns.

1. In the simple present tense, verbs with the third person singular subjects (*he*, *she*, and *it*) end in *-s*. (*he likes*, *she thinks*, *it does*).

2. In the present perfect and present perfect progressive tenses, all verbs with the third person singular subjects begin with **has** (*he* **has** *asked*, *she* **has** *wanted*, *it* **has** *been raining*). Verbs with the subjects *I, you, we,* or *they* begin with **have**.

3. The *be* verb is irregular in the simple present and simple past tenses.

	Present Tense	**Past Tense**
I	*am*	*was*
he, she, it	*is*	*was*
you, we, they	*are*	*were*

Note. Prepositional phrases and adjective clauses may appear between a subject and verb but do not affect subject-verb agreement.

SUBJECT   VERB

The truth about the actual cost of repairing the windows was revealed.

SUBJECT   VERB

The young man who assists the front office managers has learned the business well.

4. In sentences that begin with *there*, the verb agrees with the subject, which follows the *be* verb.

SUBJECT   SUBJECT

There **has been** a dry *wind* recently, and there **are** *wildfires* in the hills now.

If the sentence has a compound subject, the verb agrees with the closest noun.

> There **was** *one child and four adults* in the photograph.

> There **were** *four adults and one child* in the photograph.

EXERCISE 25
The following passage has <u>nine</u> subject-verb agreement errors. Find and correct the errors.

[1]Dictionaries are our best source of information about a language. [2]Dictionary writers, who are also called lexicographers, selects the vocabulary that dictionary users needs. [3]There is over 600,000 words in English, but the average dictionary does not include all of them. [4]Furthermore, each year some new words, such as *podcast* and *googling*, come into the language, while at the same time some other words goes out of use. [5]To write a dictionary, lexicographers need a collection of examples of spoken and written language. [6]Today the computer have made collecting and storing language samples from newspapers, books, speeches, and everyday conversations much easier. [7]These language samples helps lexicographers write definitions and examples because the samples reflect the actual uses of a word.

[8]In a dictionary entry, the first definition give the most common meaning of a word. [9]A dictionary entry also show syllables, pronunciation, part of speech, irregular forms, word families, collocations, and usage. [10]Collocations are groups of words that usually occur together, such as *tell the truth*, *play a role in*, and *have an effect on*. [11]Usage refer to both grammar and formality. [12]For example, a usage note can explain the difference between *its* and *it's*, or it may explain that *find out* is an informal way to say *discover*. [13]Considering all that a dictionary offers, it is safe to say that each entry is a little treasure.

■ 7. More about Nouns

7a. Countable and Uncountable Nouns

English has two categories of nouns. **Countable nouns** can be plural, and the articles *a* and *an* and numbers such as *one, two, three*, and *four* can go before them.

> We need **a table** and **four chairs**.

> Alfredo suggested **an idea** about **decorations**.

Uncountable nouns cannot be plural, and *a* and *an* or numbers cannot go before them.

> The miner found **gold** in the hills and exchanged it for **money**.

> People everywhere value **freedom**.

Quantifiers are words that come before countable and uncountable nouns and give information about quantity. Some quantifiers are used only with countable nouns, some are used only with uncountable nouns, and some are used with both.

- Quantifiers used only with countable nouns: *a few, quite a few, several, many*

  Many students brought **a few questions** to class.

- Quantifiers used only with uncountable nouns: *a little, a bit of, quite a bit of, much*

  Marilyn volunteers **quite a bit of time** and gives **a lot of help** to elderly people.

- Quantifiers used with both countable and uncountable nouns: *some, quite a lot of, a lot of, a great deal of*

  Some jobs require **a lot of skills**.

  Some work requires **a lot of education**.

Note. Many English nouns are sometimes countable and sometimes uncountable, depending on the situation. For example, *coffee* is usually uncountable, but if you are ordering it for yourself and someone else in a restaurant, you ask for *two coffees*. To find out if a noun is countable, uncountable, or both, you must refer to a dictionary.

Exercise 26

Underline the nouns in the following paragraph. Mark each one **C** *if it is* countable *and* **U** *if it is* uncountable. *Use a dictionary if you need to.*

¹ I have been a <u>backpacker</u> [C] for several <u>years</u> [C], and I have found that having the right <u>equipment</u> [U] is very important. ²First, backpackers must have sturdy, comfortable hiking boots, a few pairs of thick socks, some long pants and some shorts, and two or three T-shirts. ³Backpackers also need rain gear, sunglasses, sunscreen, and mosquito repellent. ⁴In addition, a warm sleeping bag and a lightweight tent are essential to a backpacker's comfort. ⁵Backpackers also need a stove, fuel, matches, a cooking pot, and one or two water bottles. ⁶Finally, food is essential to a good trip. ⁷Backpackers need a lot of energy but don't want to carry too much weight. ⁸Freeze-dried meals weigh only a few grams (or ounces) and are easy to prepare. ⁹Many backpackers also bring instant rice and noodles, oatmeal, dried fruit, and nuts with them.

7b. Gerunds and Infinitives

Gerunds and **infinitives** are verb forms that are used as nouns in sentences. A gerund is an *-ing* form (*studying, driving*), and an infinitive is a *to* form (*to study, to drive*).

Gerunds can be subjects, direct objects, and objects of prepositions in sentences.

SUBJECT
Reading is an important part of my life.

DIRECT OBJECT
I enjoy **reading**.

OBJECT OF
A PREPOSITION
I learn from **reading**.

Infinitives are usually used only as direct objects.

DIRECT OBJECT
I like **to read**.

Both gerunds and infinitives can be followed by noun objects, prepositional phrases, and adverbs. Gerunds and infinitives together with words and phrases attached to them are called **gerund phrases** and **infinitive phrases**.

GERUND PHRASE
I prefer **reading novels and poetry**.

INFINITIVE PHRASE
But I try **to read two newspapers in the morning**.

Certain verbs are followed only by gerunds. Other verbs are followed only by infinitives. A few verbs are followed by both. The following lists show some of the most common verbs of each kind.

- Verbs followed by gerunds: *appreciate, avoid, complete, consider, discuss, dislike, enjoy, finish, go, keep, imagine, involve, mind, miss, postpone, practice, quit, suggest*

- Verbs followed by infinitives: *afford, agree, appear, choose, decide, demand, encourage, expect, hesitate, hope, learn, manage, need, offer, opt, plan, prepare, promise, refuse, seem, tend, try, want*

  I *considered going* to the movies, but I *decided to finish* my paper instead.

- Verbs followed by both gerunds and infinitives: *begin, continue, hate, like, love, start*

  I recently *started riding* my bike to work.

  I recently *started to ride* my bike to work.

Some verbs allow a direct object before the gerund or infinitive.

- (verb) + (someone) + (infinitive): *advise, ask, choose, encourage, require, select, tell*

  I advised *my daughter* to study. I encouraged *her* to work hard.

- (verb) + (something) + (gerund): *spend* + (time or money) + (gerund)

  I spent *two months* preparing for the exam.

To find out which patterns follow a particular verb, refer to a dictionary.

EXERCISE 27

Fill in the blanks in the following sentences with gerunds or infinitives.

1. Chen Zheng decided _____ *to become* _____ (become) a doctor at age fourteen.

2. He imagined _____ (be) able to help sick and injured people recover their health.

3. His parents encouraged him _____ (take) a heavy load of academic subjects in high school including biology, chemistry, Latin, and higher mathematics.

4. Chen's high school counselor advised him _____ (maintain) high grades.

5. Chen tried _____ (be) one of the top students in his high school class, and he prepared _____ (take) China's National College Entrance Examination.

6. During his three years of high school, Chen spent all his weekends _____ (study), and he avoided _____ (watch) television.

7. Chen scored very well on the college entrance examination, and he was asked _____ (attend) an interview at several medical schools.

8. Chen was selected _____ (enter) the Beijing School of Medicine, where, after five years of serious study, he became an intern.

9. As an intern, he was required _____ (assist) in a hospital.

10. The internship involved _____ (work) long hours.

11. Chen practiced _____ (monitor) patients and _____ (keep) records.

12. During this time, Chen was considering _____ (become) a specialist, but he could not afford _____ (continue) his studies.

13. He needed _____ (make) some money, so he opted _____ (apply) for positions in hospitals.

14. The Beijing Medical Center wanted _____ (hire) Chen, so he agreed _____ (take) a position there upon graduation.

■ 8. More about Adjectives

8a. Participial Adjectives

Participial adjectives are made from verbs. There are two kinds: *-ed* participial adjectives and *-ing* participial adjectives. Look at the following examples of *-ed* participial adjectives.

> The *excited* children ran to the ocean, and their *worried* parents followed.

> The students were *confused* when they read the assignment.

In each of these examples, the children, the parents, and the students have been affected by something that excited, worried, or confused them. The children, students, and parents have experienced an *effect*. They are the *receivers of an action*. Now look at the following examples of *-ing* participial adjectives.

> We are going to see an *exciting* movie and eat a *satisfying* dinner.

> Thunderstorms can be *frightening*.

In these examples, the movie, dinner, and thunderstorms cause a reaction in someone. The movie, dinner, and thunderstorms are the *cause*. They are the *agents of an action*.

Here are some common participial adjectives and examples of nouns that they can modify.

-ed Participial Adjectives That Refer to a Receiver or an Effect	*-ing* Participial Adjectives That Refer to an Agent or a Cause
improved (+ design)	changing (+ situation)
educated (+ person)	increasing (+ cost)
disappointed (+ child)	motivating (+ story)
employed (+ workers)	promising (+ future)
expected (+ response)	rewarding (+ job)

EXERCISE 28
*Add **-ed** or **-ing** to the adjectives in the paragraph. (Remember: When a verb ends in **e**, delete the final **e** before you add -ing.)*

Marcello Rossi runs the popular Rossi Family (1) Travel *ing* Circus. Marcello and his five children go from town to town giving performances in (2) crowd _____ arenas. Marcello grew up in a circus family. He was an (3) accomplish _____ clown by age ten. As a teenager, Marcello learned to perform on the high wire. Marcello says he was not (4) frighten _____. Instead, he found the high-wire act (5) challenge _____. He taught his children Miranda, Stefano, Paolo, Federico, and Carlo this skill, and together they have created a very

(6) entertain _____ high-wire act known as the (7) Fly _____ Rossis. Miranda, Stefano, and Carlo are also (8) amaze _____ acrobats who jump, turn somersaults, and land on each other's shoulders. Paolo is the lion tamer who is (9) dress _____ in a formal tuxedo and makes the big cats sit, stand, and roar on command. Paolo says he was (10) scare _____ the first time he went in the cage with the lions, but now he finds it (11) excite _____. Miranda also has a group of little (12) train _____ dogs that perform (13) amuse _____ tricks. The two youngest children, Federico and Carlo, perform together. Federico walks on stilts while Carlo rides a tiny motorcycle around him and even circles between his legs. The Rossis are a (14) hardwork _____ family who have made an (15) interest _____ life for themselves by offering (15) thrill _____ shows to (17) delight _____ audiences.

8b. Noun Modifiers

Noun modifiers are nouns that play the role of adjectives and modify other nouns.

NOUN
MODIFIER

I am going to buy an **airline** ticket.

NOUN
MODIFIER

The city council has discussed **traffic** problems.

Noun modifiers do not have plural forms. There is no final *s* on a noun modifier.

ERROR: This is a flowers shop.

ERROR: Mrs. Vu needs a children safety seat.

Noun modifiers that contain numbers are written with hyphens (-).

A six-year-old girl greeted us at the door.

I live in a four-story apartment building.

EXERCISE 29
On another piece of paper, rewrite the first sentence of each pair and add a noun modifier to it. Use the boldface word in the second sentence.

1. In 784, the first mills were built in Baghdad, Iraq. (These mills were for the production of **paper**.)

   In 784, the first paper mills were built in Baghdad, Iraq.

2. The menu was first developed in China during the early Song dynasty (960–1279). (The menu was for **restaurants**.)

3. In Shibam, Yemen, people built the first tall buildings in the sixteenth century. (The buildings contained **apartments**.)

4. The stove was invented in 1902. (This stove burned **gas**.)

5. Douglas Engelbart invented the mouse in 1963. (The mouse was for a **computer**.)

6. Dietrich Mateschitz introduced a new drink to Europe in the 1980s. (The drink gave people **energy**.)

7. Someone invented a tiny video camera. (This video camera fits in someone's **pocket**.)

8. A new television came out in 2005. (When the television is not on, it looks like a **mirror**.)

9. A portable charger was developed recently. (This charger is for **cell phones**.)

8c. Possessives

Possession is shown in English with **possessive nouns** (*Alicia's, Mr. Kim's*), **possessive adjectives** (*my, your, his, her, our, their*), and **possessive pronouns** (*mine, yours, his, hers, ours,* and *theirs*).

> This is *Alicia's* red notebook.
>
> This is *her* red notebook.
>
> This is *Alicia's*.
>
> This is *hers*.

To make a singular noun possessive, add an apostrophe (') and **s**.

> This is my best friend**'s** paper.

To make a plural noun possessive, add only an apostrophe (').

> These are my two friends**'** papers.

To show that two or more people possess something, add **'s** only to the last noun.

> This is Halil, Ruben, and Salvador**'s** project.

EXERCISE 30
On another piece of paper, rewrite each of the following statements. Show all possible ways to show possession.

1. This is Maria's purse.

   This is Maria's. This is her purse. This is hers.

2. The teacher read Jose's composition.

3. Lee and Park's experiment was successful.

4. I lost my keys, but I found your keys.

5. Jack didn't have his car, so he rode in our car.

■ 9. More about Pronouns

9a. Pronoun Forms

Pronouns take the place of nouns in sentences and paragraphs. You can use pronouns to avoid repeating a noun and to create connections between sentences. English has four kinds of pronouns (**subject, object, reflexive**, and **possessive**). There are also **possessive adjectives**, which look like pronouns but are used *before* nouns, not in place of nouns. (See Appendix IA, page 227).

Subject Pronouns	Object Pronouns	Reflexive Pronouns	Possessive Pronouns	Possessive Adjectives
I	me	myself	mine	my
you	you	yourself, yourselves	yours	your
he	him	himself	his	his
she	her	herself	hers	her
it	it	itself	its	its
we	us	ourselves	ours	our
they	them	themselves	theirs	their

Look at these examples of pronouns.

SUBJECT PRONOUN   OBJECT PRONOUN

Mother told the *boys* not to climb the *tree*. **They** climbed **it** anyway

REFLEXIVE PRONOUN

but didn't hurt **themselves.**

POSSESSIVE PRONOUN

Ana and her brother have the same kind of sweaters. *Hers* is pink, and

POSSESSIVE PRONOUN

his is blue.

SUBJECT PRONOUN   REFLEXIVE PRONOUN   POSSESSIVE ADJECTIVE

We enjoyed **ourselves** at **our** party.

Fill in the blanks with pronouns and possessive adjectives from the chart on page 228.

I sent an e-mail to my father. The same day, my sister sent an e-mail to

(1) _____him_____. He received mine first, and he got (2) _____

later. Then he wrote one response and sent (3) _____ to both of us.

In (4) _____ message, my father said that (5) _____ and

Mother were fine, but (6) _____ were missing us. He said that they

think about us every day and wonder how (7) _____ are doing. He

mentioned that my cousin Maria was visiting with her two children. He said

that Maria's children were getting big and that he and Mom were happy to

see (8) _____. Finally, he told my sister and (9) _____ that

he and Mom wanted to send (10) _____ love to (11) _____,

and he reminded us to take care of (12) _____.

9b. Pronoun Agreement

A pronoun usually refers to a noun in the same text. Generally, the noun it refers to is in the same sentence or the preceding sentence.

I am taking a psychology class, and **it** requires a lot of reading.

Marina has three interests. **She** likes history, natural science, and music.

Pronouns must agree in number and person with the nouns they refer to. For example, because the noun *class* is singular, the pronoun *it* must also be singular. Because *Marina* is feminine, you must use the feminine pronoun *she*.

him
ERROR: I heard John sing. I enjoyed listening to ~~them~~.

It
ERROR: John's voice is a baritone. ~~He~~ is very deep.

EXERCISE 32

The following passage has <u>seven</u> errors in the use of pronouns and possessive adjectives. Find and correct the errors.

¹In 1960, at the age of twenty-six, Jane Goodall began her study of a group of wild chimpanzees in Tanzania. ²At first the chimpanzees feared ~~him~~ *her*, but she was determined to get closer to them, and eventually, it accepted her. ³That same year Goodall observed a male chimpanzee putting a piece of grass into a termite hole and then putting the grass in his mouth. ⁴It was using the grass to catch termites. ⁵This was the first time anyone had reported tool use in animals. ⁶Goodall also reported that chimpanzees use facial expressions and vocalizations to express its emotions. ⁷They live in groups that have a hierarchical structure, and they make sounds to indicate his social status. ⁸Chimps also behave aggressively toward each other at times.

⁹Goodall gave the chimpanzees that she studied names, and some scientists criticized him for doing this. ¹⁰But Goodall's purpose was to show that chimps are very much like us and that they need protection. ¹¹Goodall stopped doing research in 1986 and now devotes her time to educating people about environmental protection. ¹²Of their work, she said, "My mission is to create a world where we can live in harmony with nature."

■ 10. Comparatives and Superlatives

You can use the **comparative** form of adjectives and adverbs to compare two people, places, things, or actions.

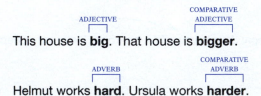

ADJECTIVE   COMPARATIVE ADJECTIVE

This house is **big**. That house is **bigger**.

ADVERB   COMPARATIVE ADVERB

Helmut works **hard**. Ursula works **harder**.

You can use the **superlative** form of adjectives and adverbs to compare three or more people, places, things, or actions. Always put the definite article *the* before the superlative form.

SUPERLATIVE
ADJECTIVE

Jericho is **the oldest** city in the world.

SUPERLATIVE ADVERB

Of the five people in my family, my brother plays chess **the most skillfully**.

Certain rules apply to the formation and spelling of comparative and superlative adjectives and adverbs.

Adjectives	Adverbs
One-syllable adjectives and adverbs: Use *-er* or *-est*.*	
fast → fast**er** → fast**est** strong → strong**er** → strong**est** Note 1. When an adjective ends in *e*, just add *-r* and *-st*. nice → nic**er** → the nic**est** Note 2. Double the final consonant after a single vowel. fat → fa**tt**er → fa**tt**est	fast → fast**er** → fast**est** hard → hard**er** → hard**est** Note 1. Most adverbs end in *-ly* and therefore have two syllables, so most adverbs form the comparative and superlative with *more* and *most*.
Two-or-more-syllable adjectives and adverbs: Use *more* and *most*.**	
useful → **more** useful → **most** useful effective → **more** effective → **most** effective	quietly → **more** quietly → **most** quietly conveniently → **more** conveniently → **most** conveniently

* Some one-syllable adjectives and adverbs are irregular in their comparative and superlative forms.

Irregular Adjectives	**Irregular Adverbs**
good → better → best	well → better → best
bad → worse → worst	badly → worse → worst
far → farther → farthest	far → farther → farthest

** When a two-syllable adjective ends in *-y*, change the *y* to *i* and add *-er*.

happy → happ**ier** → happ**iest**

easy → eas**ier** → eas**iest**

When you are unsure about the comparative or superlative form of a particular adjective or adverb, refer to a dictionary.

EXERCISE 33

Fill in the blanks with the comparative or superlative forms of the adjectives in parentheses.

1. UNESCO (the United Nations Educational, Scientific, and Cultural Organization) identifies the places in the world that have *the greatest* (great) cultural or natural value and that are *the most endangered*. (endangered)

2. A famous World Heritage Site, the Taj Mahal of India is one of _____ (beautiful) buildings in the world.

3. The Great Wall of China is _____ (large) than any other military structure in the world.

4. Damascus, Syria, is one of _____ (ancient) cities in the Middle East.

5. Lake Baikal in Russia is _____ (old) and _____ (deep) than any other lake in the world.

6. Uxmal in Mexico has some of _____ (good) examples of Mayan architecture.

7. Mount Kilimanjaro, which is _____ (high) than any other mountain in Africa, is in Kilimanjaro National Park in Tanzania.

8. Iguazu National Park in Argentina and Iguaçu National Park in Brazil share one of _____ (impressive) waterfalls in the world.

9. Shalamar Gardens in Lahore, Pakistan, are some of _____ (elegant) gardens in the world.

10. The Aflaj Irrigation Systems of Oman are some of _____ (efficient) systems for distributing water in the world.

11. Virunga National Park in the Democratic Republic of Congo has some of _____ (exquisite) scenery in Africa.

■ 11. Conditional Sentences

You can use **conditional sentences** to express various meanings: general truths, habitual activities, possible events, and imaginary situations. In most conditional sentences, the subordinating conjunction, which is usually *if*, introduces a condition, and the event described in the main clause depends on that condition.

> If the temperature rises, sugar melts.

Conditional sentences fall into two groups: those that describe **real** situations and those that describe **unreal** situations.

Real Conditional Sentences	
Example	**Meaning**
PRESENT If (when) sugar gets very hot, it turns brown.	a general truth
If (when) I **make** cookies, I always **share** them with my neighbor.	a habitual activity
FUTURE If I **make** cookies tomorrow, I **will/am going to share** them with my neighbor.	a possible event
PAST Last year, if (when) I **made** cookies, I always **shared** them with my neighbor.	a past habitual activity that may not happen anymore
Unreal Conditional Sentences	
PRESENT OR FUTURE If I **had** enough money now, I **would buy** a laptop computer. (I don't have enough money.)	an imagined event that will not or probably will not happen
PAST Last year, if I **had had** enough money, I **would have bought** a laptop computer. (I didn't have enough money.)	an imagined event that did not happen

EXERCISE 34

Fill in the blanks in these real present, future, and past conditional sentences. Use the verbs in parentheses.

1. Five hundred years ago, if people who were far apart wanted to communicate with each other, they _____*traveled*_____ (travel) or they _____*sent*_____ (send) messengers.

2. Fifty years ago, if someone in Tokyo _____ (need) to talk to someone in London, he or she used the telephone.

3. Today, if a young man in Saudi Arabia wants to communicate with his sister in Canada, he _____ (call), _____ (send) a text message, or _____ (e-mail).

4. In the future, people who _____ (want) to communicate with someone far away probably will use wireless devices.

5. Five hundred years ago, if people _____ (want) entertainment, they started to sing.

6. Fifty years ago, if someone craved entertainment, he or she _____ (turn) on the radio or television.

7. Today, if someone _____ (want) entertainment, he or she chooses between the Internet and video games.

8. In the future, if people want entertainment, what choices _____ they _____ (have)?

EXERCISE 35
Fill in the blanks in these unreal present and past conditional sentences. Use the verbs in parentheses.

1. Solar technology provides less than 1 percent of the energy we use. If we _____*used*_____ (use) solar technology more, it would be good for the planet.

2. Cars don't have solar cells. If cars had solar cells, they _____ (not produce) air pollution.

3. Denmark gets over 20 percent of its energy from wind. If other countries _____ (get) some of their energy from wind, we would be less worried about global warming.

4. There is no way to store surplus wind energy. If there were a way to store extra wind energy, wind energy production _____ (be) more efficient.

5. In the nineteenth century, the gasoline engine appeared. If the gasoline engine had not appeared, people _____ (continue) to use horses for transportation.

6. Oil companies used to burn off natural gas that they didn't want. If they _____ (not burn off) natural gas, they wouldn't have wasted so much energy.

7. U.S. automakers made a lot of SUVs, or big cars, before 2009. If they hadn't made so many big SUVs, people in the United States _____ (use) less gasoline.

8. In 2006, a man claimed that he had discovered a source of free energy, but the claim turned out to be false. If his claim _____ (be) true, his discovery would have changed the world.

■ 12. Transitions

Transitions are adverbs that show logical connections between sentences or between parts of a text. If you use transitions in your writing, readers will find it much easier to understand your ideas and to follow the plan of your paragraphs and essays.

See some common transitions on page 235.

To Show a Sequence	
first, second, third, finally	A new Brazilian capital was established in the 1950s. **First,** a location was chosen. **Second,** a city plan was developed. **Third,** construction was begun. **Finally**, in 1960, the government moved into the new capital, Brasilia.
then, after that, afterward	Kyoto was the capital of Japan from 794 to 1868. **Then/After that/Afterward**, the capital moved to Tokyo.
To Add a Related Point	
also, in addition	Shanghai is the largest city in China. It **also** has the most industry. (**Also**, it has the most industry. / It has the most industry **also**.)
	Shanghai is the largest city in China. **In addition**, it has the most industry.
second, third, etc.	Shanghai is important for several reasons. First, it is the largest city in China. **Second**, it has the most industry. **Third**, it has the largest port.
To Introduce an Example	
for example, for instance	Some cities are known for a major industry. **For example/For instance**, Milan, Italy, is known for fashion.
To Introduce a Contrast	
however, in contrast, by comparison, on the other hand	New York is the most expensive city in the United States. **However/In contrast/By comparison/On the other hand**, Memphis, Tennessee, is one of the least expensive U.S. cities to live in.
To Introduce a Result	
therefore	Cities offer many job opportunities. **Therefore**, people move to them.
To Introduce a Surprising Result	
however	People move to cities hoping to improve their lives. **However,** many migrants to cities do not find better lives after they move.

EXERCISE 36

Fill in the blanks with transitions that signal sequence, addition, example, contrast, or result.

A.   **The Effects of Being a Hydrologist**

I used to work as a hydrologist in Iran. A hydrologist is a scientist who studies water quality and water supplies in order to meet human needs and help protect the natural environment. Working as a hydrologist had three positive effects on me. (1) _____*First*_____, I spent about half of my time in the field. (2) _____, I often went to the Karaj and the Latian reservoirs to collect water samples. I enjoyed being outdoors and hiking around. (3) _____, I gained valuable experience in teamwork from this job. There were four members of my team—Jafar, Ali, Mohammad, and myself. We shared the responsibilities of collecting and analyzing data, writing reports, and working with other scientists and engineers in the government and private businesses. (4)_____, working as a hydrologist gave me a lot of satisfaction because I was able to make a difference in people's lives. If water is polluted or in short supply, people suffer. (5) _____, as a hydrologist I performed a valuable service in helping to protect public health.

B.   **Differences between the Friendships of Six-Year-Olds and Twelve-Year-Olds**

The friendships of six- and twelve-year-olds differ in two ways. (1) _____, the activity that is the basis of the friendship differs. The friendships of six-year-olds usually involve creation of fantasy games in which the children play roles such as police and robbers or mothers and fathers. (2) _____, the friendships of twelve-year-olds generally involve sharing private feelings about schoolwork, parents, and members of the opposite sex. (3) _____, the friendships of six- and twelve-year-olds differ in terms of how relationships develop and how long they last. A friendship between a pair of six-year-olds can start instantly when the children discover that they are playing the same game with the same level of interest, but this friendship can end just as quickly with a disagreement over the rules of a game. (4) _____, the friendships of twelve-year-olds develop slowly as trust is built up and often last throughout the adolescent years and beyond.

■ 13. Word Forms

The ending of an English word often tells you the part of speech of that word. This is especially true with academic vocabulary. Therefore, it is a good idea to memorize common **word endings**, or **suffixes**.

The following chart lists some common noun, verb, adjective, and adverb suffixes.

Suffixes		
Noun Suffixes	-ance, -ence -er, -or -ment -ness -ship -sion, -tion -y, -ity	annoy**ance**, consequ**ence** caregiv**er**, act**or** accomplish**ment**, punish**ment** unique**ness**, spacious**ness** friend**ship**, companion**ship** discus**sion**, institu**tion** propert**y**, prior**ity**
Verb Suffixes	-ate -en -ify -ize	cre**ate**, stimul**ate** dark**en**, bright**en** simpl**ify**, clar**ify** organ**ize**, popular**ize**
Adjective Suffixes	-able, -ible -al -ed -ent, -ant -ful -ing -ive -less -ious, -ous	valu**able**, respons**ible**, emotion**al**, benefici**al** tir**ed**, extend**ed** effici**ent**, signific**ant** harm**ful**, suspense**ful** appeal**ing**, demand**ing** descript**ive**, effect**ive** care**less**, humor**less** marve**lous**, prosper**ous**
Adverb Suffix	-ly	traditional**ly**, financial**ly**

■ 14. Irregular Verbs

Many of the most common English verbs are **irregular**. You will need to memorize these verbs in order to use them easily in your speech and writing. Here are some of the most common irregular verbs.

Irregular Verbs		
(be) am, is, are	was, were	been
become	became	become
begin	began	begun
break	broke	broken
bring	brought	brought
broadcast	broadcast	broadcast
build	built	built
buy	bought	bought
choose	chose	chosen
come	came	come
cost	cost	cost
do	did	done
draw	drew	drawn
drink	drank	drunk
eat	ate	eaten
fall	fell	fallen
feel	felt	felt
find	found	found
fit	fit	fit
fly	flew	flown
forget	forgot	forgotten
forgive	forgave	forgiven
freeze	froze	frozen
get	got	gotten
give	gave	given
go	went	gone
grow	grew	grown
have	had	had
hear	heard	heard
hide	hid	hidden
hold	held	held
hurt	hurt	hurt
keep	kept	kept
know	knew	known
lay	laid	laid
lead	led	led
leave	left	left
lend	lent	lent
let	let	let
lie	lay	lain
lose	lost	lost
make	made	made
mean	meant	meant

meet	met	met
mistake	mistook	mistaken
pay	paid	paid
put	put	put
quit	quit	quit
read	read	read
ride	rode	ridden
run	ran	run
say	said	said
see	saw	seen
sell	sold	sold
send	sent	sent
show	showed	showed/shown
sit	sat	sat
sleep	slept	slept
speak	spoke	spoken
spend	spent	spent
stand	stood	stood
steal	stole	stolen
swim	swam	swum
take	took	taken
teach	taught	taught
tell	told	told
think	thought	thought
understand	understood	understood
wear	wore	worn
weave	wove	woven
win	won	won
withdraw	withdrew	withdrawn
write	wrote	written

EXERCISE 37

The following story has <u>twelve</u> errors with irregular verbs. Find and correct the errors. (The story contains two verb tenses, simple past and past perfect. For information about these tenses, see Appendix IA, page 215.)

                           told

[1]My grandmother ~~tell~~ me a story about a young woman who made rugs. [2]When the young woman weave each rug, she made a wish. [3]One night she finished a beautiful rug and made a special wish. [4]Then she fall asleep. [5]The young woman dreamed that her wish would come true.

[6]In the morning, two traders came and bought the rug the woman had just make. [7]The young woman saw their faces for a moment. [8]They were two brothers, and the young woman knows who they were. [9]People said that the younger brother was kind but the older one was not. [10]After the young woman's father had given the brothers a price, they paid her family, took the rug, and left.

[11]That evening a messenger bring a note to the young woman's house. [12]The young woman's father read the note, sat down, and wrote an answer. [13]He send his response back with the messenger. [14]Then the young woman heard her parents talking. [15]Her father said that one of the brothers wanted to marry the young woman, but it was not clear which one.

[16]The following morning, the older brother appeared at the young woman's door. [17]The young woman thinks he wanted to marry her. [18]She got scared and run away. [19]She hide in the woods until evening, and then she went back home. [20]When she returned, her parents comforted her. [21]They said the younger brother meant to marry her. [22]The young woman kissed her parents, holds them, and began to cry because her wish had came true.

Appendix IB: Capital Letters and Punctuation Marks

Capital letters and punctuation marks make writing easy to read. They also tell readers that the writer has taken time to learn the rules of written English and has been careful to apply them. By using capital letters and punctuation marks correctly, you can let readers know that you are serious about your writing.

■ 1. Capital Letters

Use capital letters in the following situations.

1. The title of a composition.
   Always capitalize the first word. Capitalize all other words in a title except articles and prepositions.

Draft #2	
	The <u>C</u>auses of <u>S</u>tress
	With the growth of cities, many people are having
	to get used to a faster-paced lifestyle. Three aspects of

2. The beginning of a sentence or a quotation.

   He said, "There is a small park near the river."

3. Certain words are always capitalized.

   a. The first person singular pronoun *I*.

   First, I chose a quiet place to study, and I reviewed my notes.

   b. Proper names of people, places, and things.

   I saw a famous painting called the *Mona Lisa*, which Leonardo da Vinci finished painting in France in 1519.

   c. Days of the week, months, holidays.

   On January 15, a Saturday, the festival known as Pongal will be celebrated.

d. Countries, nationalities, languages, and ethnic groups.

> **B**elize is a multilingual country. **B**elizeans speak **S**panish, **B**elize **C**reole, and three **M**aya dialects.

e. The names of specific school classes.

> I took **M**ath 41, **C**omputer and **I**nformation **T**echnology 10, and **C**hild **D**evelopment 100.

> Do *not* capitalize the names of school subjects.

> I took classes in ~~M~~math, ~~C~~computers, and ~~C~~child ~~P~~psychology.

f. The titles of books, magazines, essays, short stories, movies, television programs, songs, etc.

> We read a novel titled <u>**T**he **C**all of the **W**ild</u> and a short story called "**T**he **N**ecklace."

g. The names of relatives (only if they are not preceded by a possessive adjective such as *my*).

> My sister brought **P**apa and **M**ama to the picnic.

> My sister brought my papa and mama to the picnic.

EXERCISE 1

The following sentences have errors with capital letters. Find and correct the errors.

1. ~~a~~Alna's wedding is in ~~m~~Mazatlan, ~~m~~Mexico, in ~~a~~April, and her friends ~~t~~Teresa and ~~u~~Umberto will be there.

2. new years day falls on a friday, so we will leave for tokyo on thursday.

3. in my english class, we read *to kill a mockingbird*, and then we saw the movie.

4. my mother and aunt mimi sang john denver's song "country roads."

5. I wrote a paper for my world history class called "events that led to the korean war."

6. in addition to english, pierette speaks french and creole.

7. anita has registered for biology 131, math 80, and psychology 100 in the spring. She likes biology and psychology, but she is not fond of math.

■ 2. Punctuation Marks

2a. Period

1. The period is a very important punctuation mark because it marks the end of a sentence.

   I study English**.**

In order to use periods correctly, you need to understand different sentence patterns. (See Appendix IA, pages 195–204.)

2. Other uses of periods:

   Dr.   Mrs.   A.M.

   Mr.   Ms.   P.M.

EXERCISE 2

Periods are missing in the following paragraph. Read the paragraph, and insert periods where they are needed.

Our neighbor Mr**.** Rodas is a soccer referee**.** He referees games every Saturday and Sunday from 8 A M to 1 P M To be a referee, first a person has to be physically fit because a referee runs up and down the field throughout the game Second, a person must be able to focus and make quick decisions because things happen very quickly in a soccer game A referee also needs to be able to handle players, coaches, and spectators when they get upset about a call If this happens, a referee must explain his decisions to them calmly but firmly Mr Rodas is quick on his feet, alert, and good at quieting disputes He says being a referee is rewarding for him It is his way to make a contribution to the community

2b. Comma

Use a comma in the following situations.

1. To separate independent clauses in compound sentences. (See Appendix page 200.)

   Cindy is a Web page designer**,** and she is self-employed.

2. After a dependent clause at the beginning of a sentence. (See Appendix page 201.)

   When Cindy started her business**,** she didn't make much money.

3. Before a dependent clause of contrast or surprising result at the end of a sentence. (See Appendix IA, page 198.)

> Telephone operators sit down all day, whereas salespeople stand up.

> Aldo likes driving a taxi, although it is stressful at times.

4. To separate items in a list.

> I have worked as a housecleaner, a receptionist, and an office manager.

5. After transitions and introductory prepositional phrases.

> Tony has had seven jobs. However, he has never held a job for more than ten months.

> In March of this year, Tony quit his job at the construction company.

6. Before or after a quotation. (See Appendix IB, page 245.)

> Tony said, "Driving an ice cream truck was my favorite job."

EXERCISE 3

Commas are missing in the following passage. Read the passage, and insert commas where they are needed.

[1]When the F. W. Woolworth retail stores opened in the United States in the 1870s, they were innovative in several ways. [2]First because most of Woolworth's goods were priced at either five or ten cents the company called its stores "five-and-dime" stores. [3]Earlier stores had allowed customers to bargain but Woolworth's had fixed prices. [4]In addition the Woolworth five-and-dime stores let the customers pick things out for themselves whereas earlier stores had made customers wait for a clerk to select items for them. [5]Also the Woolworth Company was the first to put lunch counters in its stores. [6]When hungry shoppers came in for toothpaste or a comb they smelled food and they were likely to buy something to eat.

[7]In the 1960s shopping centers began to appear across the United States so the Woolworth Company had to adapt. [8]It created specialty stores that sold athletic gear clothing and watches. [9]The Woolworth five-and-dime stores didn't survive but some of the specialty stores did. [10]To explain his success, the founder of the Woolworth stores said modestly "I am the world's worst salesman; therefore I must make it easy for people to buy."

2c. Quotation Marks

The use of **quotation marks** to report the exact words that someone has spoken or written is called **direct speech**. To punctuate direct speech correctly, follow these rules.

RULE 1. If a quotation is less than one sentence, don't place a comma before it or start it with a capital letter.

> Sonia said that she had "the best time of her life" at the party.

RULE 2. Place a comma before a quoted sentence, and begin the sentence with a capital letter. If the end of the quotation is the end of the sentence, place a period *inside* the quotation marks.

> Henri said, "The music was excellent."

RULE 3. Place commas, periods, question marks, and exclamation marks *inside* the quotation marks.

> Peter asked, "What was the name of the band?"

RULE 4. When reporting a quotation that is more than one sentence long, do not close the quotation marks until the end of the person's speech.

> Nina said, "I danced for three hours. I couldn't stop!"

EXERCISE 4

The following short passages are taken from compositions. Each passage contains a quotation with incorrect punctuation. Read the passages, and add quotation marks, commas, and periods where they are needed.

1. Many people like their jobs but hate to commute. My father always says, "If I could work at home, I wouldn't want to retire." I think many people share his sentiment.

2. I think that young people should finish college before they get married. My cousin Veronica got married at age eighteen, and she often says Why didn't I wait? It would have been so much easier to be a student if I had stayed single

3. I often hear people say Money can't buy happiness But I believe money contributes to happiness. If a person doesn't have money, he can't eat nutritious food, sleep in a comfortable bed, or take the time to study and improve himself.

4. When immigrants enroll in school, they learn a great deal about the culture of the country they have moved to. For example, from the curriculum in a literature class, they learn about cultural values. I was surprised when my English teacher said We are going to study Edgar Allen Poe because he is one of the greatest American writers I wondered why U.S. culture values Poe's stories, which were meant to be frightening.

2d. Semicolon

A **semicolon** can replace a period between two sentences that you want the reader to see as closely connected.

> The company is in serious financial difficulty; it owes more than it expects to receive for the next five years.

> Marvin's dream is marrying Winona; her dream is marrying Felipe.

2e. Colon

Use a **colon** to introduce a list that explains the noun or noun phrase that precedes the colon.

> On the first day of school, bring the following things: a pen, a pencil with an eraser, and some binder paper.

> To make a salad, follow these steps: take out the lettuce and tomatoes, wash them, and cut them up.

> Do *not* use a colon after a verb or a preposition.

> **INCORRECT:** I have taken: chemistry, physics, and microbiology.

> **CORRECT:** I have taken chemistry, physics, and microbiology.

> **INCORRECT:** I am interested in: physics and astronomy.

> **CORRECT:** I am interested in physics and astronomy.

Appendix II: Peer Review Forms

Peer Review Form

■ **CHAPTER 1—*Accomplishments***   **PROCESS PARAGRAPH**

WRITER: _____   READER: _____

Read a classmate's paragraph and answer the questions.

1. Did the writer use correct paragraph form as shown on page 12?   ❑ yes   ❑ no

2. Does the paragraph have a topic sentence?   ❑ yes   ❑ no

3. Does the paragraph contain supporting sentences that describe the steps the writer followed?   ❑ yes   ❑ no

4. Does each supporting point contain a transition word?   ❑ yes   ❑ no

5. Did the writer add any explanation to help you understand the steps he or she followed?   ❑ yes   ❑ no

   Would you like the writer to include more explanation about any of the steps?   ❑ yes   ❑ no

   If yes, write some questions to guide the writer.

   _____

   _____

Peer Review Form

WRITER: _____   READER: _____

Read a classmate's paragraph and answer the questions.

1. Does the topic sentence of the paragraph contain a controlling idea?   ❐ yes   ❐ no

   If yes, what is it? _____

2. How many supporting points does the paragraph contain? _____

   Did the writer introduce each supporting point with a transition?   ❐ yes   ❐ no

   Does each supporting point in the paragraph relate to the controlling idea
   of the topic sentence?   ❐ yes   ❐ no

3. Do you see any information gaps in the paragraph?   ❐ yes   ❐ no

   If yes, write questions to help the writer address them.

   _____

   _____

4. Did the writer use specific nouns, adjectives, and prepositional phrases to
   describe the place or event?   ❐ yes   ❐ no

   Write down the best descriptive phrase you see in the paragraph.

   _____

5. Is the paragraph written in the present or the past time frame? _____

   Are there any changes in the time frame?   ❐ yes   ❐ no

   If yes, did the writer mark the changes in the time frame with time signals?   ❐ yes   ❐ no

Peer Review Form

■ **CHAPTER 3—*Pastimes and Entertainment***   **REASON PARAGRAPH**

WRITER: _____   READER: _____

Read a classmate's paragraph and answer the questions.

1. What is the topic of the paragraph? _____

   Does the topic need to be defined or explained?   ❐ yes   ❐ no

   If yes, is the definition or explanation clear?   ❐ yes   ❐ no

2. Does the paragraph contain a second level with sentences
   giving supporting reasons?   ❐ yes   ❐ no

   How many supporting reasons are there? _____

3. Did the writer use transitions to mark the supporting reasons?   ❐ yes   ❐ no

4. How did the writer develop the supporting points?

   ❐ with sensory details   ❐ with examples   ❐ with explanations

   Are there any information gaps in the paragraph?   ❐ yes   ❐ no

   If yes, write questions to help the writer address the information gaps.

   _____

   _____

5. Did the writer use coordinating and subordinating conjunctions to join
   sentences and to show relationships between ideas?   ❐ yes   ❐ no

   If yes, list the conjunctions the writer used. _____

   _____

Peer Review Form

■ **CHAPTER 4—*Occupations***   **EFFECT PARAGRAPH**

WRITER: _____   READER: _____

Read a classmate's paragraph and answer the questions.

1. What is the topic of the paragraph? _____

   Does the topic need to be defined or explained?   ❏ yes ❏ no

   If yes, is there a clear definition or explanation?   ❏ yes ❏ no

2. How many effects does the paragraph discuss? _____

3. Does the paragraph contain three levels?   ❏ yes ❏ no

   How did the writer develop the supporting points?

   ❏ with sensory details   ❏ with examples   ❏ with explanations   ❏ with quotations

   Do you see any problems with unity or focus?   ❏ yes ❏ no

   If yes, explain. _____

   _____

4. Did the writer use repeated and related words to create connections
   within the paragraph?   ❏ yes ❏ no

   If yes, what are some of them? _____

5. Which verb tenses did the writer use in the paragraph?

   ❏ the present perfect   ❏ the simple present   ❏ the simple past

Peer Review Form

■ **CHAPTER 5— *Growing Up in Different Cultures***   **CONTRAST PARAGRAPH**

WRITER: _____   READER: _____

Read a classmate's paragraph and answer the questions.

1. What two things is the writer comparing? _____

   _____

2. What pattern of organization did the writer use?

   ❏ side-by-side   ❏ point-by-point

3. Does the paragraph have balanced development?   ❏ yes   ❏ no

   Would you like the writer to explain or develop any part of the paragraph?   ❏ yes   ❏ no

   If yes, write some questions to guide the writer. _____

   _____

4. Did the writer use transitions effectively?   ❏ yes   ❏ no

5. Did the writer use consistent point of view?   ❏ yes   ❏ no

   What point of view did the writer use in all or most of the paragraph? _____

   _____

6. Does the paragraph contain a conclusion?   ❏ yes   ❏ no

   If not, do you think it needs one?   ❏ yes   ❏ no

7. Did the writer use some academic vocabulary?   ❏ yes   ❏ no

   If yes, give some examples. _____

Peer Review Form

■ **CHAPTER 6—*Making Communities Better***   **OPINION ESSAY**

WRITER: _____   READER: _____

Read a classmate's essay and answer the questions.

1. Does the essay have an introduction?   ❐ yes   ❐ no

   Does the introduction have a thesis statement?   ❐ yes   ❐ no

   Does the introduction lead you to the thesis statement?   ❐ yes   ❐ no

   Does the introduction provide background information?   ❐ yes   ❐ no

   Does the introduction provide any explanation?   ❐ yes   ❐ no

2. How many body paragraphs does the essay have? _____

   Does each body paragraph have a topic sentence that identifies a supporting
   point?   ❐ yes   ❐ no

   Do the supporting sentences in body paragraph 1 develop the topic
    sentence well?   ❐ yes   ❐ no

   Do the supporting sentences in body paragraph 2 develop the topic
   sentence well?   ❐ yes   ❐ no

   If the essay has a third body paragraph, do the supporting sentences in it
   develop the topic sentence well?   ❐ yes   ❐ no

   If you think any of the body paragraphs need more information, write questions here.

   _____

   _____

   Circle the strategy that the writer used most to develop the body paragraphs.

   sensory details   examples   quotations   explanations

3. Does the essay have a conclusion that provides a summary of the main ideas? ❐ yes   ❐ no

   Did the writer use any synonyms in the conclusion?   ❐ yes   ❐ no

Index

noun modifiers, 44, 226
noun phrases, 44
nouns, 27–8, 121–2, 185
   countable and uncountable, 153, 221–2
   possessive, 227

objects
   direct and indirect, 190–1
   of prepositions, 186
   of verbs, 189–91, 212
opinion paragraphs, 155, 157
outlining, 60–61

paragraph, 7
   conclusions, 139
   connections, 106–7
   definition in, 64
   development, 17, 42–3, 71, 104, 137
      balanced, 137
      quotations as, 104
   focus, 103
   focus points, 33
   form, 12
   levels and outlining, 60–1
   support in, 7, 13, 15, 42–3
   three levels in, 60–1, 69
   topic sentence in, 7, 13
   unity, 102
parallel lists
   for comparison/contrast essays, 130
participial adjectives, 54–5, 111–2, 225
parts of speech, 185–7
peer review forms, 247–52
period, 243
phrase
   gerund and infinitive, 76
   noun, 44
   prepositional, 186, 193–4
point-by-point organization, 126–7
point of view, 144
   change in, 145
possessives, 227
prepositional phrases, 44, 186, 193–4
prepositions, 186
prewriting, 9
   brainstorming chart for, 66
   brainstorming cluster for, 35
   brainstorming list for, 10
   brief outline for, 99
pronouns, 144, 186–7, 228
   agreement, 229
   possessive, 227

point of view, 144
   relative, 205–8
punctuation, 243–6

quantifiers, 221
quotations, 104, 245–6

relative pronoun, 205–8
reported speech, 211
revising, 9, 13
run-on sentences, 202

semicolon, 246
sensory information, 30, 71
sentences
   combining, 19–20, 77, 79, 195–9
   complements, 189, 192, 212
   fragments, 203
   objects, 189
   parts, 188–9
   run-ons, 202
   subjects, 188
   types, 200–1
   verbs, 188
side-by-side organization, 125–6
specific information, 30, 42
subjects
   of sentences, 188, 190
subordinating conjunctions, 79, 198–9
   comparison and contrast, 140
such as, 73
suffixes, 27–8, 237
superlatives, 230–31
support, 7, 15
supporting points, 59
   in opinion paragraphs, 155
   organizing, 95
survey, 160
synonyms, 151

thesis statement, 165–6, 169
three-level paragraphs, 60–1, 69
time frames, 45–7
topic sentence, 7, 13, 34
   contrast paragraph, 124
   controlling idea, 34
   effect paragraph, 93
   opinion paragraph, 155
   reason paragraph, 58
transitions, 15, 41, 234–5
   comparison and contrast, 141–2
   examples, 73

unity
in paragraphs, 102

verbs, 185, 188, 190, 212
agreement with subjects, 219–20
irregular, 214, 238–9
kinds, 185, 188
linking, 212
modals, 179–80, 217–8
phrasal, 213
regular, 214

of sentences, 188
tense, 18, 45–7, 108–9, 214–6
time frames, 45–7, 214–6
transitive and intransitive, 212

whereas, 140–1
while, 140–1
word families, 4, 87
word forms, 27–8, 237
word order, 190–4